CHRISTIANITY A

KT-419-406

JM Sutton
1985.

CHRISTIANITY
AND
SYMBOLISM

F. W. DILLISTONE

SCM PRESS

1955.

—

— 1985.

334 01929 X

First published 1955 by Collins
This reissue 1985 by
SCM Press Ltd
26–30 Tottenham Road, London N1 4BZ

Printed in Great Britain at
The Camelot Press Ltd, Southampton

Contents

5

Preface

WHEN *Christianity and Symbolism* first appeared in 1955 I referred in the Preface to man's use of symbols throughout his long historical career. Yet "where could I find any sort of agreed terminology which would enable me to use such terms as sign, symbol and sacrament with the assurance that their precise connotations would be recognised and understood." Could a framework of reference be established which would show how these terms can best be distinguished from one another and how they have come to be used in various departments of human life?

The original edition of *Christianity and Symbolism* has long been out of print, but general interest in symbolism has not only continued but seems to have increased. Hardly a day now passes without the word "symbol" appearing in a newspaper report or a magazine article. Some object or event or person or pattern of behaviour is seized upon and declared to be the symbol of some wider or larger configuration. A village is seen as a "symbol of France's bitter private school row." Ronald Reagan is made the subject of a book subentitled "The Politics of Symbolism." At the inauguration of the Olympic Games in Los Angeles four thousand pigeons were released as "a symbol of peace." "Christopher Columbus symbolised to perfection those qualities without which Europe could never have achieved its scientific and technological triumphs or have remade the world in its image."

These examples are drawn from recent writings of a more popular kind, but the interest in symbols has also been evident in departments of scholarly activity. Social scientists have been at pains to show how symbolic actions throw valuable light on tribal man's relation to nature, to his fellows and to divine beings. Sir Ernst Gombrich, the historian of art, writes a book incorporating a lengthy essay on *Symbolic Images*. *Man and his Symbols* can be regarded as a summary of Jung's investigation of the human condition. In his astonishingly detailed studies of the history of religions, Mircea Eliade reverts again and again to the significance in any people's religious life of symbolic patterns of myth and ritual. Literary critics have been quick to detect symbolic references in names, characters, or events encapsulated in novel, poem, and drama. In fact the interpretation of symbols has become one of the most important exercises in many academic disciplines.

The danger is, however, that the words symbol, sign, and signal, together with their literary cognates simile, analogy, and metaphor, will come to be used so loosely and arbitrarily that they lose their power to express particular kinds of relationships within particular social contexts. Perhaps the commonest example of arbitrary exchange is that between symbol and sign. For Paul Tillich it was vital to distinguish between these two words. His whole system depended on it. For him a symbol was rich and expansive in its power to transform and elevate mind and spirit towards some higher reality: a sign was an external indicator (for example a road-sign) relating to some pattern of behaviour already recognised by a social group. There was a direct and unequivocal correspondence between a sign and that which it signified.

Though much has been written about symbols over the past thirty years I believe that the general framework of reference which I presented in *Christianity and Symbolism* is still valid. If the text could be completely revised I should try to give proper attention to some of the important books which have been published since it first appeared and to make certain adjustments. But the original text must remain unaltered. I have, however, been allowed to prepare a new Bibliography in which I have drawn attention to books on symbolism which seem to me to be of major importance. I am exceedingly grateful to Dr John Bowden and SCM Press for their willingness to re-issue a book which, I hope, still has something to contribute to the ongoing study of symbolic forms.

In the religious sphere one of the crucial issues of our time is that between the literal and the symbolic, the sign and the symbol. Admittedly there is great strength in a single vision, in following a direct path, in staying within strictly defined boundaries of thought and action. Symbolic interpretation can become so far-fetched and fanciful as to seem (as for example at the time of the Reformation) to have become trivial and remote from the central Christian gospel. Yet advocacy of *plain* interpretation and *literal* correspondences soon begets narrowness and exclusiveness. To see a scene or to hear a message as symbolic of something far greater and more enduring can be the way of true freedom.

In his fine book *The First Urban Christians*, Professor Wayne A. Meeks refers to "the crucifixion and resurrection of God's Son, the Messiah" as "destined to prove one of the most powerful symbols that has ever appeared in the history of religion." This drama, vividly depicted in word and ritual, became the central symbol of Christianity. And this symbol, Meeks continues, proved to be of "enormous generative power." Whatever other symbols may be of value in Christian worship and witness, it is my conviction that the symbol to which I have given particular attention in this book still generates power and illuminates every department of thought and life.

Oxford 1984   F. W. Dillistone

CHAPTER ONE

Signs, Symbols and Sacraments

WE LIVE in a world in which symbols have come to occupy a place of paramount importance. Outwardly the impressive phenomena are the jet-plane and the television-set and the atom bomb. But everyone knows that behind the actual production of these intricate mechanisms there lies a long process of learning and invention and calculation and skilled technique and that within this process much of the work is done by the manipulation of a multitude of mysterious symbols. When not long ago it was rumoured that Dr. Einstein had discovered a principle of unification for the whole universe, the newspapers carried photographs of the formula which was supposed to be the possible key to unlock the world's mysteries. All that the layman could see was a group of figures and letters and signs which to him made no sense at all. Yet his respect for Dr. Einstein was such that he was quite prepared to believe that this insignificant constellation of symbols held within it a whole world of potential meaning.

In the opening chapter of his important book, *Symbol and Metaphor in Human Experience*, Professor Martin Foss remarks that every age has its favourite solutions to its problems. These solutions may be shallow and premature, they may be profound and definitive. Ideally they should always prepare the way for further questioning and research. But, he goes on to say, " the favourite answer of an age is often one in which only a minimum of problems is preserved and which has been promoted to its place as favourite because it seems to render superfluous all further questioning. It closes all doors, blocks all ways, and just because of this permits the agreeable feeling that the goal has been reached and that rest is granted. One of the favourite answers of our age has been the symbol. Man has, as they say, a ' symbol-forming power,' and it is this power which makes him a man. Consequently everything that man produces is a symbol. Symbol is the slogan, the magic key which opens all doors and answers all questions. In symbolism all our thinking comes to rest. Science is symbolical, art is symbolical, even religion is." (p. 1.)

Yet, paradoxically enough, together with this recognition of the importance of the symbol, there has arisen a situation in which the ordinary man either has no symbols at all or fails to find any vital meaning in the symbols which are at his disposal. We have already touched upon the mystery which surrounds modern mathematical symbolism, but the same is also true of much of poetical symbolism. The Symbolist Movement in litera-ture has come to be associated in the mind of the layman with the confusing and the unintelligible. He is frankly bewildered as he tries to make sense of language which he suspects is expressing an important insight but which corresponds to nothing in his own tradition or experience.

But the more serious thing is that for multitudes in the world to-day old symbols have either decayed or been violently snatched away and no fresh and commanding symbols have taken their place. At the conclusion of her great study of symbolism to which I shall have occasion to refer more than once, Susanne K. Langer writes : " In modern civilisation there are two great threats to mental security : the new mode of living, which has made the old nature-symbols alien to our minds, and the new mode of working, which makes personal activity meaningless, inacceptable to the hungry imagination. Most men never see the goods they produce, but stand by a travelling belt and turn a million identical passing screws or close a million identical passing wrappers in a succession of hours, days, years. This sort of activity is too poor, too empty, for even the most ingenious mind to invest it with symbolic content. Work is no longer a sphere of ritual ; and so the nearest and surest source of mental satisfaction has dried up. At the same time, the displacement of the permanent homestead by the modern rented tenement—now here, now there—has cut another anchor-line of the human mind.

Most people have no home that is a symbol of their childhood, not even a definite memory of one place to serve that purpose. Many no longer know the language that was once their mother-tongue. All old symbols are gone, and thousands of average lives offer no new materials to a creative imagination." [1]

Thus in the world of symbolism we are confronted with a strangely ambiguous situation. On the one hand we are told by social scientists that man lives by symbols, that he is a symbol-making animal, that only through adequate symbols can he find stability and satisfaction. Further, we are aware that the scientist, in whose hands so much of our destiny seems to reside, works by means of complicated symbols which are quite unintelligible to the lay mind. Therefore it seems that the scientific symbol, important as it is, cannot meet the needs of the ordinary man. He must either renounce his symbol-making functions and allow himself to be treated as raw material by those who can interpret the mysterious language of science or he must discover symbols capable of giving him some security in a constantly changing world. On the other hand, however, we are assured by those well versed in the history of mankind that old and time-honoured symbols have disappeared, that it is useless to turn nostalgically to the past, that the very conditions of modern life make it impossible for the ordinary man to find meaning and security any longer in the familiar symbols of tradition and environment. [2] We are at least partially aware that the fanaticism of modern nationalism is inspired by this search for a symbol or symbols capable of appealing to every member of a large community. If man cannot any longer find " natural " symbols in his home and work, he must have " communal " symbols to bind him to his fellows. Thus the choice is coming to be confined to one of two alternatives—either to entrust our destinies to the scientist with his symbols of mystery or to surrender to the leadership of the fanatic with his symbols of mass-association. It is in part the purpose of this book to inquire whether any other patterns of symbolism may be found to guide man through the complexities of the world in which he lives. What are the nature and function of symbols? What are the distinctions

---

[1] *Philosophy in a New Key*, 291 ff.
[2] See D. M. Emmet, *The Nature of Metaphysical Thinking*, 100 ff.

which differentiate symbols from sacraments and signs and which distinguish different kinds of symbols the one from the other ?

SACRAMENTS AND SIGNS

Let us first look at the term " sacrament " in order to make clear in what sense we understand it and why we prefer the term symbol for general use. In the main the word " sacrament " is employed to-day either within the context of the Christian Church or by writers who are well aware of the general meaning attached to the word within that particular context. As illustrations of the latter we may appeal to the great philosophical work of Professor A. A. Bowman which he entitled *A Sacramental Universe*, or to Professor R. R. Marett's anthropological investigation which he entitled *Sacraments of Primitive People*, or to a pamphlet on *Religious Perspectives of College Teaching in the Physical Sciences* in which Professor Hugh S. Taylor declares that " somehow or other the teacher of science must communicate in his teaching, in his work, in his life, the truth that our physical universe can go down into physical death unless we can at the same time make of it a sacramental universe." In each case the writer, knowing something of the significance of the term " sacrament " within the specifically Christian context, seeks to give it a wider application and to suggest that behind the material realities of the universe and behind the ritual actions of primitive people there are spiritual and religious depths which make them in a true sense sacramental. These writers know that certain ceremonies in the Christian Church are called " sacraments " : they know that certain material elements are called " sacraments." Why then should not all religious ceremonies and all material realities be included under the same general title ?

On the face of it there is much to be said in favour of such a usage and yet it can very easily lead to confusion. The history of the word sacrament is a curious one. As has often been pointed out, it is derived from the Latin word *sacramentum* which at the time of the birth of Christianity was commonly used in two contexts. On the one hand it was a *legal* term, describing the deposit lodged in the temple by a litigant as a mark of good faith or as a pledge that a fine would be fully paid. On the other hand it was a *military* term, applied to the oath by which young recruits pledged their loyalty to the symbolic representatives of the Roman Republic. Inasmuch, however, as religious sanctions governed the life both of the law-court and of the army, it could be said that *sacramentum* was normally employed within a religious context.

In the early Greek-speaking Christian Church the natural word to use for a religious rite was the word *mysterion*. It had a certain Biblical authorisation and its general meaning was well known in the Hellenic world. But when the Church began to use the Latin tongue, some equivalent had to be found for *mysterion*. For reasons unknown the word *sacramentum* was chosen and thus it began its career of ever-increasing popularity and usefulness within the vocabulary of Christendom. Used at first to describe any rite of the Church, it gradually became the centre of more philosophical interest, especially in the time of St. Augustine, and came to be understood, in accordance with a general Platonic outlook, as being an outward and visible reality : through sacraments man could penetrate to the inner spiritual world and receive grace therefrom for his spiritual life.

From at least the time of St. Augustine onwards the term sacrament has carried the possibility of this double meaning. It might, on the one hand, be used to designate either the rite itself or some essential part of the rite. It might also be used to refer to any outward action or object which holds more of value or significance within it than at first meets the eye. To use the definition of a modern writer : " There is a sacramental sign or sacrament whenever a religious reality exists both visibly and invisibly, with a relation of causality or at least of significance between the elements, the one falling under the senses, the other unseen by eyes of flesh." (E. Masure, *The Christian Sacrifice*, p. 81.)

Again the *range* of the definition has varied. When referring to a rite the word has sometimes included seven (or even more) sacraments, sometimes three, sometimes two. Similarly, when referring to a sign, the word has sometimes been applied to any outward reality within the Christian context, sometimes it has been confined to the particular acts or elements of the rites properly called sacraments. But however widely usage has varied in the course of Christian history, the general associations of the word have been with *either* a specific rite of the Church *or* its attendant actors or elements. Thus to extend the application of the word to the *whole* universe or to every kind of action in ordinary life or to the practices of primitive people is a question- able procedure. It may, for instance, imply that the grace of God is just as much available to man through the ritual procedures of a Hindu temple as it is through the Eucharist of the Christian Church or that an ordinary loaf of baker's bread is just as truly sacramental as is the consecrated bread of the Eucharist. These are large assumptions and could only be justified by being worked out into a whole philosophy of life. Without being pedantic, then, it would seem better to restrict the term sacrament to its time-honoured usage as a specifically Christian word, associated with the rites and sacred objects of the Christian Church. This is the procedure adopted by the *Shorter Oxford English Dictionary* when it defines " sacrament " as " any one of certain rites of the Christian Church of which Baptism and the Lord's Supper are held to be generally necessary to salvation." This may be too restricted in its range, but it indicates what is the primary meaning attached to the word in current usage. To extend the use of " sacrament " in such a way that it comes to include the whole universe and any human activities within it, only leads to con- fusion of thought through the glossing over of certain pre- suppositions which belong to a particular philosophical inter- pretation of reality.

For the present, therefore, I shall leave aside the word " sacrament." Our concern is to examine man's relationship to nature and to his fellow-men in the broadest possible way, and for this purpose a wider word with a less clearly defined history is desirable. The word " sacrament " no longer carries any of its original Latin associations into common speech : it imme- diately suggests definitions and philosophical inquiries and theological battles and religious rites within the restricted sphere of the Christian Church. The term *symbol*, therefore, is altogether more suitable for our purpose. It can be used in all kinds of contexts—logical, mathematical, artistic, religious. Its original connotation, as we shall see, is quite general and, in common usage to-day, it is applied without hesitation to any one reality which represents or suggests another. Our inquiry, then, is concerned with the nature of symbolism, though before we can begin our analysis proper there is one other word which calls for consideration. It is the word " sign."

Possibly the most familiar " signs " to-day are those used in connection with man's journeys to and fro in the world. On the roads there are signs of direction, parking signs, signs at cross-roads, signs of approaching danger, signs of gradients, signs of distance, signs of speed-limits, signs of rules to be observed. These signs vary in form—some are words or sentences to be read, some are coloured lights to be observed, some are lines or arrows or circles or crosses. Some are numbers or geometrical figures. For travel by air there are signs to give height and direction, signs by which to ascend and descend, signs to indicate speed and fuel-supply. The signs may be given to the eye or to the ear but in all cases they are designed to bring about some appropriate form of behaviour in an appropriate situation and at an appropriate time. In other words, a sign as we think of it to-day is usually *practical* in its purpose. It is a shorthand way of communicating information, simply, clearly and quickly. The better the sign the more effective will it be in leading to a swift and decisive reaction.

According to the dictionary definition, a sign is primarily a gesture or motion of some part of the body, and its purpose is to convey an intimation. But man has discovered ways of constructing signs which will convey messages by proxy and any pattern in space or time which serves to distinguish or to demonstrate or to forewarn or to inspire may be regarded as a sign. M. Maritain has pointed out that it was the custom of philosophers of old to distinguish between practical signs and speculative signs but to speak of a " speculative " sign is to depart from the original flavour of the word (the Romans were a practical people and were not interested in *signa* which would arouse speculation) and to detract from the very characteristics of clarity and immediacy which it is expected to provide. We shall therefore use the word " sign " to denote a pattern, either static or dynamic, which is designed to bring about an appropriate reaction immediately and accurately. The pattern of the sign usually has a direct correspondence to the pattern of the appropriate reaction, though as soon as we begin speaking of the relation of patterns we are approaching very near to the realm of symbolism which is the main subject of our inquiry. The connection between signs and symbols raises very real problems and it is to some of these that we shall now direct attention. Nothing seems more desirable at the present time than to establish some agreed terminology in this highly important department of human experience.

SYMBOLS

In the *New English Dictionary* symbol is defined as " something that stands for, represents or denotes something else (not by exact resemblance but by vague suggestion or by some accidental or conventional relation)." At the root of the word there is to be found the idea of throwing together or putting together : through a symbol two realities are *related* to one another, for in the symbol certain elements of each are to be found. The whole problem of the symbol is to define or describe this relationship and it must be said at once that it cannot be described or defined in any single way. Is the relation natural or accidental or artificial or conventional ? Our dictionary definition hesitates between suggestion, accident and convention. It introduces the word " vague " in order to ensure that the relation should be regarded as inexact and indefinite. Can nothing more enlightening be said about the relation than this ?

To examine this relation more carefully and to state it more precisely has been the task of many different writers. One after another has recognised that there are different types of relationship between one reality and another and the attempt has therefore been made to classify these types and to give them appropriate names. Let us look at some of the more notable of these attempts.

In the field of theology a book which has attained the status of a classic in many quarters is *The Christian Sacraments* by Canon Oliver C. Quick. Very early in the book the author encounters the problem of the nature of the relationship between what he

calls " outward " realities and " inward." Taking as an example
of outward realities the material objects which man himself
constructs, he points out that they divide themselves immediately
into two classes. " Some take their character from what is done
with them ; and these we will call instruments. Others take
their character from what is known by them ; and these we will
call symbols." (p. 5.) Immediately, however, the author proceeds
to point out that every instrument is also a symbol and every
symbol also an instrument. A violin is primarily designed to
produce music, but it is also bound to suggest to the mind the
thought of music. (This is not necessarily the case to someone
who has never seen a violin in action.) A musical score is
designed to express certain patterns of music but it is also part
of the apparatus for producing music. (Again this is only the
case when the player has been instructed and trained to decipher
the musical score.) After further discussion Quick sets forth
his main distinction thus : " Instrumentality is the relation of
a thing to that which is effected by it ; significance the relation
of a thing to that which is suggested by it." (p. 12.) He touches
on a further distinction which is sometimes made between
" natural " symbols (those which by their very appearance or
sound suggest some other particular reality) and " artificial " or
" arbitrary " symbols (those which suggest other realities as a
result of custom or tradition or agreement or convention). But
his main distinction, which sets the pattern for his whole treatment of sacramental theology, is that between instruments and
symbols, between effectiveness and expression.

I believe that Quick's terminology would have been improved
if he had kept the basic word instrument to refer to each of the
possible relations which he had in mind. He himself admits that
although a symbol must always be in some sense an instrument,
it is not always so clear that an instrument is necessarily a symbol.
Could he not therefore have spoken of effective or practical
instruments on the one hand and expressive or symbolic instruments on the other ? Or, still better, could he not have made his
essential distinction between " signs " which, as we have already
seen, are primarily designed to serve some *practical* end and
" symbols " which, it might be suggested, are designed to serve
some more *expressive* or *significant* end ? Sheer direct instru-

mentality of the type which Quick illustrates by the example of the savage striking another man with a club belongs to an almost sub-human category which is hardly worth considering in the realm of symbolism. It appears, therefore, that in the main this particular author is concerned to draw the distinction between the sign, natural or conventional, whose primary function is to effect a purpose, and the symbol, natural or conventional, whose primary function is to express or suggest significance. This distinction is useful so far as it goes, but I believe that a more penetrating analysis can be made.

Michael Roberts was a remarkable combination of mathematician, poet and man of affairs. He sought to discover a comprehensive world-view within which the disciplined investigations of the scientist and the creative insights of the poet would each gain full recognition. He could not fail to see that symbols were of paramount importance in each of the two fields which he himself had explored. So in his *Critique of Poetry* we find him attempting to establish a distinction of a general kind, a distinction, however, which finds its most notable illustration in the contrast between the two fields already mentioned. His theory is that the symbols of mathematics are pure *signs*. They are manipulated according to strictly logical processes and appeal almost exclusively to the *intellectual* side of man's nature. I say " almost exclusively " because it is in my judgment quite impossible to split man's nature into watertight compartments— intellectual, emotional, volitional. A mathematician engaged in the most rigorous exercise of his logical powers still experiences a sense of delight when a neat proof or a simple solution presents itself to him. At the same time it is true that man is sometimes operating in a more rational and intellectual way, sometimes in a more imaginative and emotional way. Roberts, then, goes on to assert that the symbols of art must be regarded as belonging more to the realm of emotion. They may have the character of signs but their chief quality is to be found in the fact that they are " emotive " symbols. The man who succeeds in creating a symbol of this kind does so as the result of a deep emotional experience : those who come into contact with the symbol likewise find themselves strangely moved by the encounter.

Thus the main division which Roberts suggests is that between signs and symbols. The former are logical and appeal to man's intellect : the latter are sensory and appeal to man's emotion. The former develop out of experiences already familiar and out of assumptions already taken for granted : the latter introduce elements of surprise, of pleasure, of harmony, of resolution of conflict. The former emphasise correspondence, the latter lay greater stress on contrast. The former are constructed by the exercise of careful and sustained rational thought : the latter emerge out of the patient exercise of the imagination. Even fantasy and allegory Roberts would regard as belonging more to the realm of " signs," for often they are formed by conventional patterns being shuffled in unusual ways. Metaphor and drama, however, belong in a special way to the realm of " symbols," for in these forms the surprising and the dynamic find full expression. We shall not attempt to follow Roberts in the details of his critique and exposition. Our main object is to keep in view the interesting distinction between " sign " and " symbol " which he attempts to establish.

C. Day Lewis is a modern poet who has given us a fascinating account of the poetic experience and task. In his book, *The Poetic Image*, he sets out to examine the nature of that which is the constant in all poetry—the image—and to describe the processes by which images are brought together to form the complete image which is the poem itself. One of the striking things about Lewis's book is the fact that the word " symbol " comes up for serious consideration only once and then is quite summarily dismissed. Raising the question of what is most prized in the realm of imagery, Lewis suggests a threefold answer—freshness, intensity and evocative power. He then proceeds to contrast the image and the symbol. " An intense image," he says, " is the opposite of a symbol. A symbol is denotative ; it stands for one thing only, as the figure 1 represents one unit. Images in poetry are seldom purely symbolic, for they are affected by the emotional vibrations of their context so that each reader's response to them is apt to be modified by his personal experience. Take the word " white," for instance. It has been used often enough as a symbol of innocence, or chastity. But what should we say of Mr. Auden's lines ?

Innocence is not the immediate thing that white suggests to me there, in spite of its association with " children." My mind, transferring the epithet, has already received an image of white doves, pecking about at the foot of broken columns white in sunlight, which is the picture I compose from the second line. The general emotional tone I feel in the image is one of distance, separation, and a certain nostalgic melancholy." (40-1.)

It is evident that in this passage Lewis interprets the word " symbol " in a quite limited sense. It is roughly equivalent to the " faded metaphor." Through tradition and convention it has come to stand for one thing only. Whether even such a mathematical symbol as 1 would be regarded as a faded metaphor of the kind that " white " obviously is does not become clear in the discussion. But it is altogether plain that in Lewis's vocabulary " symbol " represents a static, denotative, unemotional sign, which can be used for a direct one-to-one correspondence and for nothing more. The " image," on the other hand, is alive, evocative, intense : it can call up a whole range of suggestions and emotions. New and striking images constitute the poet's main contribution to his fellow-men. And as we examine the book still further we find that of all possible images the *metaphor* is in Lewis's view the most characteristic and the most important. " Every poetic image," he writes, " is to some degree metaphorical." " Trends come and go, diction alters, metrical fashions change, even the elemental subject-matter may change almost out of recognition : but metaphor remains, the life-principle of poetry, the poet's chief test and glory." (18, 17.)

I shall return to Lewis's further references to metaphor, but meanwhile we are in a position to formulate his main distinction. It is between symbols and images or between symbols and metaphors. His primary concern is to deal with images and the imagination. The symbol to him is factual, denotative, conventional. But through the image the poet asserts or re-asserts spiritual control over the material ; he draws back from the actual and by coming to grips with it in a creative image, gains the mastery over it. To have a command of metaphor, Aristotle affirms, is the mark of genius—a judgment with which Lewis would be in full agreement. Thus on one side we set the symbol, on the other side the metaphorical image. Whether or not we are prepared to accept this particular terminology, we can scarcely fail to recognise that Lewis is here making a distinction which is important not only for poetry but for every aspect of human life.

So far we have encountered distinctions but no agreed terminology. A greater clarification, I believe, will emerge as we consider the contributions made by two modern philosophers to this field of inquiry. In her book, *Philosophy in a New Key*, Susanne K. Langer considers the place of symbolism in language, ritual and art, and out of her comprehensive survey certain notable distinctions begin to appear. Early in the book she affirms that it is pre-eminently through his symbolic activity that man rises above the level of the animal. " Man's conquest of the world undoubtedly rests on the supreme development of his brain, which allows him to synthesize, delay, and modify his reactions by the interpolation of *symbols* in the gaps and confusions of direct experience, and by means of " verbal signs " to add the experiences of other people to his own." (p. 29.) Thus symbolisation is the all-important activity which distinguishes man from every other known living creature.

From this beginning, Mrs. Langer goes on to point out that there is a profound difference between using symbols and merely using signs. The basic quality of a sign is that it acts as a substitute either for a particular stimulus or for the response to the stimulus. In the famous experiment with the dog and his food, the dog comes in course of time to respond to the *sign* of the food's presence, rather than to the direct sight or smell of the food itself. Similarly, if a response to a certain stimulus is accompanied by a particular sign, in course of time the sign may actually take the place of the response itself. Even animals, then, can respond to signs. Their responses may vary according to the particular structure of their own bodies and the nature of the environment in which they live. But there is nothing to prevent communication with animals by *signs* and nothing to prevent a certain response by *signs*. A dog can even associate a person with a name but only in so far as the name announces a person immediately forthcoming and produces thereby an appropriate response.

Man, however, goes beyond this. To use Mrs. Langer's terminology, man employs signs not only to *indicate* things but also to *represent* them. The thing or person or event does not need to be immediately present within the local environment. The event may have happened long ago, the person may be at the other end of the world. But it is still possible to think of or to refer to or to argue about the event or the person through the use of the characteristically human sign which is best called a *symbol*. In other words the symbol is not, like the simple sign, a direct stimulus but rather an indirect reminder or representation. This distinction between signs and symbols is most interesting and in my judgment most valuable. According to it the sign indicates, the symbol represents : the sign transmits directly, the symbol indirectly or obliquely : the sign announces, the symbol reminds or refers : the sign operates in the immediate context of space and time, the symbol extends the frame of reference indefinitely.

At a later stage in her book Mrs. Langer analyses the distinction in a still more detailed way. " A sign," she asserts, " indicates the existence—past, present or future—of a thing, event or condition. Wet streets are a sign that it has rained. A patter on the roof is a sign that it is raining. A fall of the barometer or a ring around the moon is a sign that it is going to rain." (p. 57.) These are *natural* signs and it is the characteristic of a natural sign that it actually is a part or a symptom of the wider state of affairs which it indicates. But there are also *artificial* signs—the blow of a whistle or the waving of a flag to indicate that a train is about to start. These are not part of the condition which they announce but by custom and agreement they have come to occupy the same one-to-one correspondence to a particular state of affairs as is the case with natural signs. Direct indication and one-to-one correspondence are the altogether important properties of a sign, natural or artificial.

How then are we to define symbols ? " Symbols," says Mrs. Langer, " are not proxy for their objects, but are *vehicles for the conception of objects*. To conceive a thing or a situation is not the same thing as to ' react toward it ' overtly, or to be aware of its presence. In talking *about* things we have conceptions of them, not the things themselves ; and *it is the conceptions, not the things, that symbols directly ' mean.' "* (p. 60.) Thus, whereas the sign announces or directly indicates, the symbol suggests or indirectly represents. The symbol leads the hearer or the watcher to *conceive* or to *imagine* an object or an event. It is not concerned necessarily with direct *action* in the way that the sign must always be. Rather it is concerned with thought and imagination. It is designed to represent a state of affairs. It may do this accurately or inaccurately, vividly or dully, in a complicated or in a simple fashion. But it must represent, at least in some degree, the general pattern of the configuration of which it is a symbol. There is no one-to-one correspondence between symbol and conception, but there are patterns of correspondence which govern the relation between the two and prevent the connection being purely arbitrary and ephemeral.

Such, in brief, is Mrs. Langer's exposition of the fundamental distinction between sign and symbol. There is a further question, however, which she raises and on which she has many illuminating things to say. The question is : Are there different kinds or types or modes of symbolism ? As soon as this question is raised, we find ourselves drawing nearer to the essential concern of Michael Roberts and C. Day Lewis. Is there a form of symbolism applicable to logical and rational thinking which is different from that which is applicable to emotional and imaginative activities ? Mrs. Langer recognises the difficulty of this question but she is not prepared to answer it immediately in the negative. Instead she devotes a chapter to what she calls " Discursive and Presentational Forms." Discursive Forms are employed to set forth clear and definite meanings. Symbols used in this way represent determinate conceptions and the relations between them (i.e. the symbols) are governed by definite rules. Discursive Forms, in other words, are employed within the context of the regularities and the agreed conventions of human experience. But it is obvious that this does not take care of the whole of experience. There are emotions, desires, novelties, irregularities, experiences, which do not fit into the patterns of the discursive forms already in operation. For this second group of experiences the term Presentational Forms is suggested. Here symbols represent indeterminate conceptions. They are connected and combined by less definite rules. They partake more of the quality of picture and moving pattern. They have " presented " themselves to the observer but they do not fit into any preconceived pattern.

At a later stage in her book, Mrs. Langer remarks that " Metaphor is our most striking evidence of *abstractive seeing*, of the power of human minds to use presentational symbols. Every new experience, or new idea about things, evokes first of all some metaphorical expression." (p. 141.) This, I believe, is an important clue and leads directly to the last book to which I intend to refer in this examination of terminology. But before turning to it I shall attempt to summarise the thesis which Mrs. Langer has presented so impressively. Her *first* main distinction is between " signs " and " symbols." A sign directly indicates a thing, event or condition ; a symbol is a vehicle for the conception of a thing, event or condition. Her *second* main distinction is between discursive and presentational symbols. A discursive symbol bears a recognised meaning and obeys well-established rules ; a presentational symbol is evoked by, and evokes, a *new* experience and may break certain recognised rules in order that *new* forms may be created. This second distinction serves to raise the question of the relation between symbol and metaphor, and it is on this point that the notable book by Professor Martin Föss, entitled *Symbol and Metaphor in Human Experience*, has much of value to say.

In the opening pages Foss delivers a challenge to any form of all-embracing symbolism. He will not allow that the forms of art and religion belong to precisely the same category as those of logic and science. The symbolical thinking of the scientist and the logician " has as its goal the ordering of the world into clear and convenient patterns," but this is by no means necessarily true of the prophet or the artist. There are, he judges, two approaches to knowledge and whereas it is legitimate to speak of the one as the symbolical approach, for the other he prefers the term metaphorical. He will not agree that the metaphor is to be regarded simply as a species of the scientific symbol. How can it be so when it is often highly complex and far from clear ? Yet the metaphor exercises an extraordinary power in art and religion. He therefore proposes to elucidate the character of metaphorical thinking and to determine its relationship to other forms of thought.

Having thrown down his challenge, the author proceeds to explain the meaning which he attaches to his two principal terms. He begins by contrasting two views of life which have competed for supremacy throughout the history of human thought. There is the view, generally known as Sensationalism, in which the all-important element is the image and the all-important context is the continuous flux. Man only discovers his true self by yielding himself up to the succession of sensuous images which float across his inner vision. His task is not to separate or to organise or to classify but to receive and to hold and to reflect. Again there is the view known as Rationalism. In this the all-important element is the symbol and the all-important context is the structure of relations. Man only discovers his true self as he sets to work to organise his experience by the aid of symbols which carry a clear-cut meaning. His task is not to feel or to respond but to define and to differentiate and to connect. Both these views Foss rejects as inadequate, but he takes special pains to deal with the second. By so doing he shows clearly what is his own view of symbolism.

Rationalism, he points out, in attempting to define and separate, comes near to breaking up the whole of experience into disconnected parts, and only saves itself from doing this completely by means of its use of the symbol. The symbol, he says, is the part which stands for the whole, which signifies the whole, which represents the whole. This theory can be traced back to Plato and his followers who asserted that the part actually participates in the idea of the whole. It reveals the whole; in a certain sense it is identical with the whole. Symbolism, in this sense, " is exact the more it succeeds in omitting details and abstracting from everything which could distract from the one and only route to the whole. The tendency to exactitude is a tendency to abbreviation, and at the end of this tendency stands the abstract sign, a symbol so utterly simplified that it in fact denotes nothing but itself and so negates its own destination. Surely, such an extreme symbol is no longer a real symbol; it is an empty abstraction and as such just as insignificant as the crude sense datum in its pure factuality, the detached detail in the sensuous flux." (p. 10.)[1]

What, then, does the author mean by the term metaphor? It is in large measure the purpose of the whole book to set forth the meaning of metaphorical thinking in various departments of life. But perhaps the heart of the matter is to be found in a passage where simile is contrasted with metaphor. " The Simile and the analogy," the author writes, " link the unknown to the known, in an expedient and practical way, closing the problematic unity into a familiar pattern. The metaphorical process, on the contrary, raises the problem even there where we seemed at home and shatters the ground on which we had settled down in order to widen our view beyond any limit of a special practical use." " Shatters in order to widen "—this essentially is the function of metaphor. In other parts of the book we read of the metaphor " breaking up," " keeping on the move," " drawing into the disturbing current," " negating," " blasting," " destroying." But this is never the whole process. The metaphor " widens," " transcends," " overcomes," " gives birth to the new," " creates." It is a process of tension and energy. It begins with symbols but it transcends and transforms all symbolic fixations and reductions. It is the secret of all life. It is indeed the innermost secret of the life of God Himself.

We have reviewed a number of modern attempts to bring some degree of order into the confusion which surrounds the use of the terms sacrament, sign and symbol. I have suggested that the term " sacrament " is so limited by its history and particular associations that it is hardly suitable for use in any comprehensive way. We are then left with the terms " sign " and " symbol," but our survey has revealed that even these are used in a great variety of ways by different writers. At the same time it also appears that different writers may be aware of very similar distinctions and divisions though they may express them

[1] There is a kind of entropy in the realm of symbols. This process " has sometimes gone slow, sometimes speeded up ; poetic revolutions have made it retrace its steps for a time ; in the main, however, the direction in which the changes proceed does not alter : the word, a living symbol felt to be somehow inwardly bound to the thing it signifies, tends to become an abstract sign, similar to those employed by algebra or the telegraphic code." (W. Weidle, *The Dilemma of the Arts*, p. 53.)

by different forms of speech.   Let us therefore try to work out our own scheme of classification, bearing in mind the contributions of the writers whose works we have studied and using their insights to guide us in our task.

A TENTATIVE CLASSIFICATION

Let us begin with the lowest layer of human life of which there is reasonable evidence—the area usually designated the unconscious or sub-conscious. This layer may be conceived as having two aspects—the sea of the collective unconscious and the innumerable vessels of the individual unconscious dancing as it were upon its waters. Recognising as I do the difficulty of describing this vast hidden region with any confidence or precision, I would judge that there is good evidence for the assumption that certain regular *patterns* of imagination and behaviour are to be found at all periods in the history of mankind and that they may be regarded as having arisen out of the depths of the collective unconscious. Certain well-defined images seem to occur universally in myths and dreams ; certain corporate activities recur in ways which seem to be independent of the conscious determination of any single individual. In Dr. Jung's terminology there are within the unconscious of us all certain images or archetypes which are the " psychic residua of numberless experiences of the same type " and which are transmitted to us apart from any conscious experience of our own. Or in the words of Heinrich Zimmer, " Ages and attitudes of man that are long gone by still survive in the deeper unconscious layers of our soul. The spiritual heritage of archaic man (the ritual and mythology that once visibly guided his conscious life) has vanished to a large extent from the surface of the tangible and conscious realm, yet survives and remains ever present in the subterranean layers of the unconscious."[1]

At the same time there is sufficient evidence to show that the individual also carries within his own unconscious certain highly specialised images which are derived from experiences in his own past though entirely forgotten by the conscious mind.

[1] Quoted I. Progoff. *Jung's Psychology and its Social Meaning*, p. 252.

Moreover we know that an individual may behave in unusual, even in eccentric ways, by reason, it appears, of certain forces acting in his own unconscious. Neither he nor his neighbours can interpret these particular actions in terms of purely conscious drives or motivations. Thus on the level of the unconscious we may picture a great sea over which there travel waves possessing a recognisable pattern (archetypal images). These waves inevitably influence the motion of each individual ship upon the ocean though each still possesses some small differentiating characteristic of its own. It has some guiding star, some distinctive pattern of unusual behaviour, which constitutes its own identity and governs its particular expression of the archetypal images which are ever seeking individual representation.

As soon as we move up into the daylight of conscious life, we enter the realm of the sign. Most of the writers whose works we have considered agree that man both responds to signs and uses signs himself. Some incline to despise the bare sign, to regard it as belonging to the animal part of his nature (do not animals also respond to signs?) or to look upon it as the degradation of the higher possibilities open to him. There may be elements of truth in these views but the sign appears to be an essential part of human existence and indeed the first expression of conscious life. As we have suggested, the sheer practical needs of life lead to the employment of signs. It takes very little time for a new-born baby to associate a cry with its desire for food ; equally the mother is quick to detect slight variations in baby-cries which may indicate that other needs beside food have to be met. Thus the ground work of all conscious life is the use of signs and this use is to be deprecated only when it stands in the way of or takes the place of something higher and better.

Immediately the question arises, however, as to whether there are any broad differences to be observed in the nature and use of *signs*. Do all signs belong to one general class ? Mrs. Langer has pointed out the difference between " natural " signs and " artificial " signs. Michael Roberts has spoken of signs which have an intellectual reference and those which bear some emotional stimulus. Each of these distinctions seems to me to be better covered by extending the division which we suggested for the layer of the human unconscious. Some signs belong primarily to man's *communal* life : some depend rather upon *individual* experiment and development. If this division be allowed, " natural " signs fall into the first category, " artificial " into the second ; the more intellectual referents fall into the first, the more emotional into the second. This division between " communal " and " individual " signs is, however, linked with another important division which we must now consider.

In all matters which concern the collective or the community the important quality is *similarity* : in matters which concern the ultimate establishment of individuality, the important quality is that of *dissimilarity* or *distinctiveness*. In saying this I am not inferring for a moment that these two qualities can be held in complete isolation from one another ; the community and the individual are interrelated at every point. But collective life becomes an impossibility unless certain patterns of similarity can be established ; on the other hand, the development of individuality also becomes impossible unless some scope is allowed for difference. Now it can be seen at once that " natural " signs are likely to be associated with the " similarity " class. The wet road being recognised as a sign of rain, the patter of the raindrops on the roof being recognised as a sign of a shower —these are " natural " signs because rain is a regular phe- nomenon in the natural world and one shower of rain is to all intents and purposes similar to another. Man's primary effort in relation to his natural environment is to discover similarities and reliabilities : " signs " of similarity are therefore of great importance and a source of great comfort to him. On the other hand an " artificial " sign is normally created by the unusual and distinctive behaviour of a particular individual. He initiates a method or a pattern in which one object is associated with another unlike object, one action with another which is quite dissimilar. (The association of the bell with feeding-time in Pavlov's experiment was quite arbitrary but it served to establish an " artificial " sign in that particular context.) Thus man's primary effort in seeking to develop his own individuality is to discover some distinctive mode of behaviour or some differen- tiating mark which will distinguish him from his fellows. Even the process of " naming " is an example of the sign of difference and we seem to be justified in regarding this quality of dis-similarity as the peculiar mark of individual life.

This division also holds good, I believe, in relation to the intellectual and emotional life of mankind. Speaking generally, it may be said that intellectual systems belong more to the collective life of mankind, emotional experiences more to the individual. Intellectual activities are always moving in the direction of order and order is based upon patterns of similarity. The ideal of the intellectual worker is not to be swayed by emotion (though, as a matter of fact, emotion will always enter into his labours), but to deal with his evidence coolly and dispassionately, fairly and comprehensively, seeking similarities and proportions, and thereby gradually building up a structural framework within which human experience can gain stability and meaning. In such an endeavour signs of similarity are obviously of enormous importance. They are the foundations and the ties of his structure. The more he can build by patterns of symmetry and proportion and congruent relationship, the more stable and enduring and pleasing his building is likely to be. And such a building is a necessity for any kind of ordered community life.

On the other hand, the individual who dares to do anything contrary to the accepted pattern of the society in which he lives, passes thereby through a profound emotional experience. He is defying tradition, he is challenging convention, he is venturing into the realm of the novel and the unexplored. His emotional life is shaken to its foundations. And the sign which comes to be associated with the new adventure or experience always carries with it an overtone of emotional stimulus. Emotion is contagious. If in the first instance a sign of contrast or novelty inspired a feeling of emotional disturbance, subsequent uses of the sign or encounters with it are likely to produce at least some marks of emotion also. Thus the development of individuality cannot be dissociated from emotional disturbance, and emotive signs may therefore be regarded as belonging to the overall category of signs of dissimilarity or distinctiveness. On the level of conscious life, then, we find ourselves in the realm of *the sign*, a realm which can be divided into two overlapping divisions: on the one side signs of similarity, corporeity, order: on the other side signs of novelty, individuality, emotional surprise. The very constitution of man's being as an individual within society does not allow him to make any absolute division between these two classes of signs but compels him to take account of both emphases if he is to be true to the wholeness of his nature.

Finally, there is the momentous step by which man advances from the sign to the symbol. The essential character of this step has, I believe, been adequately described by Mrs. Langer, but a deeper understanding of its significance may be gained by combining her insights with those of Professor Foss. If symbols go beyond signs by making possible the *conception* of an object rather than the direct re-action to an object, then a division amongst symbols, corresponding to that which we have outlined amongst signs, can readily be imagined. In the first place there are symbols which are primarily related to the life of the community : these symbols gain their force and appropriateness by emphasising the notes of similarity, system, order, proportion, universality. In the second place there are those which are primarily related to the life of the individual : these gain their energy and creativeness by emphasising the notes of contrast, novelty, freedom, paradox, uniqueness. Let us look at each of these classes in more detail.

Signs, as I have said, must be as simple and direct as possible. They must point the way to immediate action. Symbols, on the other hand, need not be direct, for they are not necessarily designed for immediate use. One of the main principles which determines their appropriateness is the principle of *economy*. If they are to be stored up for future use, if they are to cover a very wide area of experience, then the more compact they are the better. Further, they must build upon the already known and seek to extend it, even to universalise it, and the method they will employ is that of *analogy*. As Mrs. Langer points out : " The only characteristic that a picture must have in order to be a picture of a certain thing is an arrangement of elements analogous to the arrangement of salient visual elements in the object." (p. 70.). A similarity of pattern, in other words, is the essential characteristic ; so long as the relation of parts within the symbol is similar to that within the reality it can fulfil its proper function. Of course some symbols may be more effective than others, but the principle remains the same at all times.

Analogy and economy I have defined as the two main principles which operate in the building up of a system of effective and appropriate symbols. It will readily be seen that each of these principles tends to keep the other in check. Details of similarity can be multiplied almost indefinitely but then the principle of economy is at stake : economy can be used to the point at which a closed system of abstract formulæ becomes the ideal if not the actuality and at this point the symbol reverts to the sign and the idea of similarity becomes irrelevant. The excessive use of the principle of analogy leads to the weaving of elaborate patterns of fantasy and allegory. The excessive use of the principle of economy leads to the formulation of precise and exact systems of logic, mathematics and science. I do not deny that these patterns and these systems have their place in human thought so long as they are kept in check and provided they do not presume to impose themselves upon the whole of experience. For the general life of mankind, however, the more important tool is the pictorial and the analogical symbol. By means of this instrument of thought man brings order and proportion into his experience and gains a vision of a world which is not chaotic and insecure but which possesses stabilities and regularities which make an ordered existence possible.

The symbols so far considered belong to our first general category of the communal and the intellectual. The second category of the individual and the emotional does not yield so easily to an agreed vocabulary. C. Day Lewis, for example, disparages the term " symbol " and concentrates his discussion upon the word " image." Martin Foss also dislikes the term " symbol " as a description of the creative force which he has in mind and he therefore decides for the word " metaphor." I believe, however, that it is legitimate to retain the word " symbol " even within this general area, so long as we safeguard it by means of checking principles comparable to those suggested for the former class. The first principle to be observed is that of *intensity*. If symbols of this kind (the symbols, that is to say, of contrast and novelty) are to preserve their usefulness, they must be capable of embodying layer upon layer of creative meaning. Behind the symbol there normally lies a strong emotional experience but unless its expression be concentrated into a tightly-packed intensity, it fails to have more than a strictly limited usefulness. Secondly, symbols of this kind always express a leap towards the beyond and the unknown, and to do this they reveal some kind of *tension*. When a common symbol is suddenly taken and applied to an object or an event or a situation to which it does not properly belong there is bound to be surprise and tension. But this is the essence of metaphor. "Metaphor," writes C. Day Lewis, "is the natural language of tension, of excitement, because it enables man by a compressed violence of expression to rise to the level of the violent situation which provokes it. Images are, as it were, a breaking down of the high tension of life so that it can be safely used to light and warm the individual heart." (p. 99.) There must be distance and yet there must be togetherness : there must be contrast and yet there must be points of similarity : there must be tension and yet there must be communion. Such are the characteristics of metaphor in every department of life.

Intensity and metaphorical tension I have defined as the two essential principles of this class of symbol. The symbol which expresses the new emotion, however, may be so intense, so enigmatic, so highly individualised, that it becomes a locked mystery and then the principle of metaphorical tension is at stake ; or the principle of tension can be applied with such violence that the two contrasting parts tend to break asunder and all concentration of meaning is lost. Thus the excessive use of the principle of intensity leads to the production of esoteric forms such as the riddle, the apocalypse, the mystery story : the excessive use of the principle of tension leads to the creation of the fraudulent, the grotesque, the absurd. Even these forms may have a temporary and severely limited part to play in times of extremity, but in the hands of fanatics they become utterly destructive. For the reinvigoration of the general life of mankind the altogether important factor is the imaginative and the metaphorical symbol. By means of this expression of emotion, man gains freshness of vision and renewal of energy and sees to each of the three successive levels is the image, the sign and the symbol respectively. In the realm of the symbol I have made a division between the analogical and the metaphorical classes or types. This general frame of reference might be depicted diagramatically in this way:

	CORPORATE	INDIVIDUAL
Transcending immediate consciousness	The Analogical Symbol	The Metaphorical Symbol
Conscious	The Natural Sign	The Artificial Sign
Sub-conscious	The Archetypal Image	The Traumatic Image

My main thesis, which I shall now try to establish by examining various aspects of human existence and activity, is that only as man cultivates a constant inter-relationship between these different levels of his experience and above all only as he maintains a constant dialectic between the two types of symbolism here defined can he move towards the fullness of his destiny in relation to God, nature, and his fellow-men.

The aspects of existence and activity which I have chosen for more careful study are those which belong to the normal outward life of mankind. Man must have a *spatial* environment from which he can " suck in the orderliness " (Erwin Schrödinger's phrase) on which his very life depends. But even within this spatial environment there are rhythms and recurrences and novel events which compel attention and mould experience in terms of before-and-after or of remote-and-near in *time*. Space and time are not independent but are sufficiently unlike to justify separate consideration and indeed have normally, in man's history, been represented by different classes of symbols.

Within this space-time environment stands man himself. But man cannot exist in isolation from his fellows. His life depends upon a social as well as upon a natural environment and within this social environment it is possible to distinguish between persons-in-themselves and persons-in-active-relation-ship-with-others. A person may occupy a certain position in society by reason of tradition, custom, reputation, birth-relationship, general acclaim or consent. As such he (or she) becomes a significant figure for all those who belong to this particular social environment. On the other hand a person may make a direct impact upon his fellows in society by means of his activities. These activities may be of many varied kinds but in the main they are likely to appeal either to the ear or to the eye. Through language in its manifold forms, personal relationship is established by means of ear and mouth : through significant actions and gestures it is promoted by means of eye and limb. In other words a person's words and actions become significant factors for all those who belong to his or her particular social environment. And although a person-in-himself can never be independent of his words and activities, it is in fact the case that in human history not only have words and actions been signifi-cant as symbols but also the person himself who occupies a particular status or position in society has come to be regarded as symbolically significant for the life of the larger corporate whole.

I shall first, therefore, seek to examine man's relation to his natural environment and his creation of symbolic forms within this context. Next I shall look at various kinds of time-symbolism, giving particular attention to its development within the Christian tradition. Passing then to man's social environment, I shall examine in turn the significance of symbolic personal figures, of symbolic language-forms and of symbolic outward activities. This will lead finally to a more detailed study of the ritual dramas (including word and gesture) which have played so large a part in traditional Christian symbolic activity. The inquiry as a whole will be carried forward within the skeleton framework already presented in diagram form but no attempt will be made to confine different aspects of human experience within watertight compartments. Both in life itself and in the symbolic representation of life, departmentalisation is dangerous while isolationism spells death.

CHAPTER TWO

The Symbolism of Nature

THE VARIATIONS in man's attitude to his natural environment may be vividly illustrated by comparing the general pattern of life in the Old World with that of the New. The contrast might be developed and elaborated in numerous ways. The Old is conservative and traditional, the New is liberal and adventurous : the Old seeks ever to preserve the essential framework of its social structure, the New attempts to adapt its forms to the rapidly changing conditions of frontier life : the Old clings to the inherited wisdom of the past, the New adopts the scientific techniques which prove to be most efficient for meeting the demands of the present. These and many other differences might be noted and yet they would all, I suggest, be varied forms of a still more fundamental divergence of attitude and outlook.

Basically this divergence is to be found in man's total relationship with Nature—with the soil and the trees, with the fruits of the earth and the harvest of the seas, with the hills and the valleys, with the sunshine and the rain-storm, with the gentle streams and the swiftly flowing rivers. Is Nature a bountiful mother, a kindly nurse, a protective guardian ? Or is Nature a wild and untamed virgin, a possible partner though at present suspicious and even hostile ? Is it man's task and responsibility to cherish and even to reverence this Nature which has begotten him or is it his aim and object to gain possession of and even to subdue this Nature which confronts him and frustrates him ? Is his role a dominantly passive one, in which he receives from Nature, learns from Nature, co-operates with the long-established processes of Nature, dedicates himself to Nature ? Or is his role a dominantly active one, in which he experiments with Nature, seeks to subjugate Nature, increasingly controls Nature and gradually moulds Nature to his own heart's desire?

This contrast of attitudes may be readily illustrated by comparing, for example, the nature poetry of Wordsworth with that of Mr. Robert Frost. In Wordsworth there is the sense that Nature, being herself completely in harmony with the Divine Will, can inspire and train her human children to attain their own true destiny by humbly conforming themselves to the pattern which she reveals.

> Still constant in her worship, still
> Conforming to the eternal Will,
> Whether men sow or reap the fields,
> Divine monition Nature yields,
> That not by bread alone we live,
> Or what a hand of flesh can give;
> That every day should leave some part
> Free for a sabbath of the heart:
> So shall the seventh be truly blest,
> From morn to eve, with hallowed rest.

Here one can feel the deep confidence of a mind which does not doubt the orderliness and trustworthiness of Nature and delights to learn lessons from the forms and patterns which she unconsciously reveals.

On the other hand, as a reviewer has suggested, while Mr. Robert Frost is passionately devoted to his New England countryside, he is aware that there are elements of disorderliness and wildness in nature which man has not yet conquered and which he must never forget, " The elemental spirits that wish invading man no good are still lurking in the woods of New England to the sensibility of the poet. The wolf is only in retreat. There is a certain exhaustion in man, too, as a result of the huge pioneering effort, which leaves a potentially dangerous situation—dangerous to human integrity. There is a reflection of it even in such an apparently artless poem as the often quoted *The Pasture* :

I'm going out to clean the pasture spring;
I'll only stop to rake the leaves away
(And wait to watch the water clear,
                                        I may):
I shan't be gone long.—You come too.

Is there not, as an undertone of this poem, the fact that he *may* be gone long—may be gone, in fact, for ever?" (*Times Literary Supplement*, March 9, 1951). Elsewhere one can feel the sense of wariness and watchfulness, the remembrance of a bitter struggle not yet completed, the love of that which has been won coupled with the haunting fear that the unsown and the untamed might once again recover that which it has so recently lost. Wordsworth was aware that sternness and retribution were parts of Nature's orderliness and because of this he sometimes regarded Nature with awe and even fear. But this is different from the irrational and unpredictable elements in Nature which Mr. Frost dreads. These can threaten and even terrorise. Man must watch the signs and remain on his guard.

As soon as this general distinction has been established, certain obvious qualifications must be made. No longer, for instance, is the Old World a coherent unity. Since the outbreak of war in 1914 a spirit of nihilism has been abroad and this belongs to neither of the outlooks which I have sought to define. It must, moreover, be admitted that in large sections of Europe the links with the past seem to have been totally destroyed. The continuity of social life has been broken and even Nature itself has been so mutilated and deformed that it is desperately hard to regard it with the same feelings as hitherto. On the other hand, there are now large areas in the New World where man has lived so long with Nature that he has come to share much of the outlook which we have associated with the Old. When a particular section of land has been tended and cared for over a period of more than three centuries, it begins to be regarded with the same affection and devotion as is felt in the Old World towards time-honoured places and customs. In Massachusetts and Virginia, as Mr Frost suggests in another poem, men now not only possess—they are possessed by the land. Above all, it must be admitted that the two attitudes which I have attempted to define will rarely, if ever, be found in complete isolation the one from the other. Within any society there will be those whose attitude to Nature will lean more heavily in one direction than the other.

Yet when all qualifications have been made, it remains true that whereas in any wide view the *typical* attitude of the European towards Nature may be described as one of filial love and devotion, of responsibility for due care and preservation, of semi-religious reverence and regard, the typical attitude of the North American may be described as strong and masterful, as inspired by a sense of responsibility to mould to a particular purpose, as relatively indifferent to any spiritual forces which may be operating within the Nature which has to be conquered. I have set out the contrast somewhat starkly and crudely in order to illustrate the possibility of holding sharply contrasting views of the natural order in which we live. For it is the case that different peoples at different periods have been governed by varying attitudes to Nature ; and these divergent outlooks have determined in no small measure the place allotted to symbolic forms in their communal life. The way in which a man or a social group regards Nature soon manifests itself in and through the value attached to signs and symbols. Let us then seek to gain some idea of the most notable attitudes to Nature which have emerged during the course of man's historical development.

INDIA

Prior to the impact of Western ideas upon Indian culture, a relatively homogeneous civilisation had maintained a steady pattern of attitude and outlook for more than two millenia. There were invasions by foreigners and these brought new ideas in their train but the main characteristics of the Hindu way of life were but little disturbed. This is not altogether surprising when it is remembered that India consists of a kind of basin bounded by the Himalayas on the north and by the sea on the south-east and south-west. Within this basin conditions are extraordinarily regular and even uniform. Nature seems to be entirely self-sufficient and self-contained. The seasons are chiefly determined by the coming of the monsoon. Month after month the long dry season continues with the burning heat of the sun by day and the brilliant shining of the stars by night. Then when all is parched and weary the monsoon arrives, bringing torrential rains and a miraculous revival of life to the barren earth. In the sultry aftermath Nature luxuriates but man wilts in the damp heat. There is a hot haze which spreads its garment over all natural phenomena and these tend to lose all marks of distinction and to merge into one another. Existence is vegetative and organic and the teeming life of the jungle becomes the symbolic representation of all that is. Every phase of the annual cycle recurs with absolute regularity and the very changes of Nature seem only to be aspects of its eternal change-lessness. So man does not seek to conquer Nature, nor does he try to modify its course in any way. He is a part of the life of Nature and his wisdom is to identify himself with her, to learn her ways, to be enfolded within her embrace, to realise his essential union with this universal mother to whom he unreservedly belongs.

In such a view of the universe no particular form or con-figuration can be regarded as more significant than any other. Man may create forms or change forms but this does not indicate any variation in his total interpretation of life. Vegetation is prodigal in its production of forms : they come into existence, decay, die, are reborn. All alike may be regarded as expressions of the vital essence of the universe. (Atman.) " The atman is the same in the ant, the same in the gnat, the same in the elephant, the same in these three worlds . . . the same in the whole universe." (B. Heimann quoting from the Brhadaranyaka-Upanisad in her book, *Indian and Western Philosophy*.) So " any individual shape whatever, even that of a personal God and of a single world, is considered purely accidental and transitory." (*Ibid.*, p. 38.) The stream of life flows on unceasingly and man's salvation lies, not in creating forms nor in controlling his environ-ment, but in being completely absorbed into the undifferentiated flux of existence. " The highest state man can attain is when the senses, mind, intellect, do not move, all desires in the heart cease, all attachments are cut, and the individual is joined to or absorbed in the universal." (G. Phillips, *The Gospel in the World*, p. 136.)

What then is the significance of the religious sculptures and art-forms which abound in India ? If Nature is all, if one Divine life pulsates through all phenomena, if all particular forms are devoid of special significance, if God and Nature and Man are ultimately indistinguishable, what place is there for symbolism of any kind ? The general answer to these questions seems to be that *all* temples, *all* images, *all* sculptures, *all* phallic symbols, are archetypal expressions of the one ultimate cosmic reality, that all outward manifestations of form are to be regarded merely as undulations upon the sea of Brahman, the Universal Soul, the unchanging divine consciousness. The carved and sculptured images are entirely continuous with the life of nature within which they are set. They are designed, not to point beyond themselves, not to suggest relationships of a transcendental kind, but rather to act as wave-forms, playing, as it were, upon the surface of the universal unconscious. The ideal is that all particular forms shall be absorbed into the universal All.

Such a view of Nature allows no real place for symbolism or even for signification in the sense in which we are interpreting those terms. Nature is the ultimate reality : men, animals, trees, plants are illusory forms within that reality : the only function of outward images is to express this truth more vividly and to draw man back into the universal unconsciousness within which his true salvation lies.

GREECE

The all-important difference between the Greek view of Nature and the Indian is to be found in the emphasis which the former lays upon the operation of *mind*. In the main, the Indian has been indifferent to consciously determined form or orderliness. Nature is a luxuriant profusion of images, all of them surface-movements upon the ocean of a single cosmic life. But the Greek, as to some extent the Egyptian before him, could not rest content with such a conception. He was convinced that there was a principle of world-order and that this principle could be discovered, or at least comprehended, by the human *mind*. He was not concerned to subdue Nature or to conform it to a preconceived pattern. That would have seemed to him not only undesirable but impossible. Rather he desired to conform his own thinking to the inherent pattern of Nature itself and to allow his own mind to develop in the way that the inner mind of Nature directed.

This point has been excellently stated by Professor R. G. Collingwood in *The Idea of Nature*. " Greek natural science," he writes, " was based on the principle that the world of nature is saturated or permeated by mind. Greek thinkers regarded the presence of mind in nature as the source of that regularity or orderliness in the natural world whose presence made a science of nature possible. . . . They conceived mind, in all its manifestations, whether in human affairs or elsewhere, as a ruler, as a dominating or regulating element, imposing order first upon itself and then upon everything belonging to it, primarily its own body and secondarily that body's environment."

In their view the whole world of nature was alive and intelligent. " The life and intelligence of creatures inhabiting the earth's surface and the regions adjacent to it, they argued, represent a specialised local organisation of this all-pervading vitality and rationality, so that a plant or animal, according to their ideas, participates in its own degree psychically in the life-process of the world's ' soul ' and intellectually in the activity of the world's ' mind,' no less than it participates materially in the physical organisation of the world's ' body.' " (pp. 3-4.)

This view may be designated an " organic " view of Nature and Collingwood himself uses the term " intelligent organism " as a convenient description of it. He points out that in its developed form it rests upon a simple analogy. Just as the human body consists of many parts, all in motion and performing different functions, yet held together in a delicately balanced harmony by the mind which controls and directs them all, so it is inferred that Nature itself, with its infinitely many parts performing their several operations, is constituted a harmonious whole by a cosmic mind whose inner principle is that of perfect regularity and orderliness. Thus the famous saying of Protagoras which has been regarded as an apt description of the Greek view of life : " Man is the measure of all things "—is entirely applicable to the Greek view of Nature. Man is a body, informed by mind : so also is Nature. Man's true end is to live in conformity with the logos of his being : Nature does, in fact, operate in conformity with the logos of its being. In other words Nature is an " intelligent organism " whose inner principles of organisation are changeless and eternal. Man is an " intelligent organism " who through the exercise of his intelligence comes to know the law of his own being and makes it his aim to conform himself to it.

What then may be said of the religious art-forms and ritual-actions which formed so distinctive a part of Greek culture ? In essence these were all intended to express the logos of Nature and thereby to strengthen and fulfil it. Man himself in the development of his own life trains and disciplines his body, forms regular habits, organises his pattern of living, according to a certain rhythm and orderliness. The Greek was well aware that a life which is without form is insignificant and ultimately inhuman. So he set before himself the ideal of " *Mens sana in corpore sano* " and made the balanced development of the human body one of his highest aims. But if the logos of the human body could express itself in this way, could not the logos of Nature also express itself symbolically through human art-forms and artifacts ? There was in all this no thought of subduing or dominating Nature but rather of attaining such sympathy with Nature as to be able to co-operate in the expression of those perfect forms which Nature itself is always embodying in the material with which it works. So we find in the art forms of Greece some of the most remarkable attempts ever made to express in wood and stone those forms which were believed to be immanent in Nature itself.

As I have already suggested, the dominant notes within the Greek concept of nature were regularity and orderliness. The movements of the heavenly bodies, the recurrence of the seasons, the rhythm of the tides, birth and death, day and night—all these impressed upon the inquiring mind the importance of proportion, symmetry, balance, rhythm, harmony. So we find these notes determining the construction of his temples, the sculpturing of his images, the performance of his rites, the creation of his dramas. Even the games, in which athletes sought to excel one another in achievement through the disciplined movements of the human body, had a cosmic character. In all these ways the Greek was seeking to represent the life of Nature and at the same time to support and renew the life of Nature. He was not unaware of the forces of disintegration and disruption which threatened the ordered life of Nature at all times. His task was to forestall the operation of all such destructive influences and to employ his own mind and imagination in constructing visible objects of beauty and order. In the main he does not seem to have conceived of the possibility of repairing actual breakdowns of the cosmic order though Plato and the great dramatists were moving in this direction. To represent or at least to suggest the Divine perfection and to promote cosmic harmony through the construction of beautiful forms out of the materials of mundane existence—this was the supreme aim of the Greek and this has been his legacy of inexhaustible value to later generations of mankind.

EARLY SEMITIC NOMADS

Let us now look at a very different area of the world and a very different philosophy of life. It would be hard to exaggerate the importance in human history of the vast tract of country bordered on one side by the valley of the Nile and on the other side by the valley of the Tigris-Euphrates. Within this area three of the great religions of the world had their origin and these religions have without question inherited certain basic attitudes and outlooks which belonged to the earliest dwellers within this particular section of the earth's surface. Probably before any considerable settlements were made in the more fertile lands, there were nomad clans wandering in the desert spaces of Arabia and the arid steppes of Sinai and it will be of value to gain some idea of their general religious outlook before coming to the Hebrew view of the natural world which is our chief concern.

The first and most obvious thing to be said of this early

nomadic life is that it was hard, ruthless and even savage. Man was engaged in a never-ending struggle with Nature, with wild beasts, with hostile tribes, with demonic forces. He could never settle down—his very security depended upon constant movement. He could seldom relax except on the occasions when he had gained some signal triumph over his enemies or had concluded some league of friendship with a formerly hostile clan. He had always to struggle to maintain his food-supply and water was a constant anxiety. Moreover, the tension under which he lived was made the greater by reason of the fact that the places from which he had the greatest chance of replenishing his stores of food and drink were normally the most dangerous to approach. The place where he was safest and happiest was the wide open desert and yet that was the one place where he could never make a permanent dwelling.

In a deeply interesting examination of the character of the life of these early nomads, Robertson Smith has shown that the special objects of their fear were the evil spirits and the wild beasts which inhabited the places where water was to be found. The evil spirits were conceived in realistic fashion as capable of assuming many forms but as having their lairs or houses in particular trees or caves or springs. They were believed to be in league with the animals which were man's inveterate enemies and his only hope was to attack them and drive them out of any locus which he desired to use for his own purposes. But this was a task which he could not possibly perform in his own strength. Only by dependence upon his own tribal god, the god of his ancestors and the personal protector of his clan, could he hope to expel these hostile forces from any particular spot. The most notable events of his historical existence, then, came to be those in which through the help of his god and of his fellow clansmen he succeeded in clearing a tract of ground of evil spirits and unfriendly beasts and making it a sanctuary for the habitation of his own god and a place for his own refuge.

In a graphic description of the conflict between the gods and the demons, Robertson Smith points out that the altogether distinctive characteristic of the gods was their relationship to men. Each god had a band of human dependents and wor-

shippers whereas the demons had no friendly intercourse with
men but dwelt with wild beasts in deserted places. "The
demons," he writes, "like the gods, have their particular haunts
which are regarded as awful and dangerous places. But the
haunt of the *jinn* (i.e. the demons) differs from a sanctuary as
the *jinn* themselves differ from gods. The one is feared and
avoided, the other is approached, not indeed without awe, but
yet with hopeful confidence ; for though there is no essential
physical distinction between demons and gods, there is the
fundamental moral difference that the *jinn* are strangers and so,
by the law of the desert, enemies, while the god, to the worshippers who frequent his sanctuary, is a known and friendly
power. In fact the earth may be said to be parcelled out between
demons and wild beasts on the one hand, and gods and men on
the other. To the former belong the untrodden wilderness with
all its unknown perils, the wastes and jungles that lie outside
the familiar tracks and pasture grounds of the tribe, and which
only the boldest men venture upon without terror ; to the latter
belong the regions that man knows and habitually frequents,
and within which he has established relations, not only with
his human neighbours, but with the supernatural beings that
have their haunts side by side with him. And as man gradually
encroaches on the wilderness and drives back the wild beasts
before him, so the gods in like manner drive out the demons,
and spots that were once feared, as the habitation of mysterious
and presumably malignant powers, lose their terrors and either
become common ground or are transferred into the seats of
friendly deities. From this point of view the recognition of
certain spots as haunts of the gods is the religious expression
of the gradual subjugation of nature by man. In conquering the
earth for himself primitive man has to contend not only with
material difficulties but with superstitious terror of the unknown,
paralysing his energies and forbidding him freely to put forth
his strength to subdue nature to his use. Where the unknown
demons reign he is afraid to set his foot and make the good
things of nature his own. But where the god has his haunt he
is on friendly soil, and has a protector near at hand ; the
mysterious powers of nature are his allies instead of his enemies,
' he is in league with the stones of the field, and the wild beasts

of the field are at peace with him.' " (W. R. Smith, *The Religion of the Semites*, 2nd Ed., pp. 121-2.)

In this picture certain features stand out clearly. First and foremost we observe two principles confronting one another in a life-and-death struggle. On the one side there are the gods of the light, of the high places, of the clean and open uplands ; on the other side there are the demons of the darkness, of the abyss, of the wild and desolate places. On the one side there are civilised men with friendly animals and fruit-bearing trees and springs of fresh water ; on the other side are barbarians and wild beasts and untamed jungles and poisonous waters. A second feature of interest is the conception of the relation of gods and demons to natural phenomena. There is nothing to suggest that these supernatural beings are regarded as vague, shadowy, insubstantial spirits. Rather they are thought of as possessing a fluid-like life-substance which can pass in and out of human beings, animals, trees, springs, rocks, etc. Thus natural phenomena may become the temporary residence of gods or demons and may be used by them for particular manifestations as they see fit. There is little speculation about what these supernatural powers may be doing in their disembodied forms of existence. What is of paramount importance for man is that he should be aware of those places which are frequented by friendly gods and those which are the haunts of the demons. He has little regard for or concern for nature as such. What he wants to know is how and when and where the friendly divine beings are operating through the medium of natural forms and how the places under the dominion of the evil powers may be cleared of their influence and made the manifesting place of the god to whom he owes his allegiance.

Thus the general attitude towards nature is vastly different from that of the civilisations which we have hitherto considered. There is little sense of dependence upon nature as such or of reverence for nature. Certain highly individual freaks or excrescences of nature are regarded with awe because through them the divine has been manifested on some occasion. They must therefore be treated with due carefulness, even with reverence, as being, as it were, " charged " with divine potency, as being images of the numinous. Where natural phenomena are under

the dominion of evil powers, man can only move under the
guidance and direction of his own divine leader in any attempt
to set them free. His great source of safety and strength is to be
found in co-operating with gods, humans, and other animate
beings who are on the side of the " good." Any forms or
practices which will promote the spirit of co-operation and mutual
aid are worthy of a high place in his scale of values. So far as
the forms and patterns of nature are concerned, there is little
disposition to copy or reproduce them. They may be " good " :
they may be " evil." Everything depends upon the kind of
divine being who is inhabiting them or using them for his own
purposes.

Among these early nomads of the deserts and open plains,
no attempt was made to construct sacred buildings or sculptures
or images or to establish a regular cultus. A rough heap of
stones might be erected, a rock of unusual shape and size might
be visited and anointed, a ring of trees or stones might serve
as a sacred enclosure, an isolated tree might be regarded as the
abode of a numen, acts of homage and obeisance might be
performed. But in all this there was little regard for regular
natural forms, or for artistic human designs. Man's chief concern
was to maintain friendly relations with his own god and with
his fellow tribesmen and to extend, where possible, the area over
which his god could rule and through which he could bestow
benefits upon his worshippers. His own traumatic experiences
largely determined his religious behaviour.

ISRAEL

The early traditions of the Hebrews show that their ancestors
belonged to the nomadic or semi-nomadic tribes who ranged
the open deserts of the Middle East. Even after the settlement
in Canaan, men looked back nostalgically to the days when their
fathers lived in tents, and in the stories of the patriarchs we are
given a vivid picture of the customs and ideas which belonged
to this earlier age. Sometimes we may recognise a tendency to
idealise the life of the desert dwellers but we may believe that
the witness to their general attitudes and outlooks is substantially

correct. It is altogether probable that many of their underlying assumptions about their god and his relations to the world and to men were carried over unchanged into the thought of subsequent generations.

The first thing which must strike the reader of the early narratives is their intense interest in the personal actors in the various scenes. The *setting* is of quite secondary importance. What matters most is the words men spoke and the actions they performed. The chief characters are men of dignity and honour and a rugged independence. The central figure is usually the father of the family and he it is who has a direct personal relationship with the family of God. God appears to him and speaks with him ; he on his part orders his own life and that of his family in obedience to the revelation which he has received. The commerce between the deity and the patriarchal family was exceedingly intimate, the god being regarded as the supreme father or leader of the clan, the patriarch as his son, his representative, his friend. The god on his part covenanted to watch over the family of his choice, to give them a secure dwelling-place, to protect them from their enemies and to bless them with fertility in the home and in the folds. They on their part covenanted to keep themselves separate from peoples serving other gods, to bring gifts to their own deity, to obey his commands, to consult him in all their plans. The god and the patriarchal family, in fact, were bound together within one living society.

What, then, was the view of the world within which the commerce between man and his god took place ? Actually little is said in the narratives about happenings in the world of Nature. The patriarchs were more concerned about their flocks and their herds and their chance encounters with other tribesmen than about the structure of the world around them. Yet they were aware that unusual happenings in the world of Nature—the storm, the fierce wind, the thunder and lightning, the long drought—were all in some way manifestations of the power of their own deity. In the early stories little attention is paid to the regularities or the orderliness of Nature—that emphasis was to come later. Instead the general attitude seems to have been one of gratitude for the gifts which God had provided through the natural order for the needs of men, together with a sense of awe and wonder in the presence of uncommon events when it appeared that God was manipulating nature in order to set forward His purposes or to make known His will.

This general attitude comes to clearer expression in the narratives which tell of the deliverance from Egypt and the settlement in Canaan. The relatively simple life of the nomads has been left behind. Now the Hebrew tribes find themselves exposed to the complexities of civilised life and the oppressive influences of peoples stronger than themselves. In this new situation they are more dependent than ever before upon the protection and guidance of superhuman powers. So in the records of the struggle with Pharaoh in Egypt, of the passage through the Red Sea, of the wilderness wanderings, of the conflicts with the inhabitants of Canaan and Syria, the control which Yahweh exercises over the phenomena of Nature is acclaimed with far greater emphasis than had been called for in quieter days. He has chosen Israel to be His people, He has called them to fulfil a particular purpose. He will therefore use the forces of Nature to hinder and distress the enemies of Israel, He will use them also to succour and protect the people of His own choice. So far we find little interest in Nature as such. There is no evidence that Nature was regarded as an independent entity, having laws and structures of its own. Rather there is the confidence that the demons and false gods who have exercised control over the powers of Nature at particular places and times are being dispossessed and that Yahweh Himself is bringing even the stars in their courses to the assistance of the people of His choice.

This fundamental subjectivity, as Elmslie calls it,[1] persists, it appears, until the time of the Exile. It is true that when the Kingdom was established in Palestine and life became more settled there began to be a greater interest in the life of Nature in the fields and the vineyards. The religion of the Canaanites was dominantly a nature-religion : the festivals and ceremonies were designed to maintain the fertility and the abundance of the vegetable and animal kingdom. All too readily the Israelites were inclined to adopt the ritual-forms of their neighbours

[1] Cp. W. A. L. Elmslie. *How Came Our Faith?* pp. 52-3.

even though they sought to employ them with a different reference. Yahweh thus came to be associated in fuller measure with the immanental life-processes of Nature and in this way there were approximations to forms of religious expression which we have considered in other contexts. But ever and anon prophetic voices would recall the people to their true faith and they would acknowledge again the God of the Covenant who had done mighty acts in the world of nature for their benefit and who at all times reigned supreme, controlling Nature, operating not so much *in* Nature as *through* Nature, for the benefit of His people.

Torn from their own land and forced to live in the midst of a strange civilisation, the Jews touched hitherto unknown depths of earthly sorrow and despair. Yet some of their number mounted to hitherto unknown heights of spiritual confidence and hope. These latter knew that Yahweh had not been defeated, that He held in His hands all the corners of the earth, that the hosts of heaven were under His control. They saw Him exalted above the universe as its creator, preserver, controller, fulfiller. Not yet do we find evidence of interest in Nature itself, its beauty, its variety, its structural forms. But there is a new sense of the majesty and the graciousness and the wisdom of the God who sits upon the circle of the earth and spreads out the heavens like a curtain. There is a dawning sense of the regularity and orderliness of Nature, though even this is seen primarily in its human reference. The earth has been created with all its resources and potentialities so that man may inhabit it and have dominion over it. The regularity of the seasons, seed time and harvest, cold and heat, day and night, are ordered and sustained for man's benefit. " No doubt," writes H. Wheeler Robinson, " this continued maintenance of Nature is effected through established ordinances and inherent energies, as the reference to the seed-containing fruit of Genesis 1 implies. But these ordinances and energies are nowhere conceived as in any sense rivals of God, or limitations of His will ; they remain wholly dependent on His constant support." (*Inspiration and Revelation*, p. 24.)

In the latest period of Judaism, the emphasis upon the almighty power of God to control and even to transform Nature receives its fullest expression. "God is not only the sole creator of the world, He alone upholds it and maintains in existence by His immediate will and power everything that is. . . . The maintenance of the world is a kind of continuous creation. God in His goodness makes new every day continually the work of creation. The history of the world is His great plan, in which everything moves to the fulfilment of His purpose, the end that is in His mind." (G. F. Moore, *Judaism* I, p. 384.) And in the final fulfilment of His purpose He will so transform Nature that the desert will blossom as the rose, the wild beasts will be tamed, there will be everlasting light and the days of mourning will be ended.

Summarising the results of this survey of the Old Testament, we may say that from first to last Nature occupies a position of secondary importance. It is the background, the scenery, the setting, but in the forefront are the actors themselves. Without exception the Biblical writers bear witness to God as the chief actor in whatever event or pattern of events they are describing. Next in importance are the human actors, who are described in their relations with God and with one another through dramatic stories of great insight and power. Finally Nature itself is described with evidences of quick observation and sometimes of delicate sympathy but always with the sense that its function is to serve God and man and in particular to be the medium through which God can act for man's succour and advantage. In the earlier narratives it is the extraordinary in Nature, the signs and portents, the mysterious and the awe-inspiring, to which reference is usually made. In the later portions of the Old Testament greater attention is paid to the regular and ordered, the movements of the heavenly bodies and the seasonal variations on earth. But all through the order is from God to man through Nature and the emphasis lies upon Nature's function as a medium of communication through which the energy and the bounty and the guidance and the protection of God may be made available to man.

What, finally, were the implications of this view of Nature for man's construction of symbolic forms? In the first place it meant that the meeting itself was more important than the place of meeting, the pattern of the encounter was of greater signifi-

cance than any natural objects employed within the encounter.
To talk together, to eat together, to have direct personal contact
was of primary importance and the human leader who could
mediate the Divine will through word or deed was accorded a
place of greater eminence than any natural phenomenon. This
primacy of the meeting, the covenant, the instruction in the
Divine will, the pledging through solemn word and act, continued
throughout Israel's history in varying shapes and forms.
Communication from God to man and from man to man was at
all times the pre-eminent concern.

At the same time it is evident that from earliest times men
recognised that particular places and particular objects and
particular events in the natural order had a special religious
significance. There were trees and rocks and springs through
which Yahweh had manifested His power : there was the sacred
fire through which He was specially wont to make Himself
known—in fact, there is good reason to think that the fire was
at one time regarded as an actual form of Yahweh's being. In
course of time a sacred tent was set aside as Yahweh's dwelling-
place and a luminous cloud which sometimes overshadowed it
became the symbol of His special visitation. Gifts from the
flocks and herds were presented to Him and feasts were shared
in His presence. Under the influence of Canaanite and Phœnician
forms, a temple was built with towers, altar, carved figures and
a regular cultus, and later still, in the post-exilic period, elaborate
regulations were made to provide an ordered priesthood and
daily sacrificial worship.

It may be questioned, however, whether these latest developments represent the particular genius of the Hebrew view of
life. They sought, as it were, to baptize these extraneous symbolic
forms into Judaism by insisting that every detail of the temple
construction had been ordered by Yahweh and that all the ritual
forms and offerings were carried through in direct obedience to
His command. In all this, however, there was at least an element
of rationalisation and this was proved to be the case when the
temple was destroyed and animal sacrifice was discontinued. It
was in and through the worship of the synagogue that the Jews
retained their identity and transmitted their particular outlook
to succeeding generations. And the genius of synagogue-

worship is to be found in the double emphasis upon the transcendence of God Almighty and upon His will to communicate His laws to man. The all-important function of Nature is to declare the glory of God and to express His righteous judgments. Neither natural forms nor artificial symbols are of any account unless they serve to promote these ends.

THE RISE OF MODERN SCIENCE

A survey of the history of Western thought reveals the fact that there was no radical change in man's view of Nature from the time of the classical Greek thinkers until the seventeenth century A.D. It is true that the advent of Christianity led to certain important developments and modifications but it is doubtful whether it really altered the basic structure of thought about the natural order. As we have already seen, the Greeks held the view that the cosmos is an intelligent organism, the logos of whose essential being is at all times governing the operations of its constituent parts. In the thought of both Plato and Aristotle there were significant movements in the direction of regarding the logos as in some way *transcendent* to Nature and it was with these movements that the early Fathers and the scholastic theologians sought to align themselves. They knew that God had revealed Himself through His logos, Jesus Christ, and they believed that the whole universe was upheld by Him and that all things were moving towards a goal determined by Him. Nature revealed the glory of God and served the purpose of God. Inquiries about Nature were in a very real sense inquiries about the nature and purpose of God.

Symbolically the conjunction of the Christian faith with Greek natural theology and Roman technical skill reached its finest and fullest expression in the Gothic cathedral of the thirteenth and fourteenth centuries. In this magnificent symbolic form the Middle Ages produced a notable example of the Roman genius for collecting and shaping and organising the necessary materials on a grand scale: a noble example of the Greek genius for expressing itself in organic wholeness, in balance and proportion, in the analogical extension of natural processes through the symbolism of stone and space : an inspiring example of the Christian concern for prayer, aspiration, faith, confidence and above all for that eternal world of which all terrestrial symbolic forms are representations or precursors. The cathedral was the setting for the constant re-enactment of the drama of redemption just as Nature itself had been the setting for the critical redemptive work of the Logos within the historical order.

But from the fifteenth century onwards, discoveries and inventions of far-reaching importance began to fill men's thoughts and imaginations. The printing-press, good clocks, and optical lenses, affected man's capacities of observation and communication in a quite revolutionary way. Above all, man began to be aware of the machine—an instrument which could be constructed by the human intelligence and made to operate by the inflow of an energy from a source outside itself. Once the model of the machine had firmly established itself in the human imagination, it was an easy step to regard man himself as a machine, to regard the whole universe as a machine and to regard God as the almighty machine-maker and machine-operator. In the words of Professor Collingwood : " The Greeks and Romans were not machine-users, except to a very small extent ; their catapult and water-clocks were not a prominent enough feature of their life to affect the way in which they conceived the relation between themselves and the world. But by the sixteenth century the Industrial Revolution was well on the way. The printing-press and the windmill, the lever, the pump, and the pulley, the clock and the wheelbarrow, and a host of machines in use among miners and engineers were established features of daily life. Everyone understood the nature of a machine, and the experience of making and using such things had become part of the general consciousness of European man. It was an easy step to the proposition : as a clockmaker or millwright is to a clock or mill, so is God to Nature." (Op. cit. pp. 8-9.)

What, then, were some of the results of adopting this new model of the universe ? So long as the universe had been viewed as an " intelligent organism," man himself had been regarded as *within* the organism and even the Divine had been regarded as *within* the organism in the sense of animating and directing it. In patterns of thought which had begun to stress the transcendence of God, a full allowance had still been made for His immanence within the universe through His logos. But now there could be no thought of God or man dwelling *within* the machine. Man, it was assumed, stood over against the world, observing it, measuring it, learning its laws of motion and above all gaining knowledge of "how it works." So, too, God stood over against the world which He had made. He had designed it, He had provided energy for its proper functioning. He had set it in motion, He had established Himself as the guardian of its smooth operation. But His relation to it was altogether less intimate than had hitherto been the case and it was not long before men were tending to ignore His connection with this mechanical universe altogether.

A second consequence of the adoption of the new model was the rapid deterioration of the idea of " telos " which had from the time of Aristotle been dominant in the Western world. What need was there for the scientist to concern himself with questions of ultimate ends ? He wanted to know how the universal machine worked, how a particular cause would produce a particular effect. But it was not his business to ask questions about transcendent goals so long as he knew the laws by which matter was set in motion and by which desired effects could be produced. He found, indeed, that by careful observation he could in many cases forecast the behaviour of particular parts of the universal machine and this only strengthened his confidence that the cosmos was one great system of cause-and-effect and that there was no necessity to postulate purposes or meanings of a transcendent character. Hence, in the words of Professor W. T. Stace, " science from the seventeenth century onwards became exclusively an inquiry into causes. The conception of purpose in the world was ignored and frowned on. This, though silent and almost unnoticed, was the greatest revolution in human history, far outweighing in importance any of the political revolutions whose thunder has reverberated through the world." (*The Atlantic Monthly*, Sept., 1948.)

A third consequence of this new conception was that the possible separation between mind and matter, which had been lurking in the background since Plato's time, now became an actuality. If the universe is regarded as a machine, then the material out of which it is made does not appear to have any necessary connection with the mind that conceived it and controls it. The mind may decide what material is most suitable for a particular instrument but having done so its only concern is to build the material into the necessary shape. The man who uses the machine has only to learn the laws of its operation—his mind does not need to be attuned in some mysterious way to the pattern of the material out of which it has been made. Moreover, a machine may be taken apart and analysed into its smallest elements. So the analysis of the universe went steadily forward until it seemed that the fundamental constituent—the atom— had been discovered. Then it came to be assumed that in some way the mind—a vague and ghost-like creation—could take quantities of atoms and so arrange them in relation to one another that an efficient machine would emerge. Thus as long as the model of the machine held men's imaginations in thrall, mind was conceived as controlling matter by well-defined laws, though how the precise connection between these unlike entities could be made was never clearly shown.

What, then, does this conception of Nature imply for the construction of significant forms and symbols ? For a long time man used his new instruments within the traditional setting of ancient symbolisms and no important attempt was made to construct dramatic representations of the new model of the universe. Great changes had indeed come to the Western world through the Reformation, changes which loosened men's attachment to ancient forms and which made them more ready to consider the adoption of new symbolism. But at first the overwhelming concern for a return to the Bible and to the Biblical world-view meant that the focus of interest was in the relationship between persons and in the ordering of social groups rather than in the structure of the world of Nature and in man's relationship to it.

In many cases existing religious buildings were taken over and used as places of assembly, though the inner arrangements and furnishings were drastically altered in order that the notes of communion and universal participation might receive proper emphasis. Much stress was also laid upon the proper hearing of the Divine word, the medium through which the Divine will was made known to man. In other cases new buildings were erected to serve as "meeting-houses," the distinctively new structure of the post-Reformation period. This particular form was in no way intended to symbolise the natural order within which man made his habitation nor were his activities inside the building in any way related to the world of Nature outside (except on very rare occasions). The meeting-house was designed, rather, as a place of convenient assembly and of separation from the world—a place where members of God's covenant-community could celebrate their togetherness and learn of His will. Design and decoration were of little account. The minimum of arrangement was necessary to make possible the continuance of the two Gospel sacraments. Otherwise the all-important requirements were freedom of access to all members of the covenant-community and full opportunity for all to hear and respond to God's holy word.

Thus with Catholic Christendom retaining the traditional symbols belonging to the conception of the one universal organism and with Reformed Christendom focusing attention upon the meeting and the hearing rather than upon the structural setting within which these activities were carried on, it was left for the secular world to develop forms and symbols appropriate to the new view of Nature which steadily gained ground through the eighteenth and nineteenth centuries. In the new mechanistic age the factory took the place of the temple, the machine became the object of veneration to be protected and nourished and cared for, the operatives became the liturgical ministers, efficiency of production became the test of ultimate value. The depletion of natural resources and the deterioration of the universal machine were rarely considered. Mind was all-powerful and in some way matter would be moulded and shaped to enable the necessary mechanical functions to continue.

So the Industrial Age brought about an efficiency of the technique of production unparalleled in the history of mankind but it was accompanied by no comparable advance in the realm of the spirit. There were innumerable attempts to recapture the artistic genius of former generations but the mechanical model itself failed to inspire creative adventures of the imagination. It was not the case that the model was a sheer misrepresentation or a tragic mistake : the extraordinary results which followed from its adoption were adequate testimony to the large degree of truth which it contained. But it was an exaggeration, a heresy, a one-sided representation, a limited model. It bore witness to an exceedingly important element in Nature's design and to an equally important aspect of human psychology. Erected into a self-sufficient and all-sufficient system, however, it made of Nature a vast soulless machine, devoid of feeling or of meaning. Man's only possible relationship to it was that of apprentice or operator. By learning its laws and utilising its energies he could promote the greater efficiency of his own mechanical existence. Beyond this there was little that he could either say or do.

THE TWENTIETH CENTURY WORLD-VIEW

One of the most remarkable developments of thought in the twentieth century has been the virtual abandonment by scientists of the mechanical model of the universe. This does not mean that the amazing discoveries of the previous three centuries have been set aside or that any large-scale displacement of the mechanical model has taken place in the popular mind. But it does mean that scientists and philosophers are describing man's relation to Nature in new ways and are seeking models and symbols which will more adequately portray the whole structure of the universe than any that have hitherto been used. Seeing that the enterprise is still in process it is not easy to make a true assessment of the present situation. I shall, however, seek to call attention to some of the new factors which have led to new patterns of thought and action.

Perhaps the most important change which has taken place has been the increasing recognition that it is impossible to think of the universe as standing over against man—a self-contained entity whose laws can be discovered and formulated by any student if he will only observe carefully and measure accurately. Actually the situation is far more complex. As a great biologist has pointed out, " our physical science is not just a set of reports about an outside world. It is also a report about ourselves and our relations to that world, whatever the latter may be like. . . . We no longer speak of a world of matter, nor of particles, properties or forces. Physics is no longer materialistic. Instead it speaks of what we may call a man-world of observers and the relations between them and the reports of what they observe." (J. Z. Young, *Doubt and Certainty in Science*, pp. 108, 111.) In other words, it is no longer possible to draw a blue-print of the universe as one would of a steam-engine. The scientist's primary dependence is now upon mathematical formulæ or symbols which can express the findings of different observers and the relations between them.

Coupled with the emphasis upon the personal equation has come a new recognition of the importance of *time*. There is no static configuration which can be set up as a model of the universe : space cannot be thought of as independent of time : matter cannot be thought of as independent of motion. Scientists no longer seek to conceive the smallest element of space as an atom at rest in a particular place. Rather their concern is to plot in some meaningful way what an element of matter is doing at a particular time in relation to another element, what is, in fact, the nature of its motion at any particular instant. There may be different doctrines in modern science of the relation of space to time but that it is no longer possible to speak except in terms of a space-time universe is generally agreed.

In the third place—and this consideration follows rather naturally from the new concern for the personal equation and the time factor—there is a strong disposition to view the whole universe as evolving by a process similar in type to that of the human species. The qualities of the universe upon which attention is focused are neither its unchanging structures nor its efficient mechanisms, but rather its patterns of change, development, growth, decay, its rhythms of movement, the ebb and flow of its mysterious life-processes. More and more the attempt is being made to sketch a comprehensive world-picture in which Nature and history, man and society, are conceived within one single pattern of thought.

In every branch of study devoted to this pursuit the key-word is " evolution." In every part of Nature, it appears, a process of evolution is at work. Plants, animals, men, societies, maintain certain *continuities* through successive generations. At the same time they clearly exhibit certain *differences*. Man to-day is so akin to man of 20,000 years ago that it is natural to apply the name "man" to each. At the same time, man to-day is so different from his predecessor 20,000 years ago that it seems only right to speak of him as "higher" or "further advanced." Thus he is the same and yet different. There is a continuity of life-pattern and at the same time a difference of organisation and function. The same is true in a measure of the life of the single individual. A man of fifty is the same as he was at five years old in certain respects : in others he is altogether different. The same is also true of a particular society. If now this model of continuity of identity and change of organisation or function can be made to cover many areas of life : if it is useful in the fields of anthropology, of biology, of psychology, of sociology, even of history : may it not be the most useful for the description of the whole universe in the light of present-day knowledge ? May not the universe itself be in process of evolution, maintaining a certain continuity of identifiable pattern and at the same time moving ever towards the achievement of a higher or more advanced form of organisation ?

The most obvious defect in this model is the uncertainty which attaches to the words "higher" and "more advanced." Each word is a metaphor, taken in the one case from man's experience of climbing upwards, in the other from his experience of moving forwards. These experiences have always been associated with a certain sense of achievement and the words, therefore, have proved to be convenient metaphors for describing conditions which are in some way to be preferred to those which preceded them. But in what sense is man to-day "higher" or "more advanced" or "better" than he was 20,000 years ago ? In what sense is the man of forty "higher" or "more advanced" or "better" than the boy of five ? These questions are difficult to answer in any single way but in the Reith Lectures to which we have already referred, Professor J. Z. Young makes an interesting attempt to include all experience under one category.

The essence of real progress or advance in any areas of life, he suggests, is to be found in more successful *communication*. The altogether determinative mark which distinguishes man from animals is his power of speech and symbol formation. The chief characteristic of a mature and well-integrated individual is his power of communication. The supreme achievements of the twentieth century have been in the realm of the discovery of new forms of communication. The brain, the most highly-organised instrument of which we have knowledge, is concerned all the time with the process of *communication*. To receive stimuli, to communicate them to the proper nerve-centres, to re-communicate them through channels leading to appropriate action—these are the functions of the brain which it carries forward by a process of immense complexity and yet of amazing efficiency. Does this mean, then, that we shall be well advised to conceive the whole universe as a vast evolutionary process, operating in many ways like the human brain, ever seeking through the process of trial and error, of testing and rejecting, to achieve some new efficiency of communication and thereby to raise the whole of life to new levels of organisation and achievement? There is much to commend this view and it may be that at our present stage of knowledge it is the best model that can be conceived.

That it is determining the most obvious symbolic forms of our time there can be little doubt. In place of the Industrial Age we find ourselves in the Age of Rapid Communication. We measure in terms of the speed of light, we observe by means of devices capable of recording the slightest movement in an infinitesimal period of time. We move from one place to another so rapidly that now no part of the earth's surface is more than thirty hours' flying distance from any other part. For the rapid communication of news the press telegram has been succeeded by the telephone which in turn has been superseded by the radio and television. The aeroplane attains ever-increasing speeds and even these are to be surpassed by the rocket-ship. Long-range detection and long-range control become ever more efficient and there seems to be no limit to the variety of waves and rays which permeate the universe. Most remarkable of all, perhaps, is the invention of the electrical brain which can far outstrip the human brain in the rapidity of its operation in certain fields and which can be used in the construction of robot-men to act as rivals to *homines sapientes*. In every one of these areas the chief agent is the force of electricity and we find ourselves living in a world honeycombed by electrical waves and circuits.

The symbols of this new age are again to be found in the secular rather than the religious world. The shrines of revelation are the laboratories and the institutes of technology : the oracles are the research scientists : the media of revelation are the scientific journals couched in highly technical language : the dominant aim is the achievement of ever more successful methods of communication. May not the universe as a whole be conceived as a vast evolving system in which the key process is effective communication ? May it not be man's chief end to organise his whole existence in accordance with this central principle ?

The dangers of this most recent model of the universe are as ominous as were those of the mechanical age. This view, if made the sole canon of the interpretation of Nature, becomes an exaggeration and a heresy. It is perhaps less dangerous than the machine model in that it is less rigid and impersonal : it is perhaps more dangerous in that it gathers man himself up into the clutches of the model and gives him significance solely as a channel of communication. The concept of communication is a noble one and the change of emphasis from man as a self-contained unit confronting a mechanical universe to man as a link in the chain of universal communication may be welcomed up to a point. But the simple yet altogether crucial question remains : *What* is being communicated ? Of what value is rapid communication unless there be something of supreme importance to be communicated ? Even the electrical brain is dependent upon a constructor and a stimulator—it does not create its own problems and work them out. Is not the universe also dependent upon a creative Mind who constructs it and has some purpose of infinite significance to be conveyed and realised through it ? Thus even if the mechanical model is abandoned in favour of the evolutionary, this does not mean that we can accept the process of evolution as an entirely self-enclosed system. The patterns and processes and means of communication can be viewed as *signs* of the Divine activity, but they are not of themselves sufficient to communicate to us the nature of the Divine purpose or the full range of the Divine operations. A revelation of a different character is needed to make clear to man the nature of God's *personal* activity and the range of His reconciling grace.

THE CHRISTIAN VIEW OF NATURE

In the course of our inquiry we have encountered differing views of Nature and of the symbolism of natural forms and objects. In one culture man seeks a complete union with Nature and pays little attention to particular symbolic forms : in another setting he seeks to gain the mastery over Nature through the aid of heavenly powers and accords a special significance to those loci or objects which are associated with dramatic divine inter- ventions. Or again man seeks to discover the laws of Nature's working and either to co-operate with them or to use them to his own advantage by the aid of models in which the *sign* is the characteristic phenomenon. Still further there is ever the possi- bility that man will seek to observe both the regularities and the revolutionary changes in the natural order and will come to view them as *symbols* respectively of a Divine order which over arches human life and of a Divine activity which is ever operating for man's final good.

The Greek was surely right to seek in Nature those forms and patterns and correspondences which are the symbols of a harmonious and ordered universe. Still more were the Greek men of genius right in seeking to penetrate beyond Nature to those eternal ideas, values, ends, which the forms of Nature may symbolise but never fully express. In the proportion and balance and ordered growth of Nature they saw intimations of a beauty and a perfection of design which are eternal and unchangeable. In the Logos of Nature they saw a symbol of the Divine Logos. And with all the advances of scientific knowledge there is still no reason to reject this ancient insight that patterns and structures in Nature can be regarded as *analogical symbols* of the perfect design which has originated in the creative mind of God Himself.

In the Christian tradition the Greek view is regarded as incomplete and defective at one crucial point. It had no central symbol of reference such as has been provided by the human life of the Incarnate Christ within the natural order. Inasmuch as God is the Creator and Sustainer of all things, it is indeed unthinkable that no other symbols of the Divine are to be found in the created order. The symmetries and proportions and harmonies and organic wholenesses in Nature are at least in a partial sense symbols of the Divine Nature. But it is only in Christ that these all find their criterion and their fulfilment. He is the perfect symbol both of Nature's origin and of Nature's goal. Natural structures and natural processes can all become symbols of the Divine Nature in so far as they are related to the perfect symbol, in so far as they are striving towards Him, growing up into Him, Who is their meaning and their goal.

But the Hebrew was also right in recognising that the apparently irregular and abnormal and unusual operations of Nature were under the control of the transcendent God Who was using them in the working out of His own gracious purpose. When Nature was charred or darkened or torn asunder by fire and tempest and earthquake, the judgments of God were abroad in the earth. When Nature was cheered and refreshed and transformed by breezes and showers and sunshine the mercies of God were being renewed. The Hebrew was convinced that in some way the singularities and discontinuities of Nature occupied a place of vital importance in God's purposes for mankind and again with all the advances of scientific knowledge there is no reason to reject this ancient faith that

> God moves in a mysterious way
> His wonders to perform.
> He plants His footsteps in the sea
> And rides upon the storm.

and that the combinations of storm and calm, of drought and rain, of flood and fertility, can be regarded as *metaphorical symbols* of God's purpose of redemption which can only be achieved through travail and purgation and even death.

The Hebrew view was incomplete in that it gave insufficient attention to created structures and to beauties of form. Moreover, it lacked the central symbol of reference which the death and resurrection of the Messiah were to provide. For it is the Christian claim that the death and resurrection of the Christ is no isolated phenomenon, without parallel, without suggestion, without correspondence in the natural world. The grain falls into the ground and dies in order that it may spring to new life and bear much fruit; vegetation fades and dies in the autumn but the garment of Nature is renewed in the spring: the storm leaves destruction in its track but often it is the prelude to the outburst of new vitality. Symbols of gain-through-loss and of life-through-death abound in the realm of Nature but, as is all too evident, man can take these symbolic forms and use them to justify deeds of cruelty and sadism rather than acts of devotion and self-sacrifice. Only by yielding himself to the hard wood of the Cross and by making his grave in a rock-hewn tomb could the true Servant of the Lord provide the symbol which would stand for all time as the perfect example of gain-through-loss and of life-through-death. In His death and resurrection even the ultimate disruption and discontinuity of Nature—Death —was recapitulated and redeemed. "O Death where is thy sting? O Grave where is thy victory?" It was by a supremely daring leap of faith that the Apostle Paul saw in the Death and Resurrection of his Lord the sure promise of the consummation of the age-long travail of Nature and the shining symbol of the fulfilment of the eternal purpose of God.

Finally it may be suggested that whereas the house of God, the sanctuary, the temple, the basilica, the cemetery-chapel, the cathedral, represent, at different periods of history, the view of Nature which comes to its fulfilment in the Græco-Christian tradition, the meeting-ground, the tent of meeting, the synagogue, the schola, the meeting-house, the auditorium, represent more adequately the view of nature which comes to fulfilment in the Hebraic-Christian tradition. In the former case the building is the symbolic representation of the framework of Nature within which the Divine presence is located or the regular Divine activity takes place. Sometimes the emphasis lies upon the temple as the earthly home of the god, the place where his worshippers may visit him and make their appropriate homage. The particular shrine is the symbol of the universal shrine within which the god has his eternal abode. Sometimes the emphasis is rather upon the building as providing the setting for the ritual of the divine drama. The effectual sign is enacted before the eyes of the assembled worshippers and thereby the universal life of the natural order is renewed and sustained. Within the Christian setting the Church is either the earthly symbolisation of that universal structure within which the mutual self-offering of the eternal Godhead is for ever being enacted or it is the earthly sign to mark off the place where the Divine presence is manifested and the Divine *opus* is performed.

In the latter case the meeting-place is the symbolic memorial of the setting within which the deity has, on some notable occasion in history, actually met with his people. Sometimes the emphasis is upon the meeting-place as the symbolic framework which provides the setting for the re-enactment of this encounter, which provides indeed the essential outline of the setting of the eschatological meeting of final reconciliation. Sometimes the emphasis is rather upon the meeting-place as providing simply a locus of assembly for the proclamation of the news that the deity has acted within the historical time-series and that at any time he may so act again. Within the Christian context the first emphasis calls for a setting where the worshippers can gather together *around the Lord's Table* and there renew the covenant with Him and with one another; the second emphasis calls for a setting where as many as possible can *hear* the testimony to what God has done in Christ and can respond by dedicating their wills to His service.

In the mid-twentieth century the mechanistic view of Nature is still strongly entrenched and the tradition which looks upon its symbolic structures as, in the main, the particular loci where the Divine miracle takes place is likely to make a wide appeal. On the other side at a time when the world has come to be viewed very largely as a field for the rapid communication of information, the tradition which looks upon its symbolic settings as, in the main, the particular loci where the Divine word can be proclaimed is also likely to gain many supporters. These traditions, however, can never adequately represent the full

Christian emphasis upon the *continuous* work of God within the created order and upon the primacy of *personal* structures and values in man's interpretation of his universe. For such an emphasis we await new symbolic structures which will both express the splendour of organic growth and fulfilment within the Divine creation and will at the same time provide an appropriate setting for the repeated renewal of the covenant between God and His people in Christ.

CHAPTER THREE

The Symbolism of Time

THE AGE in which we live is so time-conscious that it is hard to recapture in our imagination an age in which man was relatively unconscious of the passage of time. Yet it is probably true that the concern with time which is so marked a feature of our contemporary Western world is a relatively recent phenomenon in the history of mankind. We know that even to-day time is far less important in the East than in the West. Eastern man, writes Emil Brunner, " always has time, because time for him is no reality. Eternity alone is real, and the temporal world is mere appearance. If for the Western man material temporality is everything, for the mystical Eastern man it is nothing. That is why time is worthless for him. It is unreal. Why should he bother about time when it is *maya*, illusion ? " [1] Even when allowance is made for the fact that such a view of time belongs mainly to certain schools of Eastern philosophy, it still is true that the average peasant of India or China is far less conscious of the significance of measured time than is the industrial worker of Europe or America. And what is true of the Eastern peasant to-day is roughly true of primitive man in every other part of the world.

It is a fascinating exercise to inquire how exactly man first became conscious of the concept of time. One of the most thorough examinations of the question has been made by Professor S. G. F. Brandon in his book, *Time and Mankind*. In his opening chapter he refers to the evidence of the paintings and sculptures which have been discovered in the Pyrenean caves, to the earliest burial customs of mankind, to the witness

[1] *Scottish Journal of Theology*. March, 1951. p. 7.

of the evolution of human speech and to the evidence which we possess of the use of calendars in very ancient times. With regard to the first, it is notoriously difficult to interpret the significance of early cave-paintings with confidence, but there is some reason to think that they were connected with man's desire either to perpetuate the past or to anticipate the future. A successful hunt was recalled to mind and retained in the memory by means of a representation of the scene : or the wish for a repetition of fortune was projected into future realisation by the actual depicting of the desired end. Thus the primitive artist may have wished to perpetuate the past (to use Brandon's term) or to anticipate the future. At least he seems to have been aware of certain patterns of experience which were out of the ordinary and which were worthy of being expressed objectively either as a commemoration of the past or as a talisman for the future.[1]

So far as burial customs are concerned, it is a remarkable fact that even as early as the Cro-Magnon period certain cere-monial practices were being carefully observed. These indicate that there was a dawning recognition of the possible extension of human life into some other form of existence. Those who performed the funeral rites were evidently anxious to supply the deceased with food and tools and comforts such as they might need in their new environment. Such a desire could only have been entertained by those who had already established a certain pattern of ordered existence which they regarded as worthy of being extended into another world. They evidently believed that in certain important respects the life after death would be *similar* to the life before death. It was certainly not a *direct* continuity. But the pattern of existence in the future world was analogous to the pattern of existence in this world. Thus we can see in these early funerary customs an elementary recog-nition of the fact that life as experienced in the present is a symbol of life which is to be experienced in the future. Beyond this general awareness, however, the evidence does not allow us to go.

The main point of interest in the evolution of speech is that

[1] Dr. Rachel Levy, however, claims that the supreme object of the painting was to participate in the splendour of the beasts *in the present*. *The Gate of Horn*, p. 20.

of the development of verb tenses. Here we are dependent upon *written* records and these in themselves cannot tell us when the distinctions between past, present and future began to appear in spoken language. What is clear, however, is that in the earliest written material we possess, such distinctions are only beginning to be made. Man is concerned with the *duration* of time rather than with divisions in time. He knows that some experiences are so short as to appear momentary : others seem to continue indefinitely. His primary task in language, then, is to reveal this distinction, though by so doing he naturally opens the way for other refinements of time-structure to be gradually made. As Brandon has said : " Man's primary concern is with the duration of the phenomena which he experiences, viewing it, of course, from the standpoint of his own personal interest. But it is inevitable that the momentariness or continuity of that experience, together with the abiding witness of his memory, soon rendered some form of temporal distinction necessary, although the subtlety of its distinction came in time to depend upon the mental acumen of the various historic peoples." (Op. cit., p. 21.)

Fourthly, there is the witness of early calendars. This is perhaps the most important evidence of all. It has been computed that a civil calendar was being used in Egypt as early as the 5th millenium B.C., the chronological observations of the Babylonians are famous, and the achievements of the Aztecs in measuring time by aid of the movements of the heavenly bodies constitute one of the most remarkable features of the early life of the Western World. It seems that quite independently, in different parts of the world, men gradually became aware of the fact that the movements of sun, moon and stars were *regular*. Moreover, they recognised that these movements were in some way connected with the changes of the seasons and the recurring phenomena of Nature. In this way the concept of revolutionary importance emerged that there are regular patterns of movement in the universe, cycles, phases, repetitions, and that these are of fundamental significance for bringing order into human life.[1]

[1] The " long and patient observation of the regular recurrence of certain groups of celestial or natural phenomena must soon have suggested to him (sc. man) that the life of the universe follows a regular predestined plan or pattern ; that, though the passage of Time brings change, the change is not really new since it is but an

In addition to the evidence of these external phenomena it is legitimate to take into account the instinctive reactions which seem to belong to the basic psychology of man as such. In certain respects man to-day is little different from his ancestor of ten millenia ago. He cannot fail to be aware of a certain rhythm in his life—waking and sleeping, working and resting, expanding and contracting, breathing in and breathing out, birth and death. His existence is not a flat monotonous continuity but a succession of regular rhythmical beats. At the same time the regular rhythm may be disturbed and even broken by the impact of unforeseen events. Something suddenly happens : if it is pleasant man wishes to hold on to it as long as possible ; if it is unpleasant he is eager to pass it by and banish it from his mind. Such an experience, however, cannot fail to make him conscious of the passage of time which either threatens to rob him of the pleasantness he seeks to enjoy or prevents him from escaping immediately from the unpleasantness which he would fain leave behind. It is obviously impossible to know when these instinctive feelings became conscious or when man began to formulate a definite progression of past, present and future. But at least we can see that there have been experiences in his life from time immemorial which have provided the basic material for the construction of a philosophy of time in terms of continuity and change.

ANCIENT CIVILISATIONS

The great civilisations of the past all took their rise in river-valleys. The Nile, the Tigris-Euphrates and the Indus were the primary sources of fertility and advances of every kind were possible to those who lived in close proximity to them. But the rivers were not only the providers of food and fertility—they also became the natural symbols of life itself. For is there not in man's own experience a certain rhythm of birth and death,

abiding feature of an ever returning cycle. Of course, this feature of Time's flux was only gradually and dimly apprehended ; but its logic must soon have been felt by those who eagerly watched each morn for that rising of Sirius which would foretell the advent of the mysterious increase of the sacred Nile, or by those who waited in awful silence amid the mystic circles of stones for the first-tip of the mid-summer sun over the grey Hele Stone." (Brandon op. cit., p. 23.)

growth and decay, activity and rest ? This rhythm, however, also belongs to the great river : it rises and falls, it sweeps down with new force and energy and then becomes calm and listless and seems to lose its vitality and strength. Yet its flow never finally ceases. It is the supreme example of a form of life which rises and falls, ebbs and flows, and yet which always continues to move steadily along.

How far the river came to acquire full divine status in these ancient civilisations is hard to say. In Egypt certainly the popular god Osiris was closely associated with the Nile and it is in a measure true to say that Osiris *was* the Nile. But there were Osirian myths which personified the god and which may have had their foundation in actual historical events of the past. Be that as it may, the Egyptian peasant venerated Osiris and believed that through union with this god he could escape from the clutches of the twin forces of decay and death which constantly threatened his existence. This belief may scarcely have been conscious. The inner rhythm of his half-conscious life instinctively sought the support of a more abiding rhythm in the wider world around him and this it found in the great symbol of the River, Nile, Osiris, the ever waxing and waning, the unbroken continuum, the one natural phenomenon which seemed to be untouched by the force of change and decay. So he sought to be united with Osiris and thereby gained assurance of a renewal of life even after the onslaught of physical death.

The dying and rising god in Babylonian mythology was Tammuz and his connection with the river was not perhaps so close as that of Osiris. There is, however, the legend which tells of his drowning in the river at the midsummer season and it would seem that it was through union with the river that his life was renewed. In India the River retains even to-day its sacred character and to bathe in its waters is to renew life. Its steady flow, interrupted only by a regular rhythm, forms an almost exact enlargement of the pattern of man's own life. By yielding himself therefore to this more expansive and more abiding rhythm, man satisfies his fundamental urge to extend and perpetuate his temporal experience. He is vaguely conscious of being hemmed in by time but in union with the River or the genius of the River he rises above his present experience and feels himself part of that eternal rhythm which nothing can damage or destroy.

There is one other natural phenomenon which shares with the river the property of possessing a regular rhythm within its deep, unbroken continuity. This is the sea with its surface-motions caused by wind and storm ever controlled by the depths of its own rhythmic pulsations. The ancients found little attraction in the ocean as such and it is perhaps only in modern times that the movement of the sea has come to be viewed as an image of the rhythmic movement of Time in human life. In Mr. T. S. Eliot's poem, *The Dry Salvages*, Time appears as the ocean on the surface of which there are innumerable sounds vying with one another, clashing with one another, and producing only disharmony and confusion.

> The sea howl
> And the sea yelp, are different voices
> Often together heard ; the whine in the rigging,
> The menace and caress of wave that breaks on water,
> The distant rote in the granite teeth,
> And the wailing warning from the approaching headland
> Are all sea voices, and the heaving groaner
> Rounded homewards, and the sea gull ;

But there is another deeper sound, the sound of the tolling bell whose movements are controlled by the ground swell underneath. This represents the abiding rhythms of the universe which are older than the time of chronometers, older than time counted by anxious worried women lying awake, calculating the future, trying to unweave, unwind, unravel

> And piece together the past and the future,
> Between midnight and dawn, when the past is all deception,
> The future futureless, before the morning watch
> When time stops and time is never ending ;
> And the ground swell, that is and was from the beginning.
>   Clangs
>   The bell.

In other parts of the cycle of poems to which *The Dry Salvages*
belongs, the poet reveals his conviction that man needs to be
united with this deep rhythm of the universe in order that he
may be revitalised and renewed. He needs a further union, a
deeper communion with the sources of his being and not least
with that regular heart-beat of pulsating Time of which the
movement of the river or of the sea-depth is an archetypal image.
In such a view there is little place for the notion of patterns of
time in history or for the significance of special times of crisis
and decision. In Egypt, in India, in China, and in the whole
tradition of Western mysticism, the chief concern has been with
unity and continuity and changelessness. In so far as there has
been any recognition of Time it has corresponded to those
fundamental rhythms which are an integral part of ordinary
human existence. The Centre of Being is conceived as One and
yet as subject to the rhythm of breathing in and breathing out,
of expanding and contracting. This rhythm may be extended
into more or less detail, but the final implication is that only as
man withdraws himself from the superficialities of his existence
in time and becomes united with the deep ground-swell of the
rhythm of the universe can he find his ultimate satisfaction and
eternal peace.

GREECE

One of the great advances in man's conception of Time was
his discovery that beyond the regular and simple rhythm of
Nature there is a regularity in the universe which belongs to
the movements of the heavenly bodies. Man observed the path
of the sun and noted the way in which the shadow cast on the
ground moved with it. He watched the moon in its variant
phases and found that its behaviour was the same in each of its
successive cycles. He saw the stars appearing in the same configuration from night to night and so, by gradually recording
his observations, he was able to lay the foundation for a
symbolism of time. He began to think in terms of days and
months and years and in this way he constructed a collection of
signs which corresponded directly to the patterns described by

the heavenly bodies. The day represented the period between one sunrise and the next; the month the period between one full moon and another. Through this representation of the passage of Time by means of recognised *signs* the scientific approach to the problem of Time may be said to have begun. Man has become aware of the regularities of motion and of the periodicity of certain phenomena. This enables him to construct a calendar and thereby to introduce such a measure of order into his corporate existence as has never been possible before. He can calculate the times for sowing and reaping and can establish a regular succession of festivals. These divisions of Time have been elaborated and corrected in later centuries : they have never been superseded in all the long history of mankind.

But although the construction of a sign-language to represent periods of time took place, it appears, in different parts of the world, it was the Greek who first attempted to inquire more deeply into the significance of Time and to consider its place in the structure of the universe. Yet it is a striking fact that the Greeks were concerned to only a very limited extent with the ideas of continuity or progress in time. They were aware of the past—but the past was chiefly of interest as providing examples of how best to live in the present : they were aware of the future —but the future was unpredictable and man had plenty to occupy him in the present without spending time in speculating about an unknown future. In other words, throughout the long history of Hellenic culture the all-important consideration was the *Present*. There had been great heroes in the past and it was always pleasant to hear about them, but the immediate duty was to build up an ordered existence in the present and to leave the future to the gods or to Fate who held it under their control.

In the writings of the great philosophers there is indeed a much deeper inquiry into the significance of Time, but in the end the intense concern with the Present remains unchanged. In the thought of Plato, for example, Time is the supreme principle of *order* in human life and that which brings order is most certainly good. Time is not an enemy seeking to deprive man of his treasured possessions : nor is it a neutral having no significance for human life : rather is it a friend, bringing order out of chaos, a measure of unity out of multiplicity, the beauty of form and rhythm out of formlessness. Before time was created there was only the confused notion of pure becoming. Space, it is true, existed already, for becoming demands on environment. But it was chaotic becoming, a state of existence regulated entirely by sensation and appetite. " All changed with the introduction of Time, which, as a moving image of eternity, renders the notion of the sensible universe harmonious and intelligible. The universe now resembles true being so far as this is possible for anything in the realm of becoming." (J. F. Callahan, *Four Views of Time in Ancient Philosophy*, p. 190.) [1]

Thus Time is the highest principle of order. It is, as it were, the graduated ring of an outer circle revolving around the inner wholeness which is eternity itself. Through the regularity of Time the broken and dispersing fragments of human existence are reduced to order and drawn towards that perfection of harmony which is in the nature of the Living Being itself.

If we desire to look for examples of ordered time in the universe as we know it, the nearest approximation to perfection is to be found in the motions of the heavenly bodies.[2] In fact, the most fitting symbol of eternity is to be found in a complete cycle of these bodies. Such a cycle represents the wholeness of eternity and every lesser cycle known to us—a month, a day, a revolution of a wheel, a musical pattern—is a part representing symbolically this larger whole. It is through Time that order is brought into the world of becoming and that the universe begins to partake of the likeness of the Eternal. It is through relating himself to Time-symbols that man can transform his changeable

[1] This view is succinctly expressed in a famous passage in the *Timaeus*. " When the father who had begotten the world saw it set in motion and alive, he rejoiced and being well pleased he took thought to make it yet more like its pattern. So, as that pattern is the Living Being that is for ever existent, he sought to make this universe also like it, so far as might be, in that respect. Now the nature of that Living Being was eternal, and this character it was impossible to confer in full completeness on the generated thing. But he took thought to make, as it were, a moving likeness of eternity ; and at the same time that he ordered the Heaven, he made, of eternity that abides in unity, an everlasting likeness moving according to number that to which we have given the name Time." (p. 37, C.D.)

[2] " Each of the heavenly motions," writes Callahan, " such as that of any planet, when set in relation to the others, gives rise to a set of numbers : thus each of the motions can be called a time, and the whole of time comprises many individual times. When these individual motions complete a cycle and the heavenly bodies return to their original relative position, the perfect number of time is fulfilled." (Op. cit., p. 191.)

and mutable existence into one in which order reigns and in which he can approximate ever more closely to the perfect movement of the eternal Whole.

As always, Aristotle's approach to the matter is more matter-of-fact, more down-to-earth, than that of Plato. His starting point is the fact that Time is inextricably bound up with the observable phenomenon of motion. If we are unconscious of any movement in our immediate environment we are unconscious of Time : it is as we become conscious of actual change, that we become conscious of Time. Thus it is only when we have become aware of a " before " and an " after " in some form of motion that we say that time has elapsed. And this leads to Aristotle's famous definition : " Time is number (or measure) of movement (or motion) in respect of the before and after." In reality everything in the universe is in flux and time and movement together form a single continuum. Every seeming end is only a new beginning : every seeming beginning is only an end. At no place in the universe is there a resting-point. Only the pure changelessness of the Unmoved Mover is independent of Time. He is the Eternal One Who lives in contemplation of Himself and Who, being outside the realm of time and becoming, draws the whole universe into union with Himself.

Perhaps the outstanding difference between this view of Aristotle and that of Plato is that whereas for the latter Time is essentially good, the supreme principle of order and harmony, for the former, time and motion constitute the defect of the universe or at least its imperfection. Man finds himself in a world which is unending and which is continuously in motion. He experiences no sense of urgency or of crisis, for all things are moving irresistibly towards the goal and centre of their beings in the One. But it is open to man to seek a certain emancipation from this steady onward flow of time and change and he can do this by achieving through the exercise of his intellect a momentary experience of the timelessness of God Himself. As a distinguished interpreter of Aristotle has written : " The highest gift of man is reason and this is most itself when it has won freedom from the importunities of daily life and action and contemplates, with no external interest but as a mere spectator, the eternal order of the real." (J. L. Stocks, *Aristotelianism*, p. 102.)

Aristotle, then, recognises that time is the measure of motion and time-symbols are therefore to be regarded as direct representations of movements of material bodies. The standard of measurement is defined as the rotation of the heavenly spheres and by using this standard a system of appropriate symbols (in our terminology these are more accurately " signs ") can be constructed to represent any kind of motion. If, however, the attempt is made to go beyond these direct time-symbols to something suggestive of the ultimate unity of the whole, the only possible way seems to be through the concept of the " timeless moment," the moment when through the purification of reason or through the enhancement of vision man enters into the experience of Eternal Timelessness. Even in the world of external phenomena there seem to be " still points " when, for a moment, one movement comes to an end and another begins. Yet in the life of Nature this stillness is imaginary. Every end is in reality a new beginning. Only if the timelessness of the Divine can somehow be interjected into the moving flux of the temporal can man enjoy the experience of the timeless moment. It is an important part of the message of T. S. Eliot that such moments of Annunciation do take place, moments which are in truth symbols of the eternal timelessness of God. The moment when the sound of children's laughter is heard, the moment when the lightning pierces the darkness, the moment when the Angelus rings out, the moment when everything is still in the noontide heat : such moments are symbols in the midst of time of the eternal unchanging life of God Himself.

The supreme contribution of Greek thought to man's speculation about Time has been his insistence that the *present* is man's chief concern and that a heightened or concentrated experience of the present is of more importance than remembrances of the past or anticipations of the future. Time as such can be measured by referring to the motion of the heavenly bodies and in this way a degree of order can be established within the flux of human experience. But even more important than the signs of measurement which represent the passage of time are the symbols which point to the extension of man's present within the timelessness of eternity. Eternity, as Thomas Aquinas was to say later, " contains no trace of past or future." The completed cycle of the stars in their courses, the completed movement of a musical composition—these are analogical symbols of the eternal life of God according to the tradition which stems from Plato : the moment of maturity in any form of growth, the moment of critical turning in any form of motion —these are symbols of the timelessness of the unchanging Divine Being in the tradition which stems from Aristotle. To gather together the wholeness of time into the concentrated immediacy of the present is the supreme aim of every form of ritual celebration which is derived from the practice and outlook of Greece.

ISRAEL

The tradition of the Semitic tribes reveals a very different attitude to Time. In their remote past it was not so much the phenomenon of a deep and steady rhythm which captured men's imaginations. Rather it was the great victory of order over chaos, of the emergence of a cosmos out of a primal formlessness, of the imposition of form upon material which was " without form and void." One of the most notable signs of this victory was the existence of the sun and moon and stars, all of which acted as governors or controllers of time as they pursued their majestic courses. The sun ruled the day ; the moon ruled the night. Each luminary left its impress upon everything which it controlled. " ' Morning ' is everything connected with the sun's driving away the darkness with its rays ; ' high light ' is everything which happens in connection with the clear noon-day sun . . . ; the ' breeze of the day ' is the time of the day which is characterised by the cool evening breeze of Palestine. The colourless idea of ' hour,' measuring time in a purely quantitative way, is far from the old Israelite conception.' " (J. Pedersen, *Israel*, I-II, p. 489.)

This deep sense that different times were under the control of different " powers " and thereby took on different characters persisted throughout the historical experience of the Hebrew people. This does not mean that they were without means of measuring time in regular periods. There is good evidence that a calendar was being used in Mesopotamia at a very early date and in all probability the Hebrews took over a simple framework of calendar-time from one of the early cultures with which their ancestors had been associated. At least we have no record of any stage in Hebrew development when the people did not govern their lives by a simple reckoning of days and months and years. But unlike the Greeks who were ever anxious to gather together the wholeness of time into an integrated present experience, the Hebrews were conscious of more radical differentiations in time, differentiations which not only marked out certain times as properly belonging to certain purposes but also distinguished some times as favourable and others as unpropitious, some as good and others as definitely evil.[1] Thus man needed to be exceedingly careful in his attitude to time. It was not so much that every moment of the day had to be accounted for but rather that man was expected to conform to the proper times and seasons in all his behaviour. The right thing must be done at the right time if it was to achieve the full purpose for which it was intended.

Putting the matter in another way, we may say that the Hebrews regarded time primarily in terms of quality or of the characteristic use to which it must be put. For example, in the simplest household routine there was a time for waking and a time for sleeping, a time for eating and drinking, a time for feeding the flocks : moreover, in the wider social perspective, there was a time for communal festivities or for mourning, a time for hunting and campaigning, a time, in fact, for everything under the sun. So, as we see from numerous passages of the Old Testament, the Hebrew was constantly anxious to know whether the propitious time had come for him to embark upon a certain enterprise. He was likewise anxious at all costs to avoid performing on such a day as the sabbath any action which did not rightly belong to that particular time. In short, for the

---

[1] " For the Israelite time is not merely a form or a frame. Time is charged with substance or rather, it is identical with its substance ; time is the development of the very events. When the Israelite speaks of evil or good days, then it is meant literally, because the character of the time is always determined by that which happens." (J. Pedersen, *Israel*, I-II, p. 487. See pp. 487-490.)

Hebrew the matter of supreme importance was not time in its mathematical measurement but time in its actual content and moral quality.

But how was the *quality* of a particular time to be evaluated? Originally, it appears, this determination was made on the basis of unusual experiences having been associated with particular times. A frightening appearance in the heavens marked off a time as unpropitious : a discovery of unexpected treasure marked a time as favourable. Gradually a calendar of ordinary and extraordinary days was constructed. Man celebrated the days of good fortune as festivals, the days of ill-luck as fasts or times of lamentation. But in addition to events in the natural order there were events within the context of human relationships. Times of confusion and discord were evil, but no times were more propitious than those in which the purposes of one individual or group coalesced with those of another. These were times of meeting, appointed times in which soul was joined to soul and peace and harmony created. Normally such a time of meeting issued in a solemn covenant and thus it came about that the most favourable of all times were covenant-times. Such times must needs be celebrated with due ceremony and in this way the festivals associated with the renewing of covenants became the times of supreme symbolic importance and significance.

As can readily be seen, the view of time which regards the unusual event as marking the significance of a time for good or evil leads to a concentration of interest upon the past in its relation to the present. The past is of immense importance. What happened on a particular occasion can happen again. It may be in the present, it may be in the future, but the possibility is always there. Man's responsibility is to keep ever in mind the great event of the past, to recall it, to celebrate it, to look for its recurrence in still more striking form. The fact that it happened once means that it can happen again. It is the symbol which joins the past to the present or the past to the future which is all-important in man's struggle to interpret the meaning of the time sequence of which he himself forms a part. So the symbols of *history* begin to gain their significance. The celebration of notable events of the past by means of dramatic action and heroic tale becomes the supreme symbolic way of affirming that time is not simply a monotonous regular continuum but rather a context within which outstanding events happen and through which abiding purposes are fulfilled.

Such was the general outlook of the nomadic peoples of the Near East. Where the Hebrews went beyond this view of time, however, was in their conviction that the altogether significant events of the past took place at those times when God Himself intervened in the affairs of mankind. Just as man chooses particular times in which to perform a particular task, so, it was believed, God chooses times in which to fulfil His special purposes. It only remained to take the leap of faith and declare that God's time had coalesced with the time of a certain chosen people, that He had seen this people in their time of need and had brought to bear upon them all the resources of His time of mercy and grace. In other words, history to the Hebrews was first and foremost a pattern of *covenant-times*. They celebrated these times with thankfulness and rejoicing and looked forward to the time of the new and determinative covenant when the past and the present would find their fulfilment in the final Day of God.

So far as the Old Testament itself is concerned, its framework is not so much chronological as theological. The critical turning-points in the narrative are God's encounters with chosen men, and His bringing of them into union with His saving purpose. The covenant with Abraham, the deliverance of the tribes from Egypt and the establishment of the covenant at Sinai, the covenant with David and the settlement of his kingdom, the renewal of the covenant at the time of Josiah's Reformation—these are the times of crisis which mark the successive stages of the Old Testament narrative. Yet it was never easy for the Hebrew people to maintain this perspective, especially when they found themselves surrounded by those whose calendars were graduated according to other scales. In Canaan, for instance, they were immersed in a civilisation whose times were determined by the recurring cycle of Nature. The rising and setting of the sun, the phases of the moon, the growth and decay of vegetation, the seed time and the harvest, the turn of the year—all these were celebrated with appropriate ritual observances. There were regular sacrifices, there were pilgrimages to shrines, there were

festival banquetings and rejoicings. How could the Hebrew
faith that the all-important times were the times of God's intervention in history and of His meeting with men have any hope
of surviving in the midst of so different an outlook on life ?

So far as we can judge, the two most effective means by
which Israel's distinctive faith was preserved were first the telling
and recording of the stories of God's encounters with His people
in the past and secondly the insistence upon the due observance
of two symbolic times—the annual Passover-festival and the
weekly Sabbath. The stories did not so much focus attention
upon particular *moments* in time as upon critical *clusters of events*
within which the active intervention of God had been clearly
revealed. At the very centre of the nation's history there was
the period during which God's overwhelming compassion had
been joined to His people's uttermost need. Their time of
despair had been God's time of mercy. He had chosen a man,
equipped him to be a leader, and had brought the tribes out of
the bondage of Egypt into the new covenant relationship at
Sinai. This was the crucial victory of all time, the manifestation
in time past of God's triumph over all the powers of darkness.[1]
But it was also the promise for time present and for time future.
What God had done before He would do again. The blacker
the night the nearer the dawn. God was only waiting for human
wickedness and oppression to reach its climax : then He would
intervene again to vindicate His righteousness and to deliver
His people out of the hands of their enemies.

As regards the two symbolic festival-times, it is certain that
these were observed in some form before the entrance into
Canaan and probably before the time of the Exodus. The Passover was connected with the spring-equinox and the Sabbath
with the phases of the moon. They were significant seasons,
for they were turning points of calendar time, but at some period
in Israel's history they became much more than calendar signs,
more even than celebrations of mythical happenings in the
world of the imagination. They became the supreme means both of
holding in remembrance the great events of the deliverance from
Egypt and of entering afresh into the covenant-relationship
through which man's time had been gathered up into God's

[1] J. Pedersen, *Israel*, III-IV, p. 657.

purpose. Passover and the Sabbath were in very truth times of meeting. While they were being celebrated the past became the future in the faith of the present. What God had done He would do again on an even wider and grander scale. Time present was a time of celebration and of waiting, but in the perspective of faith every time of celebration, whether sabbath or passover, was a time of enjoying the blessings of the promised Day of God.

The contact with other civilisations through the settlement in Canaan and the exile in Babylon inevitably brought greater complications into this relatively simple time-perspective. Other nations had their times and seasons and these could not long be ignored by those who lived in their midst. So it came about that a number of secondary festivals were gradually, as it were, baptized into Israel's faith and made a part of their regular yearly celebration. The New Year Festival, the beginning and end of the spring harvest, the final ingathering of the fruits of the earth, sunrise and sunset, birth and death, the enthronement of a king and the consecration of a priest—all these were notable events. Were they to receive recognition only by means of pagan rites and ceremonies? Or could they be given a new significance within the faith of Israel? It was not easy to strip these festivals of their pagan associations but in the end most of them were given a place in the Jewish calendar and were somehow related to the Covenant (though in post-exilic times the Covenant came to be regarded more as a constitutive agreement than as a drama of personal encounter).

The most sacred times were those in which the Covenant was brought afresh to the attention of the people and their response of obedience was signed and sealed in some outward form. The sign of Circumcision, on the pattern of the story of Genesis 17, sealed the Covenant at birth; the morning and evening sacrifices renewed the Covenant daily; the sabbath became a perpetual Covenant; the Ark was the permanent symbol of the Covenant; the Feast of unleavened bread was associated with the Passover, the Feast of Weeks with the Covenant-bond given at Sinai, the Feast of Tabernacles with the safe journey of the Covenant-people through the dangers of the wilderness. Every important ceremonial occasion became in this way a means of recalling the requirements of the covenant and of renewing the pledge of loyal obedience to Him by whom the Covenant had been given to men. The danger was that life in Israel would become too strictly ordered and regimented and that the symbolic days would gradually lose their freshness of historical reference and would become nothing more than formal occasions for re-submission to a rigid moral code.

Thus the Hebrew saw the regular succession of days and months and seasons and years as a sign of God's gracious ordering of His universe while at the same time he recognised the significance of past, present and future within the one ongoing purpose of God. He believed that in spite of the fact that the most High ruled in the affairs of men there were times of darkness, times of travail, in which the powers of evil exercised a temporary sway. But he believed still more firmly that God had determined times and seasons in and through which He would accomplish His purposes of redemption and bring His elect people to their final destiny.

SABBATH AND LORD'S DAY

The Christian faith inherited two immensely significant views of time—the Greek and the Hebrew. On the one hand it was invited by the cultural outlook of Hellenism to focus its attention upon the Present, the Timeless, the Eternal Now, the Divine Nature which transcends all distinctions of temporal successiveness. On the other hand, it was driven by its inheritance from the Old Testament Scriptures to recognise the importance of History, the Past and the Future, the critical turning-points of Time, the significance of special seasons, the Divine Purpose working through the processes of history to achieve its final end. So already in the New Testament we find one strand of Christian teaching emphasising the fact that it is possible to enter into the enjoyment of eternal life here and now, that communion with God is relatively independent of time distinctions, that the glory of God shines forth in moments of timelessness : concurrently we find another strand emphasising the fact that there are times when God visits men in altogether exceptional ways, that the Past has a determinative significance for the Present and the Future, that it is through a definite sequence of events that God's purpose for mankind is being fulfilled. To hold these two views together in creative tension has been one of the major tasks of Christian teachers throughout the history of Christian thought. Let us look at some of the attitudes to Time which have emerged and in particular at the way in which these have been illustrated in and through men's celebration of Sunday.

At one extreme there has been the attitude characteristic of monasticism—that *all* time is ideally sacred and that the ordering of the day on earth should be a direct reflexion of the ordering of eternity in heaven. Do not the visions of the Bible reveal a heavenly form of existence in which the servants of God adore Him day and night in His temple? Is not the life of ordered worship the highest known to man? Can there not then be approximations, even under the conditions of earthly existence, to the perfect regularity of the praise and worship of heaven? This has been the monastic ideal—to carry through an unceasing round of vigil and prayer and praise within the sanctuary. The monks act as vicarious representatives of nature and society by constantly relating the rhythm of time to the eternity of God.

Traditionally the task of the sanctification of all time has been performed symbolically by means of the recitation of the Divine Office. "The Office is, ideally, the ordained form within which the whole Church performs from hour to hour, by night and by day, that unceasing praise of God which is the chief purpose of her existence." (E. Underhill, *Worship*, p. 114.) It is essentially a corporate act and it seeks to draw together the wholeness of temporal life into one united rhythm of adoring worship. In its complete form it "consists of eight parts, sanctifying before God that recurrent cycle of night and day, in which our lives are passed. It is best understood when regarded as a spiritual and artistic unity; so devised, that the various elements of praise, prayer and reading, and the predominantly poetic and historical material from which it is built up, contribute to one single movement of the corporate soul, and form together one single act of solemn yet exultant worship. This act of worship is designed to give enduring and impersonal expression to eternal truths; and unite the here and now earthly action of

the Church with the eternal response of creation to its origin."
(Underhill, Op. cit., pp. 116-17.) Within such an ordering of
life the Eucharist does not play an *essential* part (though, of
course, it has come to be included within the monastic day);
nor do Sundays or Saints' Days have any *essential* significance
(though, again, they have been included within the monastic
cycle to heighten interest and to provide variety). The aim is
to make *every* day an ordered round of adoration and contemplation—a direct representation of the perfect life of heaven.

At the other extreme we may set the attitude characteristic
of Puritanism—that *all* time is evil except the one sacred day of
each week which has been given by God as the token of what
the life of the elect will be in heaven. In this conception, which
is obviously derived from the strict sabbatarianism of post-exilic
Judaism, the six days are specially associated with labour and
travail and the curse of earthly existence, the seventh with rest
and holiness and the bliss of heavenly existence. Man must
engage in secular labour for that is both his penalty and his
duty; on one day of the week, however, he must desist from
all labour, in order that he may set his mind upon heavenly
things and be spared from the exhaustion which increasing toil
would bring. Generally speaking, the outlook is dark. All time
is evil and the passage through time is only to be regarded as a
pilgrimage towards a better land. Yet God in His mercy has
given man a light in the darkness, a sabbath-rest at the end of
his weekly toil, a place of refreshment in his journey, a breathing-
space for the renewing of his own soul while the world in its
wickedness moves on towards its doom.

Traditionally, this one day in seven has had as its central
activity the declaring of the law of God and the renewal of the
submission of the elect to its commands and ordinances. Special
days such as Christmas or Good Friday have no *essential* part to
play in this view of time (though they have gradually won their
way into even the strictest circles of Puritan orthodoxy); the
celebration of the Lord's Supper has no *essential* place within the
observance of the sabbath day (though it, too, has found its
way into most forms of Puritan worship.) But so long as God's
law which separates the good from the evil, the sacred from the
secular, is declared and strict obedience is renewed, the grand

purpose of the day is achieved and the souls of the elect are saved from a complete immersion in unholy time. The one day in seven is in a certain sense a symbol of the life of heaven, though chiefly in a negative way. Heaven is not earth; it is associated with rest and not labour; it is under the direct authority of God and not subject to the control of evil powers; it is conducive to the life of the soul and not of the body. But there is little symbolism of a positive kind. Man's time and God's Time have broken completely asunder and man's only hope is in the coming of the *Eschaton* when evil time will be replaced by the sinless time of the eternity of God.

In the wider stream of Christian thought and practice stemming from the Greek view of time and eternity, a more clear-cut division has been made between the Lord's Day and other days of the week than has been the case in monasticism. The central distinguishing mark of Sunday has been its relation to the Divine Liturgy. Christians have used daily forms of prayer and have assembled together whenever possible for the strengthening of the bonds of fellowship. But the world has made its demands and secular duties have had to be performed. Sunday then has been the traditional day for corporate worship, for participating in the Liturgy through which all the concerns of daily life can be offered up to God and thereby sanctified. In general there has been no suggestion that the mundane affairs of daily life were evil or that time itself was unholy. Rather the thought has been that all time belongs to God and is potentially sacred, but that in order to bring man's secular days into the sphere of the direct Divine provenance, it is necessary to symbolise the sanctification of the whole by consecrating a representative part to the service of God alone.

In the view of the Eastern Orthodox Church, the Liturgy is really in progress continuously. Christ is for ever manifesting Himself in time and is for ever passing through the cycle of incarnate life, death, resurrection and ascension. It is, however, through the celebration of the Liturgy at particular times that man and nature are sanctified by being actually united to the Son of God in His movement of salvation. Both the cycle of the liturgical year and the progress through Holy Week and

Easter are forms through which Time is sanctified but the regular weekly celebration of the Divine Mysteries is the supreme means by which the workaday week is cleansed and lifted up into the symbolic series of events in time which represent the very life of God Himself.

Anglican writers such as Archbishop Temple and Canon Quick have insisted that we do not observe Sunday because of a conviction that it is radically different from the other days of the week. Rather, they have said, our purpose is to show that *all* time belongs to God and that through a symbolic day this relation may be effectively represented and realised. Thus, in considering the definition of a sacrament, Quick has suggested that a distinguishing feature of sacramental realities is this : " that in them the outward consists of one member of a class or one part of a whole, which is severed and differentiated from the other members or parts, in order both to represent the true relation of the whole to God and to be the means whereby this relation is more effectively realised." (*The Christian Sacraments*, p. 105.) But this applies exactly to Sunday. It is the one day in seven which represents the true relation of Time to God and is the means by which this relation can be more effectively realised.

This, however, does not take us far enough. Sunday would not represent the true relation of Time to God simply by being emptied of all secular activities or by being filled with activities bearing no particular form or pattern. Sunday must bear upon it the stamp of the Liturgy, it must be moulded according to the sequence of the Liturgy. It must receive the Christ afresh as He enters into human history, incarnates Himself within it, passes through death to the fulness of the Divine Life.

Ideally the whole day should be conformed to this pattern. It should be a moving likeness of the life of the eternal Son of God. It should gather into its embrace all the secular affairs of the past week and lift them up to God. It should pre-sanctify the affairs of the coming week by including them also within its outreach. The pattern of the day attains its most concentrated form of expression in the actual celebration of the Liturgy when time is almost forgotten in the experience of the movement of the whole drama. But the day fails of its full purpose if the celebration of the Liturgy is the only means by which Time is sanctified. Still more it fails of its purpose if, as tends to be the case in the Roman tradition, one special moment becomes the centre around which the whole day revolves. Sunday only attains its true form as a sanctifying day if all its activities, all its pursuits, can find their place within a pattern which reflects the entire movement of the self-oblationary life of the Divine Son of God.

In the wider stream which flows from Hebrew thought and practice, a less radical separation has been made between the Christian Sabbath and the other days of the week than has been the case in the extremer forms of Puritanism. The central distinguishing feature of Sunday has been the coming of the Divine Word in judgment and mercy. This has been the day on which Christians have turned aside from the immediate practice of their secular vocations and have submitted all their activities and accomplishments to the searching judgment of the Word of God in Christ. They have come to see that the very framework of time within which they live is broken and disordered by human sin. Men rush hither and thither, seeking to break through the time pattern which God has established. Or they indulge themselves by dissipating the opportunities provided for them in the same framework of time. So man's time becomes spoiled and degraded. He stands under the judgment of Him Whose time is ordered in righteousness as He moves towards the fulfilment of His purpose.

Yet this is not all that Sunday proclaims. It is the Day of redemption, of resurrection, of new life. It is not simply a day of negation, a day to refrain from all mundane pursuits and to listen to the law of the Lord. It is rather a day whose pattern has been determined once for all by the resurrection of Jesus Christ from the dead. It is a day for despair to be joined to hope, for bondage to be joined to freedom, for monotonous clock-time to be joined to a time of festal rejoicing, for the threat of death to be joined to the promise of life. This pattern will reach its fullest expression in the great drama of the breaking forth of the Gospel of the Resurrection. By the proclamation of the Word of God's forgiveness through Christ and by the visible dramatisation of the Word in sacramental rite, the people of God will be renewed and strengthened and their time of travail will be turned into a time of joy. And not only will the present be joined to the past through the celebration of the victory of the Redeemer ; the present will be joined to the future as the Lord's Day becomes the metaphorical foreshadowing of the day of the final triumph of God.

Thus in the wholeness of the Christian tradition there is a place both for the Lord's Day as the representation of the full life-cycle of the Incarnate Son of God and for the Christian Sabbath as the celebration of the triumphant vindication of the Redeemer of mankind. All too easily the day can sink to the level of becoming either an occasion for the formal sanctification of time or an opportunity for relaxation from labour with a possible exposure to an edifying discourse. In this way it loses its essential quality of distinctiveness and becomes little more than a conventional sign. The time is even now ripe for the re-discovery of Sunday as the analogical symbol of the eternal movement within the life of God Himself and as the meta-phorical symbol of the junction of man's past with God's future in the resurrection of Jesus Christ from the dead.[1]

THE SYMBOLISM OF TIME

Two simple geometrical figures have been used again and again in human history to represent man's conception of Time. One is the circle, the other is the straight line. Poets have elaborated and embellished these figures : in particular the circle has sometimes become a celestial orbit, the straight line a terrestrial river, but the basic images have remained the same. Plato depicts time as the moving image of eternity and his thought receives exquisite expression in the seventeenth century poem of Henry Vaughan :

> I saw Eternity the other night,
> Like a great ring of pure and endless light,
> All calm, as it was bright :

[1] For a suggestive treatment of " The Sanctification of Time," see Gregory Dix, *The Shape of the Liturgy*, Chapter XI, pp. 303-96.

> And round beneath it, Time in hours, days, years,
> Driv'n by the spheres
> Like a vast shadow mov'd ; in which the world
> And all her train were hurled.

Heraclitus speaks of never stepping twice into the same stream and the picture of Time as a River (an image which supplies the necessary idea of motion to the straight line) receives dramatic expression in the eighteenth century hymn of Isaac Watts :

> Time like an ever rolling stream
> Bears all its sons away ;
> They fly forgotten as a dream
> Dies at the opening day.

and more subtle expression in the twentieth century poem of Walter de la Mare :

> With each *Now* a rivulet runs to waste,
> Unless we pause to stoop ; to sip ; to taste ;
> And muse on any reflex it may cast.
> Its source a region of mountains, east to west,
> High snows, crags, valleys green and
>   sunken fens—a region called the Past.

The point moving in a circle or the point moving on a straight line—which is the more adequate representation of the movement of Time ? The wheeling of the heavenly bodies or the flowing of the river from the mountains to the sea—which is the more adequate representation of the wholeness or the fulfilment of Time ? These are questions to which, it seems, no final answers can be given. The universe is such that viewed in one way it appears as a cyclic movement of repeated phrases, viewed from another angle it appears as a forward-movement from a source towards a goal. Can it be that both are true from the limited standpoint of human observations and that the possibility of any final reconciliation is to be found only in the mind of God Himself ?

This double view of time receives further illustration in the nature of the methods by which men seek to measure time. The rotation of the earth and the movements of the heavenly bodies are circular in form. The shadow cast by the sun on the dial describes a circular path. For this reason the cyclic motions of natural phenomena have for long provided convenient standards of measurement and when artificial clocks came to be constructed it was natural that they should conform to the same pattern. " The seventeenth and early eighteenth centuries were pre-eminently the age of clocks. This was the era of the scientific revolution when the abstract study of time was supplemented by outstanding practical advances in chronometer design. What were the typical natural and artificial clocks of that age ? The fundamental laws of classical dynamics were based on an abstract scale of time to which the rotation of the earth provided an excellent natural approximation. Similarly the artificial clocks and watches of the clock-makers all incorporated some rotatory or other periodically repeating mechanism. These cyclic clocks, whether natural or artificial, served to define the uniform rate of flow of Newtonian mathematical time, without origin or termination. In principle, at least, like Tennyson's brook, this time can ' go on for ever.' " (G. J. Whitrow, *The Listener*, Apr. 20, 1950, p. 693.)

But, as Whitrow goes on to point out, during the last two centuries a great change has taken place. Men have become deeply interested in the past, even in the remote past. New methods have been devised for measuring time and the emphasis has changed from periodicity to irreversibility. " When we examine the methods now used to chart the various stages of prehistory, we find that the natural clocks employed, whether they be a sequence of tree rings or fluorine absorption by fossilised bones or radioactive decay in geological deposits all differ fundamentally from cyclic clocks. They display the linear irreversible property of time's arrow." (*Ibid.*) This does not mean, however, that the cyclic method of measurement is obsolete or outmoded. The radioactive clock is never likely to be employed by large numbers of people and tree-rings are of little use to measure small periods of time. Cyclic clocks provide an altogether convenient measurement of the structure of *public* time within which men live. They give true recordings within their own particular framework of reference. But for a more accurate measurement of the distances between events in the history of the world, other time-scales are needed. The development of scales of this kind has been one of the most notable achievements of science, though one of the chief problems in the modern mathematical theory of time is that of ensuring that any two observers shall possess clocks identically graduated.

This problem can only be solved if it is possible for the observers to communicate with one another and this has led to the conclusion that the new approach to time consists in using it as the foundation of a new science of *communication*. Much remains to be done within this field of investigation, but for our present purpose the main point which emerges is that when the linear time-scale is being used it is essential that any pair of observers shall be in communication with one another in order that their scales may be identically graduated. Cyclic clocks are more easily adapted to general corporate use for they are graduated by the standard of a great public phenomenon—the movement of the heavenly bodies : they are, in fact, more public but less accurate. Linear clocks depend more upon the inter-communication of interested observers ; they are less impersonal but more accurate. There seems to be no means of dispensing with either standard of measurement. In one case signs provided by the motions of the heavenly bodies are used to represent time periods in all their divisions and sub-divisions ; in the other case signs adapted by observers from the regular forward movement of the world-structure are used to denote distances between events and to provide a means by which the phenomena of history may be seen in their true relationship to one another.

Such are the *signs* which have been used to represent the *movement* of time. The question now arises whether there are time-*symbols* which represent the *wholeness* or the *fulfilment* of time. Let us take first the wholeness of time. Again and again the attempt has been made to isolate particular ages or periods and to regard them as symbols of the perfect wholeness of time. Usually such a symbol takes its pattern from the cycle of a living organism which comes to birth, grows, advances to maturity, declines and at length dies. So a civilisation is regarded as rising, growing in power, reaching its zenith, declining and disintegrating. Or it may be a nation in a particular period of its history or a tribe or a family. Or it may be a representative and symbolic individual such as a father or a king whose life-cycle is regarded as the symbol of the whole. In some way similarities of pattern are detected between different periods of corporate existence and the inference is drawn that this identical pattern is, in fact, the pattern of the whole.

It is this view of time which inspires the interpretations of history associated with the names of Oswald Spengler and (to a modified extent) of Arnold Toynbee. In a more specifically Christian context it may be found in the sacramental theory of Canon O. C. Quick. For him, the incarnate life of Christ is a perfect expression of Divine beauty and truth; the death and resurrection of Christ constitute a perfect enactment of the victory of good over evil. The whole career of Christ may be regarded as the perfect sacrament, expressing the ultimate truth of nature and interpreting the ultimate value of time. The time-reference may be seen, for example, in the following passage:

"When it is asserted that the Atonement wrought by the Cross of Christ is universal and all-sufficient, we desire to understand that the Crucified Saviour is in space and time the one perfect sacrament of the power by which in the end, or in the whole, all evil is redeemed, and the rational perfection of the universe vindicated and fulfilled. It follows then that the life and death of Christ, thus considered as the instrument of God's power, are again seen as unique among all the events of time; but again they sum up in themselves and interpret the ultimate significance and value of the temporal process as a whole, and also are the visible embodiment of the power by which that process is directed to its end. And we shall confirm and interpret our faith in the Cross of Christ as the sacrament of God's effective operation, if we can illustrate how the essential principle of the Cross penetrates everywhere the life of the temporal world as that which lifts existence on to higher levels, until man finds himself in presence of the truth that *every* outward good must be given up and pass away in the end, if the one pearl of great price is to be possessed. We shall verify our belief that we have dimly divined the principle which explains the temporal world as a whole in relation to eternity, if we are able to find that same principle at work in the stages by which the highest values have been reached in the temporal world itself." (*The Christian Sacraments*, pp. 84-5.)

The implications of this view are clear. Everywhere in the time process a principle of redemption is at work ; but only in one cycle of events does the principle receive full expression. The death and resurrection of Christ bring the inner principle of His whole career into focus and form the unique symbol of the redemption or sanctification of all time. This event (or cycle of events) may be said to be unique and yet it is quite clear from Quick's exposition that other events (or cycles of events) in time approximate very closely to it. Always the redemption of time is in process, but in the Cross and Resurrection it receives its fullest implementation. This means that within the time process there are innumerable patterns which symbolise the essential structure of the wholeness of time but that the central symbol, which acts as their standard of reference and interpretation, is the whole career of the Son of Man which finds its perfect expression in the submission to the Cross and in the resurrection from the dead. The symbol of time is circular rather than linear, though the thought of direction towards an end and a fulfilment is not altogether absent.

What, then, of those systems of thought which focus attention upon the *fulfilment* of time ? In these the attempt has been made to isolate a notable event or a particular series of events and to regard it as symbolising in some way the ultimate fulfilment of the time-process. Usually the symbol takes its pattern from the common experience of a man on a journey. He makes his preparations, sets out in a definite direction, encounters difficulties and obstacles, overcomes them, constantly renews his sense of direction and ultimately reaches his goal. In this pattern, the all-important ingredient is the sense of *direction*. It can only be supplied by the establishment of a relation between two situations which are separated from one another by at least a minimum of distance. In other words there must be *separation* but there must also be the *transcending* of this separation. Only through the relating of the darkness of the existential situation to some shining light in the beyond can direction be gained and with it the inspiration to move forward with confidence and hope.[1]

Within such an outlook the centre of interest is normally the career of an outstanding individual (it may occasionally be a coterie or an elite) who through some ecstatic experience becomes related to a goal of destiny. In this way he gains direction and begins his forward journey. Then comes a supreme crisis of testing, a moment in which he seems to be for ever cut off from the possibility of attaining this end. His behaviour in such a crisis is determinative. If he falters and despairs, the pattern breaks and the direction is lost. If, however, the vision holds and he goes forward into the darkness of the shadow of death and emerges victorious on the other side, a definitive symbol has been set up linking together the time of darkness and the time of light, the time of defeat and the time of victory, the time of death and the time of life. Such symbols have been rare in human history but once they have come into being they have proved to be the most powerful of all forces to move the imaginations of men and to strengthen their wills to go forward in faith towards their destiny. It is these symbols, then, which are to be regarded as the metaphorical representations of the End-Time, which is the fulfilment of all time in the Kingdom of God.

In his suggestive book, *The Interpretation of History*, Paul Tillich has employed the term " centre of history " to describe these critical moments in the passage of time which have set the direction for the lives of countless generations of men. He points out that for the faith of Israel the centre of history was the Exodus : for the faith of the followers of Mohammed it was his journey from Mecca to Medina : for the faith of Christians it was the events of Calvary and the Resurrection : for the faith of Communists it is the appearance of the proletariat as a social class. Yet there are certain difficulties both in the phrase, " centre of history," and in the particular examples which Tillich gives to illustrate his thesis, though I believe that in the main his interpretation is valid. I shall suggest certain

---

[1] This has never been expressed more vividly than in the opening sections of Bunyan's *Pilgrim's Progress*.

modifications, and these may serve to indicate what is the exact nature of the symbolism here in view.

The difficulty of the term " centre " is that it does not imply any necessary sense of direction. It can be used appropriately in the context of a cyclical interpretation but is apt to lead to confusion in a more linear context. For the determination of a line, direction through a point is the essential factor. Hence, in speaking of the critical determinant of history in the several frameworks which Tillich enumerates, it would surely be better to speak of an *arrow* of history. In each of these contexts the really critical factor has been the movement of a pioneering individual in a particular direction. In the case of Israel it was the career of Moses which, from its earliest years, was directed towards the releasing of his fellow tribesmen from the bondage of Egypt and the leading of them towards the promised land. Moses met the maximum opposition to his purpose in the stubborn resistance of Pharaoh, but having persisted in his intention even at the risk of his own death and the annihilation of his people, he finally achieved his end and set up a symbol for the interpretation of history which has given guidance to his people from that time even until now. Similarly in the case of Islam it was the career of Mohammed which, from an early stage, was directed towards delivering his people from idolatry and uniting them in submission to the one true God. Despised and opposed by many of his fellow tribesmen, it was finally the march from Mecca to Medina which overcame all resistance and set up a symbol for the inspiration of his followers throughout succeeding ages. In the case of Communism the course of events is somewhat different, though the underlying pattern is very similar. Here the career of Marx himself has been, as it were, projected on to the proletariat and a myth built up of an inexorable movement towards the establishment of the classless society. In this movement the crisis has not yet taken place but Marx (inspired, it would seem, by memories of resistance and opposition overcome in other contexts) was able to paint a picture of a final determinative victory and it is this picture which has provided the symbol for the Communist interpretation of history and the inspiration for the life of present toil and even sacrifice on the part of those who accept it.

In the Christian view, these symbols all have a certain significance, though in the history of Christian interpretation little attention has been given to the possible arrows of history outside the Judæo-Christian tradition. In the New Testament itself there is the clear recognition that the careers of Moses and the prophets were symbols of the true direction by which, in God's purpose, history is to advance towards its goal. Moses saw the vision of " the glorious liberty of the children of God." To lead his people thither became the central aim and object of all his endeavours. Despised and rejected, he yet returned to his task. Opposed and threatened, he yet remained faithful. With the ruin of all his hopes staring him in the face, he still waited for God's vindication. He endured as seeing Him Who is invisible and thereby established a symbolic pattern of faith valid for all time. In a similar way the righteous servant of the Lord, the anonymous representative of God's servants, the prophets, saw the vision of a new justification and reconciliation which might come to his people. He was despised and rejected of men, he was wounded and bruised, he poured out his soul unto death. But again his career became a symbol which set the direction for all that was noblest and best in the later faith of Israel. Here, then, in the experience of faithful Israelites, arrows of history were provided which only needed to be checked by some decisive standard of reference to make them indicators of the direction of the total movement of Time towards its goal.

Such a standard, the Christian faith proclaims, was set up once and for all by Jesus Christ, the pioneer and completer of faith, who for the joy that was set before Him (the joy, surely, of bringing redemption and reconciliation to all mankind) endured the Cross, despising the shame, and is set down at the right hand of God. Hereby what we may call the Christ-Arrow was fashioned. The resolution of his full earthly career into one arrow of direction provides the linear symbol of the total movement of time from its origin in the mind of God to its fulfilment in His completed purpose.

To discern this symbol aright men must continue to wrestle with the documents and the traditions, ever seeking to see more clearly the *direction* which the career of the historical Jesus followed. They must seek to understand His own intentions, His own words and guidance, His own significant actions, His parables, spoken and acted, His references to other symbols of direction. Above all they must seek to probe to the depths of the significance contained in His decision to accept suffering and to become obedient to death, even the death of the cross. Just as scientific observers are engaged in a constant struggle to improve their methods of observation and their standards of measurement, so the Christian historian must seek ever to gain a truer vision of the *direction* revealed in the life and teaching and death of the historical Jesus. Yet the vision can never be final. At the end the direction is still a *symbol* and not an absolute. Our limitations are such that we can never transcend personal equations entirely. As for the scientist, so for the historian— the more the dialectic of cross-checking and inter-communicating can be sustained, the more knowledge will increase and the more accurate will the measurement of quantity and direction be.

Thus we are finally brought to the position in which we have two possible time-symbolisms available. One is relatively slow and steady—the analogical extension of certain movements of the heavenly bodies or (better) of the process of organic growth. Its characteristic quality is periodicity—growth and decay, birth and death, waxing and waning, maturing and disintegrating. It is the time-span most readily applicable to universes, worlds, civilisations, generations, nations, pointing, as it does, to an over-arching, all-embracing eternity. The other is relatively swift and discontinuous—the metaphorical projection of the process of journeying from one point to another. Its characteristic quality is direction—it is ongoing and irreversible. It is the time-span most readily applicable to flashes of light, movements of individuals, inter-communication between persons, pointing, as it does, to a swiftly-approaching end. These are the two symbolisms and there seems to be no possibility of combining the two within a ready synthesis.

So in the Christian understanding of time and eternity there must ever be two methods of interpretation. One who begins by contemplating the eternal Being of God, His life of Love ever going forth and returning to its source, sees the terrestrial order as the representation of the celestial and time as the moving image of Eternity. The symbol of the Heavenly Logos is the Son of Man in His perfect beauty and rationality; the symbol of the Eternal movement of Love is the career of the Son of Man in His descent to earth, His birth, life, death and resurrection, His exaltation and triumph in heaven. On the other hand, one who begins by seeing as in a flash the final Purpose of God, His gracious design to bring many sons to glory, regards as really significant those individuals in history who have heard God calling them to move in a specified direction and those patterns of events in which the chosen individuals have passed through defeat into victory, through death into life. The symbol of the Elect Servant of God is the Son of Man hearing the call to fulfil the past by proclaiming the good news of the Kingdom of God: the symbol of the Redemption and final Reconciliation of all things is the Son of Man passing through obedience and suffering and death into His glory. Here are the two standpoints. It ill behoves an observer at one post to condemn his opposite number as a false prophet or an impostor. Rather let him look the more carefully at his own scale of measurement and let him seek by every means to communicate to his fellow-observer the glory of the vision which he has seen!

CHAPTER FOUR

Symbolic Persons

MAN LIVES in a spatial environment, he moves in a temporal continuum and he has his being normally in a social context. He may seek to withdraw from space, but this is never finally possible ; he may seek to transcend his framework of time, but this is only conceivable in high flights of the imagination ; he may seek to dwell solitarily and alone, but even this is a maimed existence and he always remains intimately related to society in ways of which he may scarcely be aware. The individual, in fact, cannot exist apart from the community ; at the same time, the character of the community depends, in the last resort, upon the quality of the individuals who compose it. These are obvious truths but they are of great importance in any consideration of the place of symbolism in human life.

A man is related to space, to time and to his neighbours through symbolic forms. He defines symbolic loci, symbolic objects, symbolic structures in space : he sets apart symbolic seasons, days and periods in time : he recognises symbolic officials, representatives, leaders in society. This is true of man in all parts of the world and at every stage of history. Patterns of symbolism change but the phenomenon itself remains. And of all symbolic forms none are more important or more influential than those which relate man to his social context. His natural environment is a major factor in his development, but his social context is a greater influence still. Let us therefore seek to examine the main forms which this symbolism has taken. The subject is vast for the whole science of sociology is of relatively recent growth, but I believe that enough has been discovered for us to be able to discern the main lines along which this particular form of symbolism has developed.

PRIMITIVE SOCIETIES

Let us take as our starting-point the relatively settled group, living in a particular area, and possessing a recognisable pattern of social behaviour. Many small-scale groups of this kind have become familiar to us through the investigations of social scientists while the great civilisation of India provides a large-scale model of a society which has maintained this general character through many centuries of human history. The common pattern of these societies may be briefly described.

In the first place, the society is intimately related to its natural environment. Its roots are in the soil of a well-defined area and men, animals, trees and plants share a common life. Even the gods and the ancestors share this same life so that all are literally bound together in one bundle of vital existence. At all costs the life of this common existence has to be sustained and the activities of all members of the group are directed to this end. Each has his designated task to perform and this leads to a certain division of labour, organised normally on a hereditary basis. This does not mean, however, that one type of labour is superior to another : in these societies the only real criteria of superiority are those of age and of marked faithfulness in conforming to the traditional social pattern.

The government of these social groups is normally in the hands of the " elders." These men are the obvious links with tradition. They are familiar with the legends which tell of the words and deeds of the ancestors, they can transmit the myths which tell of the origins of natural phenomena ; in short, they carry authority simply because of their age and experience. The whole of existence is viewed as a continuous growth rooted in the past and stretching on into the future and the canons of correct behaviour are always derived from the past. The weight of social tradition is immense and man has no stronger desires than to foster the universal life in which he participates and to pass on to future generations the heritage which he himself has received.

To keep the life-force of society at its maximum, nothing is more important than the preservation of a steady harmony between man and man within the tribe. Thus, as it has been put, it is the " quintessence of normality " which fits a man for highest office in the tribe. The odd, the novel, the self-assertive, the emotionally unstable, are all suspected and even feared. Quarrels must be avoided if possible and if they occur they must be healed without delay. All this means that the elders, being the upholders of the regular pattern of social life, constitute the nearest approach to what may be called *symbolic* persons within the tribe. Actually symbolism is at a minimum, for all men are regarded as having descended from the same divine being or world-soul and all share in the same common life. But as authentic links with the recent past and as recognised authorities in the present, the *elders* may be regarded as the earliest individuals to occupy a symbolic status within the structure of society.

One other group of men, however, deserves to be mentioned in this connexion. To promote the unity and euphoria of this type of society nothing is more effectual than the dances and common bodily movements and regular chantings in which members of the tribe from earliest times have indulged. These common expressions of emotion are the ritual-forms of the society and partake of a quasi-religious character.[1] But although these dances are essentially corporate acts, certain individuals seem to gain the ascendancy in the actual performances by reason of their versatility or their infectious enthusiasm. Often they are subject to trances or to an almost frenzied possession and, in a primitive society, these qualities are bound to lead to an enhancement of prestige. Thus pre-eminently the *elder*, secondarily the *shaman* or master of the dance—these have always been the leading symbolic figures in tribes which have attained a certain degree of ordered stability through their attachment to a particular natural habitat.

---

[1] " It was the surrender to the mystical ' call of the blood,' expressing itself in the dance, which probably constituted the original ' act of religion ' and provided the original bond of union for the social group." (A. Coates, *Prelude to History*, p. 221.)

But there is a very different type of society—the type associated with the highlands and the open steppes and the wind-swept deserts. Tribes of this kind have ever been restless wanderers, roaming from place to place in search of food and drink. They are liable to be attacked at any time. They are in conflict with Nature, with the beasts of the field, with strangers, and often with themselves. The conflict may vary in its intensity but the feeling that life is under threat of hostile forces is never far away.

But not only is there the hostility of familiar forces to be reckoned with. There are the deadlier spirit-powers which may be encountered at any time. These powers may embody themselves in stones or trees or springs or animals : they may fly with the wind or act through the storm : they may possess with frenzied energy some fellow human being. Thus existence is divided between the familiar and the unfamiliar, between friendly spiritual powers and hostile demonic influences, between moments of exulting confidence and moments of abject fear. It is a fierce and rigorous life and yet it has its compensations and rewards.

In such an existence, where all are threatened by external powers, a close bond of brotherhood and equality is quickly developed. The women normally perform the necessary chores of the encampment while the men engage in the struggle for existence. There is little prestige attached to age as such nor is overmuch attention paid to the traditional patterns of the past. The chief criterion of excellence is prowess in the contemporary struggle of life : the really valuable heritage from the past is the collection of legends which tell of the exploits of heroes of former days. In other words, the symbolic person within this society is the killer, the champion, the victor, *the hero*. Age and heredity are of little account. The man who slays the tribal enemy, the man who is skilful in the chase, the man who can perform exploits of valour and daring—this is the man who is accorded the place of eminence in the life of society. Above all, the man who through dependence upon the good spirit-power of his own society succeeds in vanquishing some alien embodiment of evil spirit-power is raised to the highest pinnacle of fame. The legends of the slaying of giants and dragons, of the cutting down of trees and of the overcoming of water-spirits, all bear witness to this fact. Even the present day legends of the exploits of the Lone Ranger and of Superman belong to the same category. The man who can overcome enemies and slay the powers of evil is worthy of the highest honours that his fellows can afford.

One other aspect of the situation deserves to be mentioned. The only serious rival to the heroic killer in these predatory societies is the *actor*. Part of the excitement of the encounter is mediated to the tribe by means of the acting out of the conflict beforehand (this is normally the attempt to ensure a successful combat through the aid of sympathetic magic) or through the imitation of the scene when the conflict is over. In this cere- monial acting the central figure may be the hero himself, but it must often have happened that the hero was not as successful in externalising the drama before his audience as he was in actually performing his doughty deeds in the forest or on the open plain. So in course of time it was found that a substitute could perform the actions of the battle-scene even more effec- tively than the champion himself and this substitute was in consequence accorded a place of special distinction amongst his fellows. Thus pre-eminently *the hero*, secondarily *the actor*— these have always been the symbolic persons *par excellence* in nomadic and frontier tribes and indeed in restless and dynamic societies in every period of world-history.

EARLY SOCIAL FUSIONS

A society which becomes encased in its own traditional pattern ultimately stagnates and dies ; a society which dissipates its energies in internecine conflict ultimately becomes exhausted and succumbs. The only way of life and progress is through some kind of fusion or interaction between raiding clan and settled tribe, between those whose imaginations are fired by the prospect of conquest and the infliction of death and those whose minds are set on the continuity of tradition and the promotion of life. Obviously in any encounter between two societies whose patterns of existence are set in one or other of these moulds, the initial victory will almost certainly be gained by the dynamic group. The settled tribe is unversed in the arts of war and is in no way prepared to meet sudden new contingencies. At the same time, unless the marauders exterminate their victims completely, the influence of the settled group in the resultant fusion is likely to be far greater than would at first have been imagined. Its members are familiar with the ways of the land, they are well versed in the techniques of production, they know how to maintain harmonious relations with the spirit-powers who reside in their territory. In fact, their assistance and support is essential to the conquerors if they are to make good use of their new acquisition. Thus a fusion of societies, like the marriage of man and woman, leads to a new creation in which well-defined characteristics drawn from each partner in the union play an essential part.

It is, of course, impossible to define one uniform pattern as constituting the social framework of such fusions of communities. The possibilities of variation through geographical and historical circumstance are endless. Yet it can at least be said that in the fusion one set of characteristics is likely to be in the ascendant. Either the settled community proves strong enough gradually to absorb the conquerors into its own pattern of life or the raiders gather up the remnants of the original group and integrate them into the pattern of their own dynamic purpose. Moreover, two other important developments may take place in the creative encounters between societies. Threatened by external danger, several groups of the more settled kind may see that their only way of safety lies in building up some form of common life together. In this way there comes into existence a new society which is predominantly conservative in character and yet which has been stimulated to make certain creative advances through the pressure from outside. Or again two of the more dynamic societies may come to see that the only way of achieving their purposes of expansion is through uniting together in the common enterprise. In this way there comes into existence a new society which is still predominantly dynamic in character but which has recognised some of the limitations of unrestrained aggressiveness and has extended the range of those whom it regards as friends and partners in the common purpose. Thus in all these various ways societies of a more complex character have emerged, combining certain elements from each of the original types which we have considered and at the same time so constructed that their general social pattern tends to be set in the direction of the one or the other. Let us now look at actual examples, first of the one kind, then of the other.

For examples of creative changes resulting in a still dominantly settled type of society we may look to the early civilisations of Egypt, of China, of Greece and of Rome. In each case we find the locus of the new civilisation in a relatively homogeneous geographical area where originally families devoted to the soil had lived. There were divine beings associated with each of the natural phenomena on the farms, as well as with the implements and furnishings in the farmstead itself. There was a regular division of labour and the person of highest eminence in each community was the elder—the father in the family, the group of elders in the larger community. These were the men of experience who knew the traditions of the past, were familiar with the ways of the divine beings in the present and could maintain the health and harmony of communal life for transmission to the future. In other words, they were the guardians of the Law of Nature by which the soil and the flocks were nurtured and the food-supply for the community was maintained.

Due to a variety of causes, there began in time to be movements towards a larger union of social groups in each of these areas. It has been suggested that in Egypt this was largely due to the fact that all groups were dependent upon the waters of the Nile and that in utilising these waters for purposes of irrigation it became necessary to draw up common rules and regulations which could promote the wellbeing of all. Common organisation for defence, common acceptance of values for purposes of exchange, common agreements on the delimitation of territory and property—all must have led gradually to the establishment of clusters of nomes or farms or walled cities or city-states, all of which recognised certain common standards and modes of behaviour and gained a sense of a greater confidence through their integration into a common life. Taking the case of ancient

Egypt as one example, we are told by Professor Moret that as early as 2900 B.C. the dweller on the banks of the Nile had already made an enormous advance. " Coming to a country which was full of resources but demanded unwearying effort, foresight and method, he controlled the forces of the Nile and disciplined Nature, submitting himself to their laws. In the Nile, which he transformed into Osiris, the Egyptian worshipped a master, an educator and the creator of his food and his life ; he knew that the Nile had exercised a salutary constraint over him, which he translated into the beneficent kingship of Osiris, Horus and the human Pharaohs. The interdependence which the Nile had created between the dwellers on its banks, limiting every man's rights by the needs of others, had for its consequence collective labour, organised with a view to the welfare of all. So, at the very sight of Egypt, peaceful and prosperous, the Egyptian of very early times lavished his feelings of gratitude in many forms, on the divine Nile which had inspired his institutions." (*From Tribe to Empire*, pp. 144-5.)

With this enlargement of the area of common life, changes were bound to take place in the organisation of rights and duties. For a time it was possible to extend the circle of elders so as to include those of all the uniting groups, but such a body must soon have become unwieldy and the principle of *representation* offered itself as the only workable solution. Out of the body of elders, some had to be selected who were pre-eminent by reason of possessing qualities other than that of having lived through a longer span of physical life. So the enormously important step was taken of appointing men who seemed to possess outstanding qualities of *mind*. These qualities may have come through age and long experience but not necessarily so. If a man showed unusual knowledge of the law of Nature, if in particular he showed himself capable of distinguishing between the changing and the permanent, the temporary appearances and the unchanging principles of existence, he was deemed worthy to act as the *representative* of his nome or of his village in the larger councils of the community. Because of his insight into the laws by which the whole life of the universe was governed —the life of gods, men, animals, natural phenomena—he could give such counsel as would promote the life of the wider community which had now come into existence. In other words, the *priest*, in the sense of the interpreter of the Divine law and the director of the appropriate ritual actions : the *philosopher* in the sense of the man with knowledge of universal principles and the counsellor on communal organisation : the *statesman* in the sense of the man with insight to discern the proper rights and duties of every man in society—these became the symbolic figures in the enlarged community. There is no necessary distinction between the three. The same body of representatives may perform the offices of priest, philosopher and statesman. The main point is that in a relatively stable society, settled in a particular area, the symbolic person is the representative man who is versed in the traditions of the country and instructed in the laws of Nature and society and who is capable of using his knowledge to frame appropriate laws of behaviour for the community as a whole.

A notable illustration of this type of social organisation is to be seen in the early development of Chinese civilisation. As the country became unified, a hierarchy of officials was established on the basis of wisdom and knowledge rather than on that of birth or privilege. In the local cities, in the provincial centres, in the imperial capital, there were bodies of officers under the presidency of a single head and in all cases appointment was by examination. From the time of Confucius onwards, the teaching which he had propounded formed the subject-matter of the tests and in this way the pattern of the political, religious and ethical life of the land attained a remarkable degree of uniformity. The basic principle to which all ethical and ritual behaviour was required to conform was the principle of *li*. *Li* is the will of Heaven which finds expression in every department of life. In nature, in society, in the relations between gods and men, *li* is the governing principle. To know *li* and to conform to *li* is the ideal in every situation which may arise. In particular *li* governs the physical basis of existence—it is, in literal fact, the law of Nature—while at the same time *li* provides the pattern for harmonious ethical relations within the community. Thus the symbolic man is the interpreter and the promoter of *li*. He is priest, philosopher and ruler all in one and though he may not have been directly selected by popular choice, he is the real representative of the people in bringing *li* to them and bringing them into conformity with *li*.

In all societies of this type the conception of the Law of Nature is of immense importance. The symbolic man does not act as an individual or in his own right. It is true that he does not merely reflect the accumulated experience which has come to him in the course of his own life—this was in essence the way of the elder in the most primitive society. He uses his *mind* to make distinctions and classifications and interpretations. He applies general principles to particular situations. He relates social traditions to new historical circumstances. But in doing this he is dependent all the time upon the Law of Nature—*li, rita, maat, themis*—to which society must in every respect conform if it is to retain its health and vigour. Thus the representative man is a man under authority and at the same time a man who bears the responsibility for the general welfare of society on his mind and in his heart. His is never an easy task. He stands between unchanging principles and the kaleidoscopic changes of actual mundane existence. He strives towards the infinite, he aspires towards the perfect order, the law of all things as they are designed to be ; at the same time he remains in contact with things as they are, he recognises the limitations of the finite, he sees the imperfections of all earthly forms. He is deeply conscious of the passions which bind to earth as well as of the attractions which draw towards heaven. He is a man in tension. Yet by performing his task faithfully he acts as one of the twin symbolic pillars which support the whole structure of the social life of mankind.

DYNAMIC SOCIETIES

For examples of creative changes which have led to the emergence of societies of a more restless and dynamic type, we may look to the early Aryans, the Iranians, and above all to the Hebrews and the Mohammedans. In each case a nomadic and migratory form of existence was followed by one in which a particular locality became the object of corporate desire. A group or a confederation of groups made it their central object to gain possession of a country or a civilisation and to establish their own way of life in this new environment. This meant the dispossession in some sense of those who already inhabited the land though, as we hinted at an earlier point, history has seen great variations in the extent to which such dispossession was actually carried through. Sometimes the original inhabitants were virtually exterminated, sometimes they survived and actually provided the pattern of life to which their conquerors were destined ultimately to conform. Recognising as I do the width of these variations, I believe that it is still possible to give some general account of the characteristics of these more dynamic societies as they appear in history.

In the primitive forms of dynamic society the most urgent matters of concern were the food-supply and the means of protection from the threats of hostile powers—wild beasts, pestilence or spirit-forces. The symbolic man was the heroic individual who could slay these enemies and bring the spoils of his exploits as an offering to the common good. But at the next stage of development, a sheer display of individual physical prowess was not enough. More complex factors had to be dealt with. When it was a question of attacking peoples already settled in a particular location, the problem of numbers had to be faced. Almost certainly the community of settlers would be superior in numbers to those who wished to dispossess them. The geographical configuration of the land had to be taken into account, the nature of the gods of the land, the processes of Nature in the land, and so on. What was needed now was a *leader*, a man who could inspire confidence, could unite his fellows in a common purpose and could show the way by which the desired end was to be achieved. In such a situation strength of a kind was essential but brute animal strength was not enough. So again the exceedingly important step was taken of according the position of leadership to the man of *imagination*, the man who would devise a plan for doing the thing that needed to be done, not necessarily in a direct and obvious way, but rather in a hitherto unthought-of way which would, surprisingly enough, prove more effective than anything previously known. In other words, the way of victory now becomes the way of conceiving a new technique, or a new strategy, and of carrying it into effect with energy and determination.

In these new circumstances the quality of supreme importance is the power to see ahead, to anticipate in ever so small a measure the way in which new techniques can deal with new circumstances. The desire for this power appears even in the dramatic activities of the hunter or the warrior who prepares himself for the encounter by going through a mock performance of the combat beforehand and by slaying his opponent in effigy. But a great advance is made when a man rejects time-honoured methods and traditional techniques and conceives some new way by which his enemy can be overcome. It may be by calling in the aid of some superior power or by inducing other men to participate with him in a common strategy or by working out a surprise movement or by engineering a clever trap or by inventing a new instrument. In all these cases the possession of sheer physical strength is not the matter of primary importance. There must still be energy and courage and determination, but above all there must be the imagination to conceive the novel and the untried and the willingness to put it to the test whatever the consequences. A man who possesses these qualities will sooner or later attain the position of *leadership*, whatever his immediate gifts and capacities may be.

Thus in all creative movements to promote the betterment of the lot of societies whose way of life is hard and rigorous and insecure, the all-important figure is the man who can see a little beyond his fellows and who is willing to reject a relatively assured lesser satisfaction in favour of a more precarious greater satisfaction. He sees a way of manipulating Nature so that it will operate to the advantage of the group. He sees a way of persuading men to unite in appropriate action in order to secure an ultimate advantage. He sees a way of responding to the command of some transcendent power and thereby of gaining the goodwill of that power on behalf of his people. In other words, the symbolic figures in this type of community are the *pioneer*, the man who envisages new possibilities of moulding elements within the natural environment : the *political leader*, the man who conceives new possibilities of organising and increasing efficiency within the social environment : and the *prophet*, the man who has eyes to discern the Divine purpose and a mouth to declare the will of God to his own day and generation. It is possible that one man might combine all of these functions, though when life increases in complexity this is scarcely likely to happen. The point I am seeking to establish is that in a relatively dynamic society, moving towards a future only dimly perceived, the symbolic person is the heroic adventurer who, while aware of past traditions and present patterns of social organisation, yet sees ahead into the future and focuses the attention of his contemporaries upon appropriate ways and means of attaining a better form of existence.

One other thing of a general kind needs to be said about the role of the leader in this dynamic context. The true leader can never operate effectively without carrying on in some degree the function of killer which belonged to his prototype in former times. The very fact that he is striving for something *new* means that he is attempting to administer the death-blow to that which is *old*. A technique is outworn, a custom is out of date, a tradition is a brake to progress, a pattern of religious life is a hindrance to the ongoing Divine purpose. To adopt the new means in each case is to discard and even to destroy the old. But more serious than this, the old always has its living personal guardians whose very existence seems to depend upon its continuance. Any attack upon a law or a custom or a method or an institution seems to be an attack upon the persons by whom they are operated and preserved. This means, therefore, that the leader is bound in some sense to be a slayer. He may find himself seeking the death of an actual person or of that person's living deputy or of that person's symbolical representation. Further, he may seek this death either in actuality or through some symbolic means. Even to attack a man with words is a way of seeking to destroy some element of his living activities.

Thus the leader in any area of human existence is a marked man. He has seen a vision of an order of existence which appears to be more desirable than anything previously experienced. He *must* seek to realise it. He can only do so by challenging and overthrowing certain patterns of social organisation which, though not necessarily evil in themselves, yet stand in the way of any action which would spell death to their own continued usefulness. He does the fearful deed. He launches himself decisively towards the novel and the unknown and deals mortal blows at the conventional and the archaic. The issue hangs in the balance. If he has attempted too much at the first endeavour, he is likely to be crushed by the forces of reaction. Or if his technique is not really an improvement on the old, he can hardly expect to survive. But if his vision has been a true one, if he has rightly discerned the will of the true God, then no matter if the forces of conservatism are strong enough even to overwhelm him temporarily, he will arise and win supporters and will ultimately gain the victory. History offers no clearly defined pattern of this process of attack and recoil and struggle towards the attainment of new forms. All we can say is that every final establishment of the new means some form of death to that which is old and that in the context of this struggle the leader can never escape the wounds or the threat of death to himself. He who wins his way through this threat of death is the man who is certain ultimately to gain his own objective and to win the support of a worthy band of fellow-adventurers in the same quest.

So far I have spoken in general terms, but if appeal is made to the lives of the outstanding leaders in history, notable examples will be seen of the pattern of leadership just described. Moses and Mohammed were the leaders of two of the greatest religious and social movements in the history of mankind. In each case the story of the leader's career is one of struggle— struggle with the external powers which were being dispossessed, struggle with the forces of conservatism which held the reins of power within the society to which each belonged. In each case the leader saw a vision of a better land, a better order of society and a better organisation of religion. In each case the challenge to the established authorities in the place of the hero's domicile was met by ridicule and active opposition. So the hero was compelled to flee, to accept apparent failure, to pass through the valley of the shadow of death. Only after an experience comparable to death itself did he return to lead out a band of followers into what proved to be newness of life.

I shall suggest at a later point in the chapter that Mohammed's leadership was spoiled by exaggeration and fanaticism, but this was not so in the case of Moses. It is true that every man who is accepted by a trusting group to be their leader and guide is immediately subjected to fierce temptations which test his character to the uttermost. Moses was human and there is evidence that he overreached himself on more than one occasion. But in the main he exercised his leadership within the context of an absolute dependence upon the Divine Leader whom he trusted and whose agent he sought to be. He believed that God had called him to shoulder the burden of his suffering brethren and to save them from the tyranny under which they groaned. The first attempt to lead the revolt was undertaken in his own strength and on the assumption that it only needed a dramatic act of rebellion to bring the slave-labourers rallying around his banner. But Moses quickly discovered that the arm of flesh could not save his people and that they on their part had little inclination to challenge their overlords to open conflict. So it came about that he spent years in the loneliness of the desert, brooding, meditating, planning, scheming, until the determinative vision came and he returned to renew his task in a new way. Now we see a man of the same courage as before but of far greater skill and subtlety in dealing with his fellows. He is able to turn natural portents to the advantage of his cause, he is able to gain the confidence of his people by setting before them the prospect of a new land and of a new national home within it. Above all, he now stands forth as the prophet and agent of a God Who is able to break down all opposition and to support his people in every emergency which may arise. So the decisive break is made, the tribes go forth out of Egypt under Moses's leadership, and a new order is established at Sinai whereby men of varying backgrounds and traditions pledge themselves to accept certain basic moral requirements and to follow the leadership of Yahweh through his prophet.

The record of the subsequent wanderings of the tribes through the wilderness and of their attempts to gain possession of the land of their dreams reveals many vicissitudes, disappointments and failures. But the very fact that a strong and settled Hebrew civilisation was never fully attained meant that the call for leaders and prophets and reformers and saviours never ceased and that in Israel's history, as perhaps in no other, a succession of leaders

served as symbols of salvation but never as final saviours. They
varied in quality and character and capacity. Some were men
of sheer physical courage, some were skilled in the arts of war
and conquest, some were able reformers of society, some were
astute in recognising trends in world affairs. All were men of
action and often their actions were such as to provide a dramatic
prevision of the end they were seeking. But beyond all (to use
the word employed by the writer of the Epistle to the Hebrews
in his celebrated roll-call of the heroes of the past) they were
men of *faith*. They had seen a vision—the vision of a new order,
of a better country, of a city that hath foundations whose builder
and maker is God. They endured as seeing Him who is invisible,
they had respect unto the recompense of their reward, they
refused to return to the securities of the past, they gloried in
the fact that they were strangers and pilgrims on the earth, they
rejoiced in the faithfulness of Him Who had promised. Thus
they became living symbols of the promise and purpose of God.
They died in faith not having received the promises but having
seen them and greeted them from afar and having thereby
become true leaders and pioneers in the religious and social
life of mankind.

Nowhere is it clearer than in the historical record of Israel's
development that the leader's task is never an easy one. The
very fact that he had been granted a special vision means that
he is a lonely man. Yet he dare not cut himself off from those
whom he desires to lead and save. He must identify himself
with them in order that the symbolism which his own life
expresses, can be translated into a language " understanded of
the people." Moreover, the very fact that he strives towards
that which is *new*, means that he is a marked man. Those whose
very existence seems to depend upon the maintenance of the old
feel threatened and insecure. They can never rest until the
leader's voice has been silenced or his possibilities of action
annulled. Yet he must speak, he must act, he must cast himself
forward in faith towards the goal of the rule of God. He is a
man on fire. Like Moses, he sees the flame which burns and burns
and yet which never finally consumes. So he himself is constantly delivered to the flames and yet in dying he lives. Only
a society which is subject to the purging and at the same time

to the impelling attractiveness of the man on fire—the leader, the reformer, the prophet, the pioneer—can remain virile and strong and able to meet the challenges which this ever-changing world constantly supplies.

EXAGGERATION AND EXCESS

We have seen that in a society whose roots are deep in the soil of a particular area and whose pattern of life has become settled and regular, there is little disposition to single out special individuals to play the part of symbolic figures within the community. It is remarkable, for example, that in the long history of Indian religious art, the individual sculptor or painter has never been accorded any special honour or renown. He does his work anonymously with as little personal expression as possible. His task is simply to reflect the forms of Nature through his material and to help the worshipper to experience more deeply that union with the natural order which is the goal of his quest. In all societies of this kind the symbolism of the particular configuration or of the particular individual is discounted. The elder is the link with the past, the babe is the link with the future : both of these are accorded a measure of distinction. Otherwise all men are gathered within Nature's embrace and their pattern of life is determined as far as is possible by Nature's laws and structural forms.

The great change in this type of existence takes place when man begins to use his mind to plan and to organise. When men of different races and backgrounds come together and when they find themselves confronted by new problems in their natural environment, they must inevitably make the attempt to discover ways and means of establishing a harmonious form of social existence. It is now that the man of wisdom and organising ability comes into his own. He acts for a group of his fellow-men in a representative capacity and becomes the symbolic figure of that group. He knows the will of heaven and acts as mediator between his people and the heavenly powers in all that pertains to the health and harmony of the whole. As a society grows larger and more complex, the organisation of

these symbolic men themselves is likely to grow more complicated. There will need to be representatives of the first order
of representatives and so on. In this way a hierarchical structure
gradually takes shape.

In all the great settled civilisations of the past the *hierarchical*
principle has found expression. Up to a point it is imposing and
effective. The pyramidal form is one of the most stable known
to men. The danger which always arises ultimately, however,
is that of the gap—the gap which separates the figures at the
highest level of the hierarchy from those at the lowest level.
It is all too easy for those at the top to lose vital touch with those
of the lower levels, to rely inordinately on the support of those
immediately beneath them, to exaggerate their own importance
as occupying the position in the hierarchy nearest to the heavenly
ideal, to come ultimately to believe that they belong to an
entirely different order from that of ordinary human beings
and are therefore worthy of a semi-divine status within the
communal life. Usually this process does not take place consciously or by deliberate design. Once begun, the upward
movement towards ever higher hierarchical forms tends to
continue until it finally comes to rest in the one who is the last
link between earth and heaven. What more natural than that
that one should be regarded and should come to regard himself
as the son of heaven and as the altogether essential symbol of
the harmony and prosperity of the whole community.

Sometimes, as in Egypt and China, great empires have been
established on this hierarchical model and the Emperor has
actually been regarded as a divine figure. He mediates the will
of God to his subjects, he represents them before the divine
throne. When the society which he represents increases in size
and complexity, it becomes natural for him to delegate certain
of his divine functions and qualities to his subordinates. Thus
there comes into existence an elaborate royal priesthood, responsible for the preservation of order and harmony within society
at large. This whole process, however, is full of danger. Once
a particular order has been invested with an inviolable divine
status, the possibility of change is virtually ruled out and any
chance of appealing against that which has been ordained by
heaven is, of course, excluded. So the society becomes mono-

lithic, immobile, unchanging, and ultimately the onward movement of the world's life either destroys it or passes it by.

In such a society the man of superior rank is no longer a symbolic representative of those beneath him. Rather is he a *sign* to them of an authority which is from above. What this authority ordains must be unquestioningly obeyed. The response of those who are commanded must be as automatic as that given to a sign in any other realm of life. Once this happens and the symbolic representative stands secure in his official position, above criticism, above the processes of interaction, a sign of a remote control which can be responded to but never questioned—then the society becomes rigid and inflexible and resistant to all possibilities of adaptation to changing circumstances. It is bound ultimately to stiffen and die.

What, then, are the special dangers to which the more restless and dynamic society is exposed? In this type of society the outstanding individual has always been accorded a special distinction and honour. He who could slay enemies and gain booty for his tribe was obviously the most valuable man in the community. But he was only one in number and he was mortal. Sometimes it was imagined that his spirit of power could be transmitted to another member of the tribe or that something of its potency might be distributed throughout the community. But while men's ideas remained within the closed circle of the physical or the quasi-physical, the individual hero, like the athletic star to-day, could only enjoy a strictly limited period of fame as the symbol and idol of his people. Once his strength began to wane, a mightier than he could arise to displace him.

The great advance in this area of life took place when men began to recognise the place of imagination and ingenuity and inventiveness for the achievement of a desired end. A quality which belongs solely to the body can only be shared in a severely limited way. That which belongs to the realm of vision and insight can be communicated to others and can be transmitted to future generations. When therefore the immediate resources open to purely physical exploitation began to diminish, a family or tribe had either to discover some alternative way of satisfying their needs or perish. In such a situation, the man of faith and foresight and imagination came into his own. He might have

seen another possible source of supply or he might have discovered some new way of gaining the mastery over the
possessors of objects of value or he might have succeeded in
gaining the friendship of a possible ally in the struggle of
existence. Whatever his particular gifts might be, he was now
in a position to act as leader and guide and so to become the
symbolic figure of the group to which he belonged. He could
see beyond the immediate area of his tribe's experience, he could
leap ahead into the future and meet beforehand the contingencies
which might arise. He became the symbol of heroic action and
of final victorious achievement.

It is clear, then, that the man who is to be an effective leader
in any new enterprise must be not only a man of action but
also a man of ideas who can communicate those ideas effectively
to his fellows. The thing which needs to be done cannot be
accomplished by sheer physical force : it must be done therefore
by the exercise of skill and imagination. But if a man exercises
this skill in isolation, no one is ultimately benefited by it. He
must be able to communicate his technique to others, as well
as perform the necessary action himself. For this process of
communication, two main methods are available. He can either
demonstrate his technique in the sight of his chosen followers
or he can describe to them in words how the action may be
performed. Thus he must be something of an actor and of a
prophet, as well as a man of decisive action, if he is to fulfil his
task as symbolic leader within the community.

But in this area of human existence, also, there is a great
danger. It is again the danger of the gap. This time the gap is
that which separates the vision of the leader from the ordinary
realities of contemporary social life. It is all too easy for him
to leap to a point so far outside the accepted pattern of existence
that few are able or willing to follow him in the working out
of his programme of action. He is then faced with two possible
alternatives. He may choose to despair of his contemporaries,
to regard them as beyond redemption, to concentrate all his
hopes and energies on the elect few who have responded to his
own new programme, to regard himself and them as so far
beyond the unregenerate multitude that he, together with his
faithful followers, may consider themselves as sharing already

in the blessings of the promised land. Many religious and social leaders in history have taken this way and have ultimately vanished into the unknown. For a time they have achieved fame. They have acted as momentary symbols of a world beyond this world, of a heavenly society altogether in advance of earthly patterns of existence. They have been the revolutionaries, the apocalypticists, the fanatics, the enthusiasts—symbols of the beyond but of a beyond that is so remote and so separate from the present order of things that there is really no communication between the two orders. And when communication becomes impossible, when contact is broken, the symbol ceases to be a true symbol, the leader and his heroic band vanish over the horizon, and their vision perishes with them.

The other alternative is more subtle and even more dangerous. The leader may decide that his vision can be hastened by exercising his ingenuity and inventiveness to mould society into the pattern which he deems to be its proper form. He has seen the way, he believes, by which the group to which he belongs could march forward into a new prosperity. A new order could be established and new resources made available. But men are slow to start. They are attached to the traditional order and the old ways of life. Moreover, there are those who actively oppose the change which the leader has in mind. So he makes his great decision, perhaps only half-seriously. He will *compel* his people to march. He will use all the devices which he has at his command to develop a mass mind and to promote mass action. He will be a man apart but he will himself act as the personal pledge and harbinger of the new order and he will use every means in his power to mould the people according to his own image and likeness. He will openly demonstrate his contempt for the old order by destroying its symbols. He will then take the people who have in this way been bereft of their social traditions and will use the new techniques of which he is master to bring them to their proper destiny by making them his blind and submissive followers. It is not a question of communication : rather is it a question of compulsion. It is not a matter of following a vision : rather is it a matter of responding automatically to the stimulus to move in a required direction.

Every form of human dictatorship has followed this rough

pattern. Normally the dictator has envisaged an order more efficient and prosperous than the one already existing and has committed himself to the task of making that vision real in the actual social experience of his people. He has perhaps begun in a small way. Then because of opposition from without or because of growing vanity within, he has decided that the slower way, the way of relationship with his people through forms of communication which preserve their integrity as personal agents, is impossible. He cannot continue to be a symbol of communication : he must become an idol. So he sets to work to stamp the image of himself upon his people by the mechanical processes of mass-production. Sub-personal methods are justified (he deems) because they are being used for an ultimately beneficent purpose. The end must justify the means. Once the new social order is achieved men can return to their status as individual persons. But in the meantime he, the leader, must be all-powerful ; his dictates must never be questioned, his vision of the new order must never be subjected to criticism.

The great conquerors of history have all been subject to this temptation. The great religious reformers have not escaped. When a leader sees a vision of a better order and learns of techniques by which its advent can be hastened, it is the most difficult thing in the world for him to rely on methods of *personal* communication as he seeks to make his dream come true. There is so much to do and so little time in which to do it. He feels himself to be the very incarnation of the new order. He is its model and its engineer. Then why not use sub-personal and even impersonal methods in order to make people move more rapidly towards their personal destiny ? Mohammed discovered ways of regimenting his followers so that they moved in absolute unison and in absolute submission to the will of their leaders. Modern dictators have found even more efficient ways of bending their subjects to their own wills. But efficiency and dynamic energy are purchased at the cost of personal values. At length the idol crashes and though others may attempt to fill his place, the drive of the movement gradually slows down and the society adapts itself to more settled ways. Unless the leader acts as a symbol, constantly pointing his followers to the Beyond, to the Eschaton, to the Purpose of God, to " unattainable imagined light,"[1] and drawing his energies from the source where all visions are constantly being renewed and expanded, his work may achieve a phenomenal success temporarily but will ultimately slip back into the conventional and ordinary as he himself becomes simply a dimly remembered hero of a former time.

THE HEBREW-CHRISTIAN TRADITION

In the Hebrew-Christian tradition these principles gain striking expression. When the Hebrews first appear upon the scene of history, they are a nomadic people made up of clans roaming the steppes of Syria and Palestine and seeking pasture for their flocks and herds. In the records contained in the Old Testament, the symbolic figure of these early days was the *patriarch*, a man of strength and courage and faith who mediated the word of God to his people and inspired them with hope of a more settled home in the land of Canaan. He was their leader in the truest sense, sharing their lot and yet ever stretching forward to attain the better home in the country which God had promised to give them. The patriarchs were succeeded by Moses, of whom we have already spoken, and he in turn was succeeded by judges, seers and kings. There are suggestions of the establishment of a hereditary kingship and of an official priesthood, but in the main the typical figure is still the pioneer, the warrior, the captain of the Lord's host, the prophet who declares the oracles of God. Only when the tribes attained a measure of settled life in Canaan did they begin to adjust the pattern of their own social life to that of their neighbours and to think in terms of a priest-king with his circle of deputies in political and ecclesiastical affairs. The periods of the kings in Israel and Judah, however, was a troubled one and kings and priests and royal officials tended all too easily to become degenerate and corrupt. The men of greater significance in the national life were the prophets and reformers who declared the word of the Lord and sought to keep the people true to the

[1] "My blindness of leadership allowed them this finite image of our end, which properly existed only in unending effort towards unattainable imagined light." T. E. Lawrence, quoted Levy, C. R., *The Sword from the Rock*, p. 211.

God of their fathers who had called them into covenant-relationship with Himself.

The period of the exile brought the Hebrews into contact with the great civilisations of Assyria and Babylon and their hopes for the future began to be framed in a more formal and hierarchical way. In Ezekiel's vision of the restored city, the model is not unlike that of the great cities of the East. The prince and the priests with the lesser ministers maintain civil justice and sustain the ordered harmony of the whole community by their regular service in the Temple. There is no evidence to suggest that Ezekiel's vision was ever realised in detail, but its general pattern was followed in the later attempts of the restored exiles to establish an ordered community in Jerusalem. The civil and ecclesiastical rulers governed the affairs of the people and sometimes one man filled both of these offices. For this reason it can be said that the symbolic figure of later Judaism was the *Priest-King*, who represented the people before God and who sought to govern them in accordance with the law of the Lord once given to Moses. At the same time it must be remembered that in the highly important institution, the Synagogue, which seems also to date from the time of the exile, the symbolic figure was the rabbi or *teacher*, who taught the people the Divine precepts and applied them to the conduct of individual and social life. The prophets of former days were still held in honour, but the prophet as a living contemporary was no longer known or expected.

Thus, taking the Old Testament as a whole, it appears that the symbolic figures of pre-Restoration days were the patriarch-leader, the saviour-hero and the prophet-reformer. In post-Restoration days they were the priest-king and the teacher-lawgiver. There was, it is true, some overlapping, but in the main this division provides a true indication of the difference of emphasis between the two periods. And whereas those in the earlier period who looked forward to a new age saw it in terms of the emergence of a new leader, a new prince, a new prophet, a new deliverer, those in the later period who envisaged a new order saw it in terms of a new Messianic king, a new priest after the order of Melchizedek, a new divine son, a new governor who would rule in righteousness. It was at a time when Judaism

was tending to lay the greater emphasis upon the latter expectation that the great revolution took place which was to result
in the emergence of the Christian Church and the final settlement
of the Jewish community within the rabbinic-synagogue pattern.

There can be little doubt that Jesus Himself appeared among
men in the role of the prophet-reformer rather than in that of
the priest-king. He spoke and acted as a prophet and many
regarded Him as a prophet. His attitude to the Messianic
expectation is not altogether clear but it is at least evident that
He did not expect to establish any kind of earthly kingdom ; nor
is there any reference to an earthly temple or priesthood. This
does not necessarily mean that He was indifferent to the ordering
of human life through law and cultus but His primary task was
to proclaim by word and deed the Gospel of God. He was the
faithful witness, the pioneer and perfecter of faith, the apostle
of our confession, the herald of the Kingdom of God. Moreover, His earliest disciples were appointed to undertake a similar
responsibility. Indeed it could be affirmed that in the earliest
Christian community the altogether symbolic figure was the
apostolos, the leader who by word and deed was declaring the
new revelation of God. He was sent by God to challenge the
old order of principalities and powers and to lead out a new
community of those who were prepared to live by faith in the
final victory of God. The apostolos was at all times a symbol
of earthly life being handed over to death in order that the new
life of the world to come might be made manifest. He could
not accept the settled and established order which was already
in existence but in the pattern of the Cross and the Resurrection
went into the conflict in faith, assured of the ultimate triumph
of God.

Yet it would be untrue to the wider evidence of the New
Testament to suggest that the apostolos is the only distinctive
symbolic figure of early Christianity. The Synoptic Gospels
return again and again to the *teaching* of Jesus. He taught with
authority : He proclaimed new ethical principles ; He gave
instruction in the life of prayer. This does not mean that He
attempted to establish codes of conduct or to provide a definite
set of rules for the religious life. But that Jesus did more than
present a challenge calling for immediate action in the present

can hardly be doubted. He proclaimed permanent principles governing the relationship between God and man. He revealed the direction which men must take if they would walk in the way leading to life. He was, in fact, a religious and ethical *teacher*, though all His teaching was set within the context of His primary task—the preaching of the Kingdom of God.

There are also hints in the Synoptic Gospels that Jesus was performing a priestly task. Few things are more striking than their emphasis upon the prayer-life of Jesus and the references to His passion suggest that through it He would be offering Himself for the sake of the wider world of mankind. The Fourth Gospel brings this thought to open expression when it depicts Jesus as offering supplication first for His followers and then for the wider world. It crystallises the thought in one pregnant sentence when it records the words : " For their sakes I dedicate myself that they also may be sanctified through the truth." The *Epistle to the Hebrews* freely speaks of Jesus as the great High-Priest and focuses attention upon His priestly acts of intercession and sacrificial offering. Thus the New Testament undoubtedly bears witness to the Christ as *priest* though again His priestly work is ever set within the context of His primary mission—to bear witness to the saving purpose of God.

In the later books of the New Testament two leading symbolic figures emerge—the *presbuteros* and the *episcopos*. The former was probably responsible for giving instruction in faith and morals : the latter may have performed certain liturgical functions besides carrying out duties of pastoral oversight. But the evidence is too scanty for any firm conclusions to be reached. What is certain is that by the end of the second century the Church was becoming more ordered and settled in every department of its life and the chief result of this in the realm of personal leadership was that the *episcopos* had taken the place of the *apostolos* as the central symbolic figure in the life of the community. How exactly the transition took place is still a matter of debate. Probably influences derived both from Jewish-ecclesiastical and Roman-political forms of organisation combined to bring about the change. The important thing is that from now on to the time of the Reformation the *episcopos*, the overseer, the priest-ruler, was the chief symbolic person and the character of the community at large came to depend in no small measure upon the character of the man who was its *representative* both before God and in the wider councils of the Church. Actually the office of an episcopos varied a great deal in character and functions from age to age. A missionary-bishop interpreted his office in terms of apostolic labours and prophetic preaching : the Bishop of Rome soon interpreted his office in terms of imperial authority and sacerdotal power. But whatever interpretation was advocated the episcopos remained the central figure in the life of the Church and the symbol of the communion which had been established between God and man through Christ.

There were heresies and schisms in the Church in pre-Reformation times, there were times when monk and abbot almost usurped the place of priest and bishop as the typical symbolical figures in the life of the community. Yet there was no serious challenge to the system as a whole until the sixteenth century. Then out on the fringe of the Roman world there came one challenge after another to the established order. The significant thing is that these challenges were made through the words and deeds of individual men. Luther, Zwingli, Calvin, Knox—these became the symbolic figures of Reformed Christianity. They were all men built in the heroic mould, prophetic, men of action, men of imagination, men of faith. In their desire for radical reform they committed excesses but they brought to birth a new type of Christianity in the Western world, the Reformed Protestant type which is more akin to the earlier religion of the Old Testament and to the reforming faith of apostolic days. In this type the *office* as such is of secondary importance. The *quality of leadership* which the individual can give is altogether primary. He must be a man who can see a little way beyond his contemporaries, a man who can hear the word of God a little more clearly than his fellows, a man who can act a little more decisively than those who are content with more settled ways. Moreover, he must be able to *communicate* with his fellows with an effectiveness a little beyond the ordinary. His use of language and dramatic action must be creative and imaginative, never going too far beyond them and yet never content to settle into pedestrian and commonplace forms. He must be prepared to risk his very life—in many symbolic ways and perhaps even literally—in order that God's call may be obeyed and God's battle may be fought. These are the qualifications of the prophet-hero, the preacher, the missionary, within Reformed Christianity, and although no man is sufficient for these things, yet the man who has accepted this pattern as his vocation can thereby become a symbol to the group of which he is leader of the redeeming purpose of God. It is through faith and action, through conflict and victory, through death and resurrection, that God's final triumph is won.

The Reformation was followed by counter-Reformation and even amongst those countries which gave a general welcome to the reforming principle some hesitated to apply it as drastically as others. So in contrast to Reformed Christianity there have come into being new forms of Catholicism which have emphasised the wholeness of the Church rather than the responsibility of particular parts and which have stressed the need for continuity and order rather than for revival and reform. Many symbols have been taken over from medieval Christianity and in particular the priest-ruler has continued to be the central symbolic figure in the Church. Within this more Catholic tradition the *office* is given the place of primary importance. The quality of the individual who occupies it can never be a matter of indifference but it can never be as important as the *type* of representation which he is called to fulfil. He must be a true representative of his people, sharing their lot, familiar with their ways, sympathetic to their needs. He must be a man who can embrace a little more of the wholeness of life than can any one of his contemporaries : he must be a little more versed in the traditions of the Church, he must be a little more instructed in the rules of ordered living, a man of wisdom rather than of brilliance, a devoted pastor rather than a creative genius. Moreover, he must be able to represent his fellows in the presence of God with a continuity and an intensity a little beyond the ordinary. He must be able to take the burdens of the commonplace upon his shoulders and lift them up into the healing and sanctifying atmosphere of the Divine compassion. He must be prepared to give his life—in many symbolic ways and perhaps literally—in order that the life of his society may be preserved and renewed.

These are the qualifications of the priest-ruler within Catholic Christianity and although again no man is sufficient for these things yet the man who has been inducted to this office and aspires to mould his life to its pattern through the power of the Divine Spirit, can thereby become a living symbol within the Church which he represents of the ordered rhythm of service and sacrifice which belongs to the very life of God Himself. It is through descent and ascent, through identification and aspiration, through compassion and self-offering, through life outpoured in death, that God purifies and sanctifies the universal life of mankind.

Thus we are brought finally to the two most significant symbolic figures in the whole history of mankind—the *representative* and the *leader*. These two categories receive more detailed definition in particular areas of life. In education we find both the faithful instructor and the inspiring teacher; in government we find both the statesman and the political revolutionary; in art we find both the critic and the composer, the craftsman and the architect; in religion we find both the priest and the prophet, the episcopos and the apostolos. No society can be healthy which does not find a place for each of these living symbols within its comprehensive view of life. Without the stability provided by the office of representation the leader becomes a voice crying in the wilderness; without the imaginative vision provided by the individual leader, the representative becomes merely the echo of the most strident voices in the community. Each is necessary to the other. Happy is the people whose priests stand before God in the way of righteousness and whose prophets declare the word of the Lord in faithfulness and truth.

It will, perhaps, have become apparent in the course of this chapter that the elder and the revolutionary belong to the lowest level of our original framework : the authoritarian ruler and the forceful commander to the middle level : the priest and the prophet (each being conceived in the widest sense) to the highest level.

CHAPTER FIVE

The Symbolism of Language

IN THE fields of scientific studies relating to man—his physical nature, his mental capacities, his historical experience—there are many unsolved problems and many questions still open to debate. But on one point a wide measure of agreement seems to have been reached. It is that the all-important characteristic which distinguishes man from other sentient creatures is his power of speech. After considering various possible definitions of man in his book, *The Human Use of Human Beings*, the distinguished scientist, Dr. Norbert Wiener, concludes : " What does differentiate man from other animals in a way which leaves us not the slightest degree of doubt, is that he is a talking animal. The impulse to communicate with his fellow beings is so strong that not even the double deprivation of blindness and deafness can completely obliterate it." (p. 2.) And in summing up his chapter on " The Mechanism of Language " he writes : " The human interest in language seems to be an innate interest in coding and decoding, and this seems to be as nearly specifically human as any interest can be. *Speech is the greatest interest and most distinctive achievement of man.*"

This emphasis upon the supreme importance of speech needs perhaps to be qualified by the reminder that action-signs, even forms of ritual action, may have preceded the development of spoken language. In Chapter I, I sought to show the place of the sign in human life and there is nothing to prevent simple signs from being conveyed through the medium of outward action as well as through the channel of audible speech. Indeed it is at all times dangerous to make too sharp a distinction between the deed and the word, between ritual and myth,

between action-signs and language-symbols. At the basis of
each of these pairs lie instinctive tendencies towards collective
behaviour on the one hand and individual self-expression on
the other and up to a point these tendencies are characteristic of
animals as well as of human beings. Bees swarm, ants perform
complicated patterns of group activity and animals move together
in herds : in their mating activities animals reveal distinctive
behaviour-patterns of an individual kind. Moreover, animals
and birds can produce distinctive patterns of sound both in
chorus and in individual song. At the same time we are aware
that there is a point beyond which the animal does not go. Signs
and sounds, yes ; symbolic actions and connected speech, no.
And the question whether ritual preceded or followed language
actually matters little so long as it is remembered that the distinctive thing about man is his *symbol*-forming activities. Whether
these are effected through action or through speech is less
important than the fact that by their use he possesses a unique
place in the realm of living terrestrial beings. He is a symbol-
making animal and his most effective and distinctive symbol is
the spoken word.

Mrs. Langer has a striking paragraph on language which
emphasises its unique quality and at the same time its universal
diffusion. " Language," she writes, " is, without a doubt, the
most momentous and at the same time the most mysterious
product of the human mind. Between the clearest animal call
of love or warning or anger, and a man's least, trivial *word*,
there lies a whole day of Creation—or in modern phrase, a whole
chapter of evolution. In language we have the free, accomplished
use of symbolism, the record of articulate conceptual thinking ;
without language there seems to be nothing like explicit thought
whatever. All races of men—even the scattered, primitive
denizens of the deep jungle, and brutish cannibals who have
lived for centuries on world-removed islands—have their
complete and articulate language. There seem to be no simple,
amorphous, or imperfect languages, such as one would naturally
expect to find in conjunction with the lowest cultures. People
who have not invented textiles, who live under roofs of pleated
branches, need no privacy and mind no filth and roast their
enemies for dinner, will yet converse over their bestial feasts in

a tongue as grammatical as Greek and as fluent as French!" (p. 103.) In other words, man *qua* man is a symbol-making and symbol-using animal and this power, as Wiener says, is his greatest interest and his most distinctive achievement.

When we begin to ask questions about *how* man came to develop this power of speech we find far less agreement amongst the experts. Philologists, biologists, social historians, give tentative answers but these appear to vary considerably in important details. It seems, however, that two leading possibilities have won favour and these are not necessarily exclusive the one of the other.

Perhaps the most popular theory to-day is that which was outlined by Professor J. Z. Young in his Reith Lectures of 1950.[1] According to this view, language is primarily concerned with *communication*. One of man's earliest discoveries was that his only hope of survival in a difficult and dangerous environment was through co-operation with his fellows. But co-operation depends directly upon communication. The better the means of communication, the more effective the co-operation. This has been true throughout human history and above all it must have been true at the time when man first attained his distinctive manhood. It was because of his discovery of the marvellous means of communication which speech affords that he advanced far beyond his fellow-creatures and gained a supremacy which he has never lost.

This theory may be called the *utilitarian* theory. Man recognises a need—the need of co-operation. He finds through a long process of trial and error that words can act as tools to satisfy this need. He discovers that a name or a sentence can produce an appropriate reaction in a fellow tribesman ; he learns to react appropriately to words addressed to himself. But not only are words useful as a means of communicating. They also help to sharpen man's own observation, leading him to note similarities in his world between things which at first seemed to have no connection with one another. In addition, through the use of words, he can avail himself of the results gained by other observers. Thus words are the tools by which man can build up an ordered universe through co-operation with his

[1] *Doubt and Certainty in Science.*

fellows. He observes and communicates his observation by
means of words : his neighbour also observes and communicates
his observation. So gradually wider and wider ranges of
experience are fitted together and man begins to recognise his
place in the whole scheme of things. He becomes more efficient
in his practical endeavours and gains increasing satisfaction as
he takes his part in building up a truly *common* life.[1]

That there are elements of important truth in this utilitarian
view of the birth of language I do not deny, but it is questionable
whether it presents the whole truth or even the most significant
part of the truth. At least, Mrs. Langer's alternative view deserves
careful consideration. She points out that apes make sounds,
but these are not symbolic speech ; she dismisses the theory
that children, apart from any contact with others, have an *instinct*
for creating language. Further, she raises the question whether
the primary aim of symbolic speech as such is communication.
That it quickly aids communication is evident. But may there
be some prior impulse which leads to the construction of the
symbol before there is any thought of communication in mind ?
What could cause men to devise a symbol rather than a sign ?
Her answer to these questions is, I believe, exceedingly important.

" The earliest manifestation of any symbol-making tendency is
likely to be a mere *sense of significance* attached to certain objects,
certain forms or sounds, a vague emotional arrest of the mind
by something that is neither dangerous nor useful in reality.
The beginnings of symbolic transformation in the cortex must
be elusive and disturbing experiences, perhaps thrilling, but very
useless, and hard on the whole nervous system. It is absurd to
suppose that the earliest symbols could be *invented* ; they are
merely *Gestalten* furnished to the senses of a creature ready to
give them some diffuse meaning. But even in such rudimentary

---

[1] " It is not known what was the essence of the first social invention, but a
very important stage must have been the development of communication to a
point where it was possible for large numbers of people to work in harmony.
Remember that animals do not come together spontaneously ; they usually tend
to repel each other. If we modern men are different it is because we have been
trained to react to particular sign stimuli, which serve as the means of bringing
people together, of communicating. Each of the social species of animal has its
own special way of doing this ; dogs keep together by smell, ants by touch, bees
by special forms of dance. In the case of man the cement for the formation of
societies was already to hand from the use in family groups of facial expression
and of speech." (Young, Op cit. pp. 93-4.)

new behaviour lies the first break with the world of pure signs. Aesthetic attraction, mysterious fear, are probably the first manifestations of that mental function which in man becomes a peculiar ' tendency to see reality symbolically ' (a phrase already quoted from Sapir's article on Language in the *Encyclopædia of Social Sciences*) and which issues in the *power of conception*, and the life-long habit of speech." (p. 110.) In the subsequent discussion the author develops her theory still further, showing that a symbol most readily comes to birth in a situation where considerations of practical usefulness are absent but where emotional tension is strong. In such a situation man gives his undivided attention to the phenomenon which has stirred his emotions and seeks either to hold on to it tenaciously or to banish it from his imagination. But whichever course he takes the result is likely to be the formation of a symbol. By a symbol he remembers, by a symbol he seeks to destroy and thus to forget. And the material for his symbol is most likely to be taken from the actions and sounds such as gestures, dances, chants already in use in the communal life of the group to which he belongs.

It is not easy to compress Mrs. Langer's discussion but it may perhaps be summarised thus : Language as a vehicle of communication is secondary ; it is more likely that some non-utilitarian motive for its origin and growth is primary. This motive is to be sought partly in the impulse which belongs to a collective group to dance out or sing out their feeling of togetherness, partly in the impulse which belongs to an individual to retain in or to banish from his consciousness, an emotion which has seized him in a dramatic situation. These two impulses cannot be separated. The one provides the cradle, the pattern of the language-symbol; the other provides the energy, the law of its growth. In all its forms, then, language is a constellation of symbols produced by the operation of a dynamic force of emotional energy acting within a field of primary patterns of gesture and sound.[1] As soon as symbols of this kind have been produced, their use for practical purposes becomes an immediate and obvious possibility. But Mrs. Langer will not allow that symbols as such were *first* produced for utilitarian ends. *Signs*

[1] One theory of language suggests that patterns of sound were produced as a result of attempts to imitate gestures of the body by gestures or movements of the lips.

may well have been employed for those purposes. The symbol (and a spoken language must be regarded as a pattern of symbols) came to birth in other ways.

I suggested at an earlier point that there were elements of truth in the theory that language came to birth and developed as a result of man's urge to communicate and thereby to co-operate with his fellows. The fuller truth surely is that communication and co-operation can be interpreted at different levels. As Wiener has shown, it is perfectly possible for man to communicate with a machine far removed from him and to receive responses from it and in this way a real form of co-operation is possible. Man can communicate with animals and in a limited way animals can communicate with one another. But the *symbol* makes communication and co-operation possible on an altogether higher level. It is the level of truly personal relationship. It is the level at which the qualities of life held in common are objectified and perpetuated through projection into a definite pattern and at which the experiences of the individual are objectified and perpetuated by means of some rearrangement or re-formation of the elements which make up the symbolic patterns of the common life.[1] Once these objectifications have been made and recognised, the way is open to almost unlimited development and expansion in communication and co-operation.

Thus I would agree with the biologist and the engineer that the discovery and development of symbolic speech took place *within the context* of man's urge to communicate and co-operate with his fellows. At the same time I believe that Mrs. Langer is right in rejecting the view that it was purely as a result of this urge that language came into being. It was not constructed like a mechanical tool, simply in order to make some practical end possible. Rather its origin is to be found in the region of those more intellectual and emotional impulses which belong to the realm of art, ethic and religion. It is still possible for the man of faith to affirm that the symbol-forming activities which distinguish man from all other sentient creatures are in reality his ways of making response to the personal approach of the living God Himself.

[1] Through objectification *distance* is established both in space and time.

There is good reason to believe that one of the earliest forms of corporate experience known to man was associated with the power of sound. The human ear is an extraordinarily sensitive instrument. It can find harsh and strident noises so physically painful that they become almost unendurable. On the other hand it can find smooth and rhythmical sounds pleasing and even deeply moving. So it seems that a normal accompaniment of any form of ritual action such as the dance or the sacrifice was a hymn or a chant. The chant might consist only of a succession of meaningless sounds but with the gradual development of language, hymns were composed and these were taken up into the ceremonies and used on appropriate occasions. Still there was always something vaguely mysterious about these words and chants. How had they come into existence ? Whence did they derive their power to move the hearts of men ? How did special individuals learn the art of creating patterns of words and sounds and of using them in an almost magical fashion ? Nowhere in the ancient world were these questions pondered with deeper intensity than in India and as early as 700 B.C., sages were formulating theories of the word which have retained their hold upon the Indian mind even to the present day. An educated Hindu will still write at the head of a letter to a friend the sacred syllable OM. There is a rolling sound in the syllable like the deep tone of a drum : it seems to gather all sound together into one comprehensive utterance. So it stands as a magic incantation, a bringer of prosperity, an appeal to the deep heart of the universe to bestow blessing upon the writer and his friend.

The earliest known literature of ancient India is that represented by the Vedic hymns. These were composed soon after the year 1000 B.C. and are in honour of the nature deities worshipped by the Aryan invaders. With the establishment of a more settled form of life and the development of a regular priestly system of worship the hymns increased in popular esteem and became a necessary part of all sacrificial ceremonies. " The hymns were arranged by the Brāhmans in liturgical form, for it was their use in sacrifice which was all important. There was the Rig-Veda or Praise Veda for the sacrificing priest, the Sāma-Veda or Chant Veda for the Chanting priest, and the Yajur-Veda or Formula Veda containing formulæ to be mumbled by the working priest. A fourth Veda was later added (the Atharva-Veda) containing spells for counteracting misfortune. The word *Veda* means ' Knowledge,' i.e. divine knowledge. But these compositions were divine, in the belief of the Brāhmans, nor primarily because of their meaning or message, but because of the spiritual power they wielded, when used as incantations in worship." (F. H. Smith, *The Elements of Comparative Theology*, p. 30.)

After the Vedas came the Brāhmanas, complex treatises to be used in connection with the sacrificial ceremonies, and after the Brāhmanas came the Upanisads, philosophical treatises which sought to gather up the teaching of the earlier literature and present it in a more profoundly spiritual form to disciples eager for knowledge of ultimate reality. The essence of the Upanisadic teaching is that the way of deliverance from all that is transitory and illusory is for man to know himself as one with the World-Soul, Brāhman, which is immanent in the universe. But the remarkable thing is that the word Brāhman, which is used to denote the ultimate spirit of the universe, originally meant the sacred spell or utterance which exercised so magic a potency in the sacrificial rites. " Brāhman originally meant the *mana* in the spoken word wielding spiritual and magical power. The priest who made use of that power was a Brāhman, ' a wielder of spells,' and the idea of brāhman or spell came to be that of a terrible cosmic force utilised by the priests. The priestly documents taught that the magic of the brāhmanic spell generated by the sacrifices was even greater than the gods, while the later Upanisadic thinkers turned this super-theistic power into the divine principle behind all the gods." (Smith, op. cit., pp. 68-9.)

Thus the word " brāhman " ultimately gathers into itself the mystical potency of the whole universe. The words of the sacred literature are themselves sacrosanct and eternal and to learn these words or to utter them is a way of becoming united with the divine. But to be united with Brāhman is the goal of all striving. To concentrate thought upon Brāhman, to repeat the name again and again, to enter, as it were, into mystical union with the word, is to attain final bliss. This means that in the tradition of Hinduism the Word is the ultimate soul of the universe and union with the Word is the final integrative principle of human existence.

Similar philosophical discussions concerning the nature of the word are to be found in the literature of ancient Egypt. In the inscription called the Memphite Theology which may date back to the third millenium B.C. the attempt is made to describe the way in which an ordered creation came into existence. In effect it is claimed that the " thought " of the universe came into the heart of the god Ptah and that this " thought " then found expression in a " word." It was this comprehensive " word " which held all created things together in proper order and ensured their harmonious functioning. By the word of the god the universe was made and by his word it is sustained in order and harmony.

Professor H. Frankfort sums up the speculations of the Memphite theologians in the following way : " The ' word of the god ' is nothing so simple in these contexts as ' divine writing ' or hieroglyphic. It is the word or concern or business of the gods which applies to the elements which the gods have created. Not only were material elements created, but there was created for them a ' word ' which applied to them and which put them into their appropriate places in the god's scheme of things. Creation was not the irresponsible production of oddly assorted pieces, which might be shaken down in a vast impersonal lottery wheel. Creation was accompanied and directed by a word which expressed some kind of a divine order to comprehend the created elements." (*Before Philosophy*, p. 70.)

But an even greater pre-occupation with the Word and its place in the life of the universe is to be found in the history of Greek thought. From the time of Heraclitus onwards Greek thinkers were familiar with the conception of the logos as the omnipresent Wisdom by which all things are steered, but it was not until the time of the Stoics that a fully developed doctrine of the logos appeared. In their view all things came into existence through the operation of the divine reason (the *logos spermatikos*) and by this same divine logos man himself is directed and enabled to live in harmony with the universe. Harmony with the universe was indeed the *summum bonum* for Greek thinkers as well as for Indian, but whereas for the latter this goal was to be attained primarily through the way of mystical identification with the Word, for the former it was to be reached primarily through the exercise of the clear light of reason and through the process of distinguishing truth from error, order from confusion, by the aid of the Word.

All through the classical period in Greece the spoken word and reason were held together in close relationship. It was the task of the reason to bring order into man's experience by discovering patterns of similarity and laws of recurrence in the world of nature ; it was the function of the spoken word (and by extension, of the written word) to express that rational order through clear and logical speech. In the hands of the masters of the Greek language this outward expression could become rhythmical and graceful and charged with emotional appeal. But this was never the primary purpose of the Word. It was designed to convey clear ideas and by sharpening word with word in the process of dialectic the Greeks sought to fashion better and better instruments for the representation of the ultimate Reason of the whole universe.

There is, however, another and very different conception of the word in the ancient world. In this view the Word is essentially *command*, the direct utterance by which change is effected and conflict is resolved. Already in the Babylonian mythology this emphasis may be discerned though it was amongst the Semitic tribes that it came to sharpest expression. One example from Babylon is of particular interest as it may contain hints of the way in which the word came to assume its prominence in the pre-history of mankind.

In the creation-myth dating from about the middle of the second millenium B.C. the general theme is the victorious rebellion of the male gods against Ti'amat, the mother goddess, who ruled the universe. Marduk, the god of Babylon, was chosen to be the leader in the fight and after a long and bitter struggle Ti'amat was slain. From her body heaven and earth

were formed and Marduk became the supreme god of the
universe.

But before he is finally acknowledged as the supreme God
Marduk is called upon to show that his word of command really
possesses that quality which leads to immediate results.

> Then they placed a garment in their midst;
> To Marduk, their first-born, they said :
> " Verily, O Lord, thy destiny is supreme among the gods,
> Command ' to destroy and to create ' (and) it shall be !
> By the word of thy mouth let the garment be destroyed ;
> Command again and let the garment be whole ! "
> He commanded with his mouth, and the garment was
>   destroyed.
> Again he commanded, and the garment was restored.
> When the gods, his fathers, beheld the efficiency of his word,
> They rejoiced (and) did homage, (saying) " Marduk is king." [1]

The testimony of this myth to the effectiveness of the word
of command is obvious. But does it also contain a hint of some
superiority of the word as compared with the " garment " ?
Using the methods employed in the psycho-analytic interpretation
of dreams, Erich Fromm contends that the garment in the myth
represents the power of child-bearing possessed by the female
goddess and envied by the male gods. Marduk, however,
demonstrated another and a superior method of creation—the
utterance of the word. Thus, it is claimed, the myth represents
one of the critical changes in the development of mankind—the
triumph of the willed command over the natural order, the
triumph of the male purpose over the female potency, the
growing domination of the world of flesh and blood by the
world of conception and symbolic form. Whether or not this
interpretation is justified we have in this myth a clear indication
of the awe which men were already feeling in the presence of
the word of direction and command.

In the Semitic world there is a similar though accentuated
emphasis upon the word and its place in human affairs. This
attitude springs from a fundamental characteristic of the Semitic

[1] Quoted E. Fromm, *The Forgotten Language*, p. 198.

mind which (as Professor H. A. R. Gibb has written in relation
to the Arab), "whether in relation to the outer world or in
relation to the processes of thought, cannot throw off its intense
feeling for the separateness and individuality of the concrete
events." (*Modern Trends in Islam*, p. 7.) There is little interest
(at least at first) in laws of Nature, in logical sequences, in
syntheses of experience. The Semite is a man of the wide open
spaces which are often bare and monotonous and which contain
few distinguishing features. It is not unnatural, then, that the
few abnormal elements which do exist take on an extreme and
almost exaggerated importance. They arouse in him strong
feelings which find release in sharp ejaculations. Words take
on the character of separate, concrete events. The instinctive
reaction, the direct command, find expression in terse and
vigorous speech.

In Professor Gibb's book to which I have just referred, there
is a most interesting passage which brings out the fact that the
power of the Arab lies in his vivid imagination rather than in
his powers of logical reasoning and that this affects his use of
language in a quite remarkable way. "The spring of mental
life among the Arabs," he writes, "is furnished by the imagination, expressing itself in artistic creation. One often hears it said
that the Arabs have no art. If art is confined to such things as
painting and sculpture, the charge may be true. But this would
be a despotic and unjustifiable limitation of the term. . . . The
medium in which the aesthetic feeling of the Arabs is mainly
(though not exclusively) expressed is that of words and language
—the most seductive, it may be, and certainly the most unstable
and dangerous of all the arts. We know something of the effect
of the spoken and written word upon ourselves. But upon the
Arab mind the impact of artistic speech is immediate ; the words,
passing through no filter of logic or reflection which might
weaken or deaden their effect, go straight to the head. It is
easy, therefore, to understand why Arabs, to whom the noble
use of speech is the supreme art, should see in the Koran a work
of superhuman origin and a veritable miracle.

Further, the Arab artistic creation is a series of separate
moments, each complete in itself and independent, connected by
no principle of harmony or congruity beyond the unity of the

imagining mind. Western art, especially since the Middle Ages, has developed a whole series of complicating techniques,—drama superimposed on romance, mass in place of line, polyphony in place of homophony in music—which makes of the artistic creation a harmony or synthesis of multiple elements, appealing to the refined intelligence as well as to the emotions. The art of speech, on the other hand, among ourselves as well as among the Arabs, still retains its simple and discrete (we might even call it ' primitive ') character ; and because of this it exerts a far more intense power of appeal to the imagination both of the individual and of the mass, a power which may even be so great as to inhibit the capacity to form a synthesis." (pp. 5-6.)

Thus for the Arab the word is an instrument which, whether upon himself or upon others, produces an immediate reaction. He has no interest in sinking down into the warm embrace of a word expressing the universal concept ; he is relatively indifferent to a sequence of words which expresses careful, logical reasoning. The all-powerful word is that which strikes his imagination with irresistible force. The sacred word from the skies, the imperious word of his leader, the concrete word denoting a well-defined object, the word born out of strong emotion and vital experience —to these words he responds without fear and without reflection. In regard to ultimate things, he is not disposed to contemplate or to philosophise. It is enough that the Word of Allah has been spoken. To that Word he submits and thereby finds his bond of brotherhood with others who have believed the same word of the Prophet. Society, in fact, is the brotherhood of the Word, the Word of revelation, which has once for all been embodied in the sacred pages of the Koran and which is authoritative for all men and for all periods of history.

Just as the Greek attitude to the word is in certain respects markedly different from that of the Indian, so the Hebrew attitude may be distinguished from that of the Arab. As we have seen, the Arab is little interested in the context within which the word is spoken or in the word as a medium of a truly personal relationship. The word emanates from a point and, as we say, goes direct to the point. Its main function is to impose uniformity through direct command. For the Hebrew, however, at least in the pre-exilic period of his history, the word was more personal and more related to the actual historical situation. It was never fixed and static: it was living and dynamic. It was never arbitrary and domineering: it was used as an instrument to unite souls in a common purpose and concern.

To say this does not imply that the word was ever of secondary importance in the historical experience of the Hebrews. Much of the fascination of the ancient Hebrew stories is derived from the fact that they are constantly enlivened with the records of the conversations between the leading characters. Moreover, they constantly remind us that the leading actor in the stories is the Hebrew God, Yahweh, and that His words are of quite exceptional importance. He discloses His purposes, He makes His promises, He declares His judgments, He proclaims His mercy. But these words do not crush or paralyse. They inaugurate new eras, they initiate new possibilities. As man responds through the word of faith and repentance, of consecration and gratitude, life attains a new purpose and meaning and a conjunction of souls is created which constitutes the supreme blessing of human existence.

As we read the Hebrew scriptures we can hardly fail to gain a sense of the solemn import of words. Words must never be used lightly. In a very real way they are irrevocable and irreversible. It is true that the strength of a word depends in large measure upon the character of him who speaks it. Some men's words are idle chatter and have little lasting effect—though the speaker of idle words will most certainly come under the judgment of God. But the word of the leader, the man of soul-substance, goes forth with power and accomplishes great things. If, for example, the patriarch pronounces a blessing, the contents of the blessing will certainly be bestowed in due course upon the one for whom they are intended. If, on the other hand, the prophet pronounces a curse, it will only be by quite extraordinary measures that the effects of the curse can be averted. Above all, the word of Yahweh is mighty in its power to judge and to save. " As the rain cometh down, and the snow from heaven and returneth not thither, but watereth the earth, and maketh it bring forth and bud, that it may give seed to the sower, and bread to the eater: So shall my word be that goeth forth out of my mouth : it shall not return unto me void, but it shall accomplish that which I please, and it shall prosper in the thing whereto I sent it." (Isaiah 55, 10-11.) "The grass withereth, the flower fadeth : but the word of our God shall stand for ever." (Isaiah 40, 8.)

Perhaps the most characteristic of all the conceptions of the word associated with the Hebrews is that of the creative efficacy of the word within a covenant relationship. The greatest of all events is the meeting together of two representative souls within a common word of pledge, of promise, of solemn obligation. The greatest of all conjunctions is that graphically described by the modern Hebrew philosopher Martin Buber in the phrase, " I and Thou." In his book under this title there is an expression which recurs several times—" I—Thou can only be spoken with the whole being,"—and it is true that it is only as the whole person in one situation joins himself creatively to the whole person in the other situation that the metaphorical symbol of meeting comes into existence in the form of the Covenant Word. Again it is God's Covenant with man which creates the most significant metaphorical expression of all time—the Cross —in which holiness and guilt, righteousness and iniquity, life and death, love and hate are joined together to form an eternal Gospel of redemption and reconciliation.

No one has more tellingly emphasised the power of the word in the social life of Israel than has J. Pedersen in his great work, *Israel*. He shows that the blessing which the Hebrews desired above all else was the blessing of harmony, community, peace. They recognised fully that a powerful bond of unity held together those souls which share a common kinship. But a covenant by design, a joint commitment to a common purpose, was stronger and more lasting even than a union by Nature. And the supreme means by which a covenant of friendship could be established was by the uniting of solemn words in a ceremony of meeting. " The word," says Pedersen, " is the form of vesture of the contents of the soul, its bodily expression. Behind the word stands the whole of the soul which created it. . . . He who utters a word to another lays that which he has created in his own soul into that of the other and here then must it act with the whole of the reality it contains." (*Israel*

I-II, 167.) Nothing could better describe the highest Hebrew conception of the word and its place in human life. The word containing the whole of the reality of one soul uniting with a word containing the whole of the reality of another soul! In and through such unions the noblest and most enduring metaphorical symbols of mankind are created. Of such a character, in the Hebraic-Christian tradition, is the Word of God which lives and abides for ever.

Later developments in Judaism, especially from the fourth century B.C. onwards, led to the depersonalisation and the legalisation of the word so that it tended to become either the instrument by which God achieved His designs or the law by which He governed His people. It operated less within the context of living relationships, more within the framework of unchanging laws. The Word of God was raised to a position of highest eminence in the teaching of the Bible, but it was a Word expressed in finally fixed forms which chiefly called for acts of obedience in every department of life. So long as the religion of the Jews remains faithful to the Old Testament, it can never forget its heritage of the word as a dynamic and life-giving power, but whenever it interprets the Word primarily in terms of sheer Divine fiat or of human obedience to a rigid Divine code it fails to convey to the world the sense of the creative energies of the word which belongs to the earliest stories of the Hebrew men of faith in their relationships with God and their neighbours.

In this brief survey of the general movement of human history we have seen how man's verbal activity has been constantly directed towards the imposing of form upon the almost bewildering variety of his experience. One of the greatest mysteries of life is the fact that things and relationships, left to themselves, tend to lose order and to approach the maximum state of disorder. Yet man is rarely content to live in a state of formlessness and growing disorder. He desires a certain stability of form in his environment, a certain established pattern of behaviour in his society. So it comes about that he strives, however blindly and instinctively, to impose form upon ever-widening areas of his experience and if possible to integrate them into one all-embracing pattern. In this quest his more obvious needs may be met by the use of *the sign*, but it is his distinctive characteristic to pass beyond the sign to *the symbol*. Through the use of the symbol he stamps form upon formlessness and brings the objects, events, and relationships of his experience into some kind of subjection to his more spiritual purposes.

In this process of imposing form, however, a major distinction appears. Man finds himself part of an imperfect or not fully co-ordinated whole and his great desire is to amend and to improve, to adjust and to integrate, to shape and to perfect. To strive for the perfection of that which he sees only in its disjointed and disordered form is a task worthy of his highest concentration and devotion. But he also finds himself part of a situation which is actually rent asunder, broken, involved in bitter conflict. Then the man of vision cannot rest until he finds some way of mending and healing, of re-uniting and reconciling, of restoring and transcending. To strive for the reformation of that which he only sees in its strained or shattered form is a task demanding imagination and faith of the highest order. In facing these twin tasks man's most powerful instrument is the symbol and I shall seek now to indicate some of the forms which the verbal symbol takes in these different fields of human endeavour.

THE SEARCH FOR WHOLENESS

In man's search for wholeness the primary form which the symbol takes is the *analogical*. The basic function of an analogy is to provide an *extension in the same proportion*. There must always, in fact, be an identity of general pattern if two realities are to be analogous the one to the other. This quality, it is true, is also characteristic of the *simile*. The simile always suggests that a pattern of relations in one context is similar to a pattern of relations in another and once such a connection has been made in thought, a step has been taken towards the building up of a wholeness more satisfying than the mere random togetherness of a collection of individual parts. The analogy, however, is a more useful tool than the simile, seeing that it is capable of whole; the simile may do no more than compare one part of the whole with another part. Perhaps we should say that the simile is a valuable first step but that the analogy gives meaning to the step by showing it to be in the direction of the growth and expansion of the living organism.

The analogy is an extraordinarily powerful form of speech for it always bears within it the suggestion that the object or event to which it is applied is part of a greater whole. It has been the favourite tool of the great philosophers as they have sought to build systems capable of embracing the whole of experience. Particularly has this been true of the *organic* systems of thought which have flourished in the Western world from the time of Plato and Aristotle down to our own day. In any organic system the single member is related to the whole according to some pattern of order and proportion; no figure of speech is more fitted to express this relation than the analogy. Plato in the ancient world, Thomas Aquinas in the medieval world, Whitehead in the modern world, all seek to move from the known to the unknown, from the part to the whole, by the method of analogy. By means of known similarities proportion can be extended until it is possible to conceive of the whole universe in terms of analogies drawn from the common similarities of human experience.

It is true that the great Christian philosophers insist that analogy does not enable man to embrace a self-contained Whole, for God transcends every wholeness which can be reached by man by the aid of analogy. At the same time they allow that man can gain a true knowledge of his world by starting from that which he perceives, by observing and recording similarities within his sensory data, by abstracting patterns of similarity and extending them to cover ever wider areas of experience, until at length a wholeness is envisaged which is held together by recognised laws of order and proportion. Thus the essence of the analogical method is to accept the direct evidence of the senses, to scan it for significant similarities (similarities between observed phenomena or similarities to previously experienced phenomena), to abstract patterns representing these similarities, and finally to apply them to wider and more extended areas of experience, thus imposing form and order upon an ever expanding universe.

Obviously such a method is a slow and difficult one to follow. It demands patience, honesty, keenness of attention, persistence, humility. Its process is comparable to that of any living growth and indeed analogy expressed in symbol may be said to be precisely similar to the characteristic form expressed in Nature. It is the method *par excellence* of the metaphysician who is ever on the lookout for resemblances, correspondences, correlations. Having discovered one he is straightaway concerned to relate it to another, to discover groups or constellations of similarities, to move patiently forwards to a tentative embracing of the whole.

This point has been well expressed by J. V. Langmead Casserley in his book, *The Christian in Philosophy*. " Metaphysics," he writes, " is not a demonstrative science but an analogical art." " Metaphysics is a search conducted throughout the length and breadth of our experience for the most pregnant and revealing analogies." (p. 223.) " A metaphysical scheme . . . is an analogical picture of reality." (p. 224.) " The method of Christian philosophy is analogical and hypothetical but only because this analogical and hypothetical method is the true method of all metaphysics, the one approach to metaphysical problems which is fruitful in practice and valid in theory." (p. 249.) And finally in reference to the particular task of the Christian philosopher : " It is to show in each of the various philosophical laboratories—the nature laboratory, the ethics laboratory, the society laboratory, and so on—that it is a metaphysic composed of analogies drawn from the realm of what we may call biblical personalism which best interprets human experience, making sense and unity of its variety, and which at the same time, most profoundly stimulates thought to pursue its inquiries upon ever deeper levels. The Christian philosopher says, in effect, to his fellow man : ' If you really want to see life steadily and whole, come and look at it from here.' " (p. 227.) A steady advance towards wholeness through the correlation of likenesses—such a phrase admirably defines the function of the analogical symbol.

I have tried to describe the role of the analogy in the widest possible terms and to suggest that it has an indispensable part to play in any attempt to gain a vision of the wholeness of the universe. But by its very nature the analogy is capable of being adapted and extended indefinitely. Meanwhile men must live together and pray together and think together. To this end symbolic frameworks must be provided within which they can find a certain stability and from within which they can pursue the task of imposing form upon their experience with confidence and hope. Such frameworks, all of which are mainly dependent upon the method of analogy for their construction, are *the system of ethics, the system of worship and the system of thought*. Let us look at each in turn.

The normal system of ethics within which any social group lives its ordered existence is the product partly of past experience and partly of present circumstance. But the guiding principle behind any such formulation is the conviction that there is a certain analogy between the life of Nature and the life of Mankind. Man depends upon his natural environment, he is in very truth a part of his natural environment : hence the similarities and recurrences which produce form and order in the life of Nature must surely be capable of extension in certain ways to the life of Mankind. If, for example, a particular pattern is associated with fertility in Nature may it not be significant for the fertility of the human species ? If a particular rhythm is observable in the growth of trees may it not be important for the life of society ? If a certain sequence tends to recur in Nature, may not that sequence be applicable to laws of human behaviour ? In all the great civilisations of the world the idea has developed that there is a definite similarity, if not identity, between the patterns which govern the life of Nature and those which govern the life of Mankind. Sometimes this conviction may be expressed in the simplest of forms and the resultant code of ethics may include the minimum of rules of behaviour ; sometimes, as in the culture of Greece, it may be expressed through a wide-ranging interpretation of the universe which sees the same rational principle at work in Nature as exists in the mind of man and sees man's good as consisting in the maintenance of as close a conformity to the laws of Nature as he is able to achieve.

Thus the framing of laws of Nature (which are manifested primarily in the world of man's physical environment but which are capable of being extended to the life of the society in which he dwells) constitutes one of the main tasks of those symbolic men who by the aid of the analogical symbol seek to establish form and order in the communal life of mankind.

The cultic life of any social group also depends in large measure upon the observance of Nature's regularities and similarities. Through a ceremonial combination of dance and chant man relates himself to the rhythms of Nature. More important, through a ceremonial re-presentation of the fundamental motif of life-through-death he relates himself to the principle through which the life of nature around him is re-invigorated and renewed. But this ceremonial re-presentation includes not only the actions appropriate to a sacrifice of oblation but also an ordered sequence of prayers which give direction and intention to the particular offering which is being made. The development of liturgical forms has been one of the most notable expressions of the analogical method for the liturgies themselves have followed the patterns provided by the sequences and rhythms of Nature and the constituent parts of the liturgies —the prayers for purification, the declarations of absolution, the petitions for renewal, the prayers of oblation, the thanksgivings for favours received—have all been modelled in some way upon processes observable in the life of Nature itself. The same is true of the mystery play and the passion play and although, in actual experience, it would rarely if ever happen that a liturgy would be performed in which no element other than those which we have described would be present, yet in the main it is through the use of *analogical* symbols that liturgies suitable for the worship of an ordered society can be constructed. The more the liturgy conforms symbolically to the recognised processes of the space-time universe, the more appropriate and effective it will be in leading the social group towards that wholeness of experience which is the goal of human life.

The thought-life of a society, as distinct from that of an individual, is governed by certain basic conceptions which have gained general acceptance by the whole group. It is true that the individual can never escape the influence of these basic thought patterns—in fact, they usually influence him more than he knows—but he is at least freer to make adventures in ideas than is the society at large. How then are these basic social conceptions formed? Normally, it seems, they express themselves in the form of a myth or of a cluster of myths. " Myth," indeed, is a term which has been used far too loosely and it is difficult to-day to obtain any general agreement concerning the meaning of the word. Originally the mythos was simply that which was uttered by the *mouth*; but in classical Greek it had come to mean a narrative or a story of a particular kind. Above all it stood for a story which represented some aspect of the life of Nature in symbolical form. The chief stages in the life of Nature were early recognised: Creation, Struggle, Establishment of Harmony, Death, Re-creation—the sequence continuing in an endless chain. This cycle, moreover, was represented in the life of the animal creation and of man himself. In fact, man found himself in an environment in which the all-important phases were the springing to life of plants and crops, the birth of the young in the folds and in the home, the struggle with wind and storm and marauding beasts, the ordered sequence of day and night, of the changes of the moon, of the seasons of the year, and the decline of the life of vegetation and of man himself. Here was material in plenty for the construction of imaginative stories, analogous to the events with which he was familiar but expressed in a form designed to explain how the world came to be the kind of place it actually was and how its continuing life was sustained and increased.

Often the analogy took the form of personalisation. It was not difficult to transform objects and events into the names and activities of living persons and it was soon discovered that no story makes so ready an appeal as that which is expressed in terms of the deeds and adventures of living people. So myths designed to represent the whole life-cycle of Nature were framed and as men listened to the recital of these myths they gained a sense of harmony with the wholeness of their universe and a sense of mastery over those elements which seemed hostile to their own and their families' continued existence. It would not, perhaps, be far from the truth to speak of myth as a pattern of the universe expressed in pictorial language and it was myth which provided the unifying framework within which the ordinary life of thought could find its stability and within which society could find its universe of discourse.

Obviously one danger constantly threatens the use of these frameworks. It is the danger that the frameworks will come to be regarded as closed systems.[1] The method of analogy is used to build up a framework of ethical behaviour which is accepted by a particular society as its recognised standard. Such a standard brings at first a sense of deep satisfaction; men know where they stand in relation to their neighbours, they know what behaviour is expected of them, they rejoice in the orderliness of their communal life. But new generations are born, new circumstances arise, new social complications appear, and the accepted code seems no longer able to provide direction at just those points where it is most needed. What then is to be done ? Various possibilities arise. The attempt may be made to keep the framework rigid but to attach to it a succession of new rules designed to deal with new circumstances. If this is done, however, the whole structure soon becomes so unshapely and cumbrous that it no longer provides that sense of orderliness which the community needs. Or the decision may be made to break through the framework at those points where the pressure of new developments is strongest. But if this is done the structure soon begins to disintegrate and the search for wholeness loses all meaning. The third possibility is to persist in the use of the analogical method by allowing the framework to expand and develop in conformity with the principles of organic life. Its form must be so elastic that it can be adjusted to the changing patterns of its environment. It will not abandon its past but will try to be faithful to those principles of behaviour which gave stability to former generations. It will not prejudge

[1] " The systematisation of language is exactly parallel to the ritualisation of behaviour. If we confined our behaviour to ritual actions, we should necessarily find either that it lacked subtlety, became inappropriate and meaningless almost without our knowing, was stilted, arbitrary and puppet-like ; or that we could not act at all, except on certain artificially favourable occasions. There could no more be a perfectly precise and systematised language than a repertoire of rituals comprehensive enough to handle every human situation." (J. Holloway, *Language and Intelligence*, p. 189.)

the future but will be willing to proceed by the method of trial and error, gradually adapting its form to the changing conditions which it meets.

What is true of the ethical framework holds good also for the cultic and the intellectual. It is notorious that no part of social life tends to be more conservative than its forms of religious worship. Once these forms have proved themselves effective in the cementing of the life of the society which practises them, any attempt at change is bound to arouse opposition. One of the most remarkable examples of this resistance to change is to be seen in the tenacious retention of the Latin tongue within the Roman Catholic Mass. The very process of translation is such that no liturgy which is subjected to it can avoid losing some elements of its order and effectiveness. Yet, just as in the realm of Nature a seed sown in a new environment gains stores of energy which more than compensate for the loss incurred in the process of planting, so, through translation, a form of worship can gain an extension of its sphere of influence which more than offsets its loss of precision. In any case it is a universal law of life that an isolated system of any kind must move in the direction of complete homogeneity which is ultimately complete lifelessness. Hence it is only by a continuous process of gain-through-loss, analogous to that which is observable in the life of Nature, that a form of worship can renew its life and ultimately retain its hold upon widening circles of mankind. This process, of course, does not only include translation. All forms of amendment, adaptation, revision and improvement may be regarded as ways of renewing the life of a cultic framework by the method of analogy.

Similarly the myths of one age must never be regarded as completely regulative of the thought-forms of another age. The framework must be capable of embracing new knowledge and new experience. The myths which tell of the origin of the universe, of the emergence of man, of his struggles with the forces of Nature, of his struggles with himself, of his achievements and failures, of his relations with the powers of good and evil, of his attitudes to death, of the end of all things, possess many features in common from whatever part of the world they come and from whatever period of time. These common features make it possible to forge connecting links between the thought-worlds of other ages and our own and provide a basis of discourse between different peoples. But if a myth ever becomes crystallised into a final form (and because of its very attractiveness this danger is never far away ; man's confidence increases enormously when he gains a clear vision of the origin and meaning and end of the universe in which he dwells) then its usefulness as a connecting link with other periods of time tends immediately to disappear. A myth which demands to be accepted in all its details—whether it be a Homeric myth or a Biblical myth or a modern scientific myth—thereby abandons the method of analogy by which it was constructed and reverts to the status of sign. It can no longer be regarded as a living creative symbol.

Thus the re-interpretation of language forms and the re-adaptation of essential verbal structures are processes which must ever be going on as man seeks for wholeness in symbol as well as in actual life. To proceed by the way of analogy is to move in the right direction. The rate of progress can never be rapid for the great structural regularities of the universe do not alter quickly—at least not in comparison with man's span of life. A place must indeed be found for rapid changes of another kind, but they demand separate treatment. For the present I am concerned only to lay emphasis upon the enormous import-ance of the *analogical symbol* which man has it in his power to use. Through it he constructs his codes, his liturgies and his myths and through them he imposes form upon his universe of experience. But he can never rest content with the measure of order which he succeeds in establishing. The universe is never at rest and life is never stationary. Recreation and regeneration are characteristic of the life of the universe ; trans-mutation and re-interpretation are characteristic of the life of symbolic structures. Only if analogy is employed to the fullest possible extent can it remain a proper means of moving towards that wholeness which is the object of man's never-ending quest.

THE RESOLUTION OF CONFLICT

In man's recurrent attempts to resolve conflicts, the primary form which the symbol takes is the *metaphorical*. The basic function of a metaphor is to provide a *transference* from the expected to the unexpected, from the usual to the surprising. There must always be some element of unlikeness, even incongruity, in the employment of a word or a group of words in a metaphorical way. This does not mean that no elements of likeness remain ; if such were the case the metaphor would lose its power. It does mean that when a metaphor is first presented, we recognise at once that language is being employed in an unusual way. We are surprised, even shocked, by the fact that this word does not really belong to the situation in which it is being used.[1] We are compelled to ask ourselves why the word is being used in this particular context and in this particular way. Some, it may be assumed, will come to the conclusion that language is being grievously mishandled ; others, however, may well find in this new departure the unlocking of a gate into a wholly new dimension of existence.

Just as the analogy has certain links with the simile, so the metaphor has links with the *contrast*. The contrast indicates that a pattern of relations in one context is markedly different from a pattern of relations in another—though there must be some elements in common in the two situations for the contrast to have point. Now the establishment of a contrast can be a highly important act. It invites attention to the variety and openness of reality, which is neither a deadpan uniformity nor a jumble of totally unconnected parts. At the same time, the contrast never does more than link two patterns together ; it points out their dissimilarity, which is more striking than their similarity, but it goes no further. It reveals a conflict ; it does nothing to resolve it.

The metaphor, on the other hand, not only uncovers conflicting elements in reality but holds them together in a tentative

[1] It could, indeed, be claimed that this is also true of the analogy but in that case the transition is so gentle and so natural that we are not shocked : we are only conscious of a feeling of general approval and satisfaction.

resolution. The resolution is not final, for there are ever wider areas of conflict to embrace. But every metaphor which holds together two disparate aspects of reality in creative tension assumes the character of a prophecy of the final reconciliation of all things in the kingdom of God. It is the favourite tool of all the great poets—in fact, as Lewis says, it is " the life-principle of poetry, the poet's chief test and glory." Through it the imagination performs its task, the task which Coleridge describes as dissolving, diffusing, dissipating in order to re-create, as reconciling opposite and discordant qualities, as struggling to idealise and to unify. Through it the prophet leaps outside the circle of present experience, the realm of the factual and the commonsense, the typical and the regular. He parts company with those who are travelling the surer and steadier road of analogical comparison. By one act of daring he brings into creative relationship the apparently opposite and contrary and, if his metaphorical adventure proves successful, gains new treasure both for language and for life.

It has been the special merit of Martin Foss in his book about symbol and metaphor, to show that it is altogether too limited a use of the word metaphor to confine it, as books on grammar usually do, to the direct application to some object of a name which does not properly belong to it. We are often told that whereas a simile asserts that a certain man is like a lion in his acts of strength and courage, a metaphor applies to him straight away the name, " lion," leaving it open to the imagination to conceive in what ways the title is most appropriate. But this is only a minor example of a much more comprehensive process. Metaphor, as Foss suggests, challenges us at the very place where we seem to be secure in our familiarity and understanding and bids us look again. Are we sure that we have seen rightly ? Are we certain that we have taken everything into consideration ? Is our present universe of discourse capable of embracing all the discordant elements of reality ? Metaphor, in other words, is the process of the continuous enlargement of man's symbolic world and this process comes to its clearest manifestation in the activity of speech.

In the realm of speech it is the task of the metaphor " to oppose the tendency of the word toward smooth and expedient fixation in familiar fences, and to draw it into the disturbing current of a problematic drive. In a way every sentence is metaphorical, conveying to the single word a meaning beyond its dictionary sense. Every word loses in the setting of the sentence something of its ' general ' character, becomes more concrete ; but in doing this it gains another kind of generality, the generality of context, difficult to define, a lawfulness which is very individual. This seems paradoxical, and it is this paradox which the mere comparison avoids. But in order to avoid it, the comparison simplifies, becomes one-sided and unfair to the concrete object. It loses too much and gains too little. Therefore we do not compare where we are vitally concerned, that is where we love. The metaphorical process of speech does not enhance the kind of generality which is systematic, i.e. which is an addition of parts to a whole. It is the unique generality of the intentional process to which the terms are sacrificed, and it is their mutual destruction in this process out of which a new and strange insight arises. . . . In blasting the symbols and shattering their customary meaning the dynamic process of the searching, striving, penetrating mind takes the lead and restores the truth of its predominant importance. It is what Aristotle aims at when he calls the metaphor energy." (Op. cit., 59-60.)

This explosion of energy will normally be made through the individual. It is the individual who suddenly sees the new possibility, the new reconciliation ; it is the individual who struggles with conventional language to make it express his own insight ; it is the individual who flashes the word of communication which makes all things new. Let us examine in more detail how exactly this takes place.

In dealing with the analogical symbol I pointed out that men need symbolic frameworks within which to live and worship and think : hence the systems of ethics, of liturgies and of myths which human history contains. A code of ethics, as we saw, is always in danger of becoming rigid and unyielding but it can be preserved from this fate if the method of analogy continues to be vigorously employed. But the very phrase " vigorously employed " brings us to the heart of a new problem. Whence is the required vigour and energy to be obtained ? A community tends always to settle down into familiar patterns ; the products of abstract thought tend to become stereotyped and uninteresting. The influx of new energy, then, must come from the creative individual who through an intense emotional experience of tension and reconciliation discovers the new word. This word (which need not be limited to a single term) is charged with dynamic energy and when it is brought into contact with any pattern of regularity it immediately disturbs and unsettles it. But it is through creative encounters of this kind that human language is renewed and the process of constant re-interpretation carried forward.

In the realm of ethics it is *the moral reformer* who suddenly draws together aspects of human experience which had formerly been kept strictly apart. In the days of Amos the prophet the people of Israel regulated their communal life by a recognised code of conduct but other peoples were regarded as outside the pale—they had no part nor lot in the righteousness of Israel. And the result was, as the book of Amos makes abundantly clear, that the closed system of Israel's moral life was steadily deteriorating. It was the supreme achievement of Amos that he suddenly related the conduct of his own people to that of the neighbouring nations and held them firmly together under the same standard of judgment. To ignore existing distinctions and to forge a new unity of moral judgment was shocking and absurd; but it was the occasion of one of the great creative advances in ethical theory and judgment.

In the days of Jesus of Nazareth a basic legal code had been expanded and extended until it seemed that every possible contingency of human conduct had been provided for. But still the great division existed between those who acknowledged the supremacy of the Law and those who were outside its orbit. The latter were heathen, enemies, aliens, without God and without hope; the former were a chosen people, instructed in the law, heirs of the covenant of promise. It was not surprising that men's attitudes were governed by the general rule: " Thou shalt love thy neighbour and hate thine enemy." This was the recognised framework within which a stable community life could be established. But it was an altogether revolutionary message that Jesus proclaimed when He bade men love their enemies and pray for their persecutors. The coupling together of " love " and " enemy " was the startling new conception. The very foundations of morality seemed to be in jeopardy and yet it was the beginning of perhaps the greatest advance in morals that the world has ever known.

In the realm of worship it is the *liturgical reformer* who leads the way to the resolving of conflicts which arise through the attempt to relate old forms of worship to new conditions of life. Ritual-forms gradually take shape within the context of Nature's regularities and the rhythmic response of human societies. The words of the liturgy, though at first experimental and variable, gradually flow into regular sequences which correspond to the general character of the life of the society which employs them. So long as no revolutionary event occurs the liturgy can be adapted and extended to include mention of new needs which may arise in the course of ordinary historical development. But when critical tensions and conflicts develop within any society and the process of communication between different sections or different generations within the society breaks down, the situation calls for a reformer to initiate a radical break with ancient word-forms and to provide new cult-forms bearing some relation to the actual breach in the historical situation. Cranmer with his new Order of Communion, Luther with his new congregational hymns, Calvin with his new provision for the proclamation of the Word of God—each in his own way was seeking to provide a liturgical form which would hold together within a common worship those who had broken with the old yet were feeling the strain and the pain of an existence from which the old supports seemed to have been snatched away. Novel concepts such as the priesthood of all believers and the doctrine of justification by faith needed to be powerfully expressed in new liturgical forms so that the conflict between the old and the new might be resolved within a new creation. The final outcome of such a process is a new burst of energy springing from the new resolution or reconciliation and revitalising the whole of the liturgical context within which it is set.

Finally, in the realm of thought, there is a general mythical framework within which the thought-life of a society normally moves. It is governed by its view of the universe and of the processes of Nature, and it must be capable of continuous growth and extension as man's knowledge of these processes develops. But once again the slow and patient work of myth-makers and scientists and philosophers is not enough. There must also be the daring leap of the pioneering man of genius—the adventurer in ideas, the poet, the story-teller, the prophet. The product of his imagination may be expressed in poetry or in prose, depending upon the nature of his genius and the particular circumstances of his time. But the all-important quality of. his contribution will be the metaphorical tension which characterises it. He will link together words, events, situations, patterns of life in a way which has never been attempted before. The combination will startle, surprise and even repel. Men's first reaction is to cling to the familiar. Even if they are willing to advance a short distance into the unknown they prefer to be able to return to their base whenever the spirit moves them. But the man of faith and imagination insists on coupling together the immediate and the remote, the present and the future, the material and the spiritual, the ugly and the beautiful, the evil and the good. He takes a new step, utters a new word and this, says Dostoevski, is what men fear most to do. He creates a new tension, sets up a new suspense and thereby breaks through all recognised patterns and leads the way to a complete renewal of human thought.

There is a revealing section in Stephen Spender's *World Within World* which illustrates the nature of the process of which I have been speaking. He tells how at first he looked upon poetry as word-pictures or word-music outside everyday life. " You look out of a window on to a lawn ; beyond the lawn there is a stream running parallel with the house and the horizon, and, barring the horizon, rising like a pillar whose top is dark against the fiery wheel of the moon, is a poplar tree whose leaves, absorbing the darkness, are filled with the music of nightingales. My idea of a poem was the imitation of some such picture." (That there is a place for poetry made up of musical phrases and word-pictures Mr. Spender would not presumably deny). But then his ideas began to change. " I began to realise that unpoetic-seeming things were material for poetry. What seemed petrified, overwhelming and intractable could be melted down again by poetry into their symbolic aspects. The fantasy at the back of actuality could be imagined, and the imagination could create its order. What excited me about the modern movement was the inclusion within new forms of material which seemed ugly, anti-poetic and inhuman. The transformation of the sordid scene and life of the Dublin of Stephen Daedalus and Bloom into the poetic novel whose title, *Ulysses*, sets its aim beside that of the most timeless epic ; the juxtaposition of scenes of European decline with ones recalling the greatest glories of the past tradition, in Eliot's *The Waste Land* ; these showed me that modern life could be material for art, and that the poet, instead of having to set himself apart from his time, could create out of an acceptance of it." And so he began writing poems containing references to gas works, factories and slums ! (pp. 94-95.)

Instances could be multiplied. It is as the poet, the prophet, and the story-teller become the creators of the encounter that great advances are made. It may be the encounter of the past with the present or of the present with the future or of the familiar with the foreign—it is in true meeting that life is renewed. The encounter is never a flat and uninteresting event. It involves tension, excitement, suspense, fear, hope, sorrow, joy, but it is the door to eternal life and the kingdom of God.

Two final reflections arise out of this discussion. In the first place it is worth pointing out that only within the context of a wide historical perspective is it possible to envisage the full process of which I have been speaking. In the history of the development of man's moral life we see the constant interplay between the systems of ethics built upon the framework of the law of nature and the challenges of prophets and reformers ; in the history of man's religious development we see the dialectic between systems of communal rites and the dramatic creations of heroic individuals ; in the history of human thought we see the movement to and fro between systems of mythology and the new adventures of men of genius. It can be claimed, therefore, that of all verbal forms *history* is the greatest and most important. Obviously history can become limited in its vision and narrow in its scope but where there is the honest attempt to see the whole picture, to avoid no unpleasant facts, to hold together the society and the individual, to give full place to new developments as well as to established patterns, to include man's symbolic adventures in the realms of art, ethic and religion, history can become the most comprehensive of all symbolic word-structures and the most significant guide-post towards the fulfilment of human destiny.

In the second place it may be claimed that the Christian faith and tradition gives full recognition both to the Word as *Logos*, as related to the structure of creation, as groundwork and pattern of the developing organism of the Body of Christ *and* to the Word as *Kerygma*, as proclaiming the event of redemption, as constituting the leap of a living flame between God and man, eternity and time, holiness and sin. The divine meaning or principle (Logos) which existed from all eternity in the being of God, which formed the ground and the energy of all created existence and which sustains the created order and in-forms itself within the growing Body of Christ—this Logos received its supreme manifestation in the life of Jesus. This life, through its gathering together of the diverse elements both of the natural order and of human life into an unceasing movement of aspiration towards a true integration in God, became the supreme example of a living analogical symbol. The record of this life constitutes a word-symbol of determinative significance. Here is revealed a proportion, a meaning, a principle of organic development, which cannot be paralleled elsewhere. The Eternal Word takes the flesh of temporal words and moulds them to its own pattern of self-oblation within the life of the Godhead itself.

But God's Word is also Kerygma, the Gospel of Judgment and Salvation. God comes to man in a crisis of destruction and re-creation. Old forms, old words, old symbols, are crossed out ; but mysteriously and paradoxically the crossed-out word reveals a startling new symbol of power and life. And the central, determinative symbol within this series of critical events is the crucifixion of the Word of God. The Kerygma, the witness to this pivotal event, tells how the promised Messiah was taken and by wicked hands was crucified and slain. Yet in reality it was not He Who was destroyed—it was the images of messianic promises and the covenant-symbols of the chosen people of God. Out of His tomb there sprang forth a new

Word, a metaphorical symbol of unique significance. Here is revealed a promise, an assurance, a proleptic disclosure of the true reconciliation which nothing can destroy. Out from the event of the Death and Resurrection of the Servant of God a cry has gone forth to the ends of the earth : " God was reconciling the world to Himself in Christ : we pray you in Christ's stead, be ye reconciled to God."

CHAPTER SIX

Symbolic Action

THE ACTIVITIES of human beings may be divided into three main categories: Unconscious, Conscious and Symbolic. The primary movements of the human organism are instinctive and unconscious. The heart beats in rhythmical fashion, the lungs expand and contract, the eyes blink, the blood flows, the inner organs digest food and excrete waste—these activities are independent of conscious thought and, for the most part, are unrelated to conscious feeling at every stage of life. Moreover, there is little significant variation in the way in which these activities are performed by different persons. Only in the cases of malformation or disease does there tend to be irregularity in the given pattern of activity.

Besides the regular and rhythmic motions of the human organs which belong to the instinctive life of the body, there are, from time to time, movements of the limbs and muscles which are visible to others but clearly not within the range of the actor's own consciousness. A slight stimulus applied to the body may produce a momentary reaction: an individual may move in sympathetic conformity with some outward pattern of movement without realising that his body is moving at all; he may perform an involuntary action in self-defence; he may be activated by a sexual impulse; he may be caught up within some eruption of communal ecstasy and have little or no sense of what he is doing. All these are common experiences and these unconscious movements have their importance in providing the material for more complex forms of activity. But our major concern is with these more complex forms and of these I shall speak in more detail.

CONSCIOUS ACTIVITIES

If the new-born babe is to remain alive it must, within a very short time, begin to suck in nourishment from some source. It may be the mother's or a foster mother's breast, it may be a bottle or some other means of artificial feeding ; the child acts to relate itself to the source of food and quickly gains satisfaction through the activity. Before long it is relating itself or being related to other elements in its environment and gaining satisfaction or discomfort through the experiences. In the earliest period of life the child's activities are likely to follow a regular pattern and sequence with small variations depending upon the way in which it obtains its food, its warmth, its sense of security from those who care for it. It is when it begins to walk and handle things that the possibilities of conscious movement become much more numerous.

Yet it quickly finds that the actual pattern of these movements is already well-established and it is only in very minor ways that it is free to act in ways of its own. The mother or mother-substitute with whom most of its waking life is spent, is engaged in the duties of cleaning, cooking, sewing, mending, and the child naturally adjusts its own activities to the routine and the habitual forms by which it is surrounded. The father may be engaged in more expansive activities but in the early years the father's outer world is largely a closed book to the child. So far as conscious activities are concerned, its chief concern is to satisfy its appetites for food and drink and to imitate in some measure the more interesting activities in which the mother is engaged. No longer are its activities entirely instinctive and unconscious but still they are performed according to a pattern which is traditional, regular, ordered and established. The child's instrumental activities conform in general to those of the society in which it dwells.

Yet there are possibilities of small variations. The child begins to become aware of its father's world, it begins to enter into other households and to see small differences in the way things are done, it begins, above all, to sense its own individuality and to feel its own powers. But as long as the basic need of the society remain unchanged, as long as the existing patterns of instrumental activity are reasonably efficient in meeting those needs, there is little likelihood that the individual child will behave in any way which could be called radically different from the existing pattern. The boy will be admitted to the father's world and become conformed to the pattern of male society while the girl in a similar fashion will take her place consciously within the female order. In each case a craft may be learned and a particular youth may reveal special skill in its practice. But the overall pattern remains—a roughly invariable series of habitual activities with slight disturbances here and there as individual talents and proficiences find expression.

There is, however, another possible development. Certain periods have occurred in the history of mankind when the whole pattern of the activities of a society—and ultimately of the universal society—has been changed. Such seems to have been the case with the discovery of the way of making fire ; or again with the discovery of the possibilities of artificial irrigation ; or again with the construction of ships to travel across the seas ; or with the invention of the mariner's compass or the steam-engine or the aeroplane. In all these cases it is not easy to attribute the change to the work of a single individual. A small group of men may have been adventurers together ; one individual may have taken the final step in a process prepared by a host of others ; an individual may have had resources at his disposal at a particular time which another lacked. Nevertheless we are bound to recognise that the large-scale changes in the pattern of human behaviour which history reveals can be traced back to the activities of individuals or at least of minorities who have responded creatively to problems set them by their natural and social environments.

Now it is true that these problems may be of two kinds. There may be the need for adaptation to a relatively small change in environmental conditions. Slight changes in climate, in water-supply, in resources of animal-food, will almost certainly be provided for by a long series of small adaptations in the behaviour-pattern of a society. Building on past experience, men will gradually adjust their habits of life and work to meet the new conditions satisfactorily. There has been no violent break in the external environment and there need be no violent break in the internal arrangements. Men can see that the essential pattern of their existence has not been destroyed and they can therefore work by the principle of *analogy* to extend and adapt their previous habits to meet the new situation.

But it is a different matter when the pressure of the conditions is such that no solution growing naturally out of past experience any longer avails. A catastrophe of a sudden and major character in the natural world, the over-growth of population in a limited space, the encounter of two peoples or cultures within a particular area—these eventualities raise problems of an altogether new kind and traditional solutions no longer suffice. It is in these situations that the creative, the unexpected, the daring act comes into the picture. The situation is critical; it is virtually an impasse. Suddenly an individual or a closely-knit company sees the possibility of leaping to a wholly new solution. Things hitherto unrelated are brought together in a moment of vision. The water from the Nile brought by artificial channels to the dry and thirsty interior : the produce of one land brought by ship to supply the needs of another : the boiling of a kettle related to the driving of a locomotive. The creative invention of a way to meet a single emergency proves to be in time the means of changing a vast section of the pattern of human activity.

The emergence of such creative solutions in the course of human history is analysed in a most interesting way in two notable books. In a chapter entitled " Habit and Intelligence " in his book, *Language and Intelligence*, Mr. Holloway contrasts the problems which may be solved by the method of analogy with those which demand a " leap," a " flash," a jump into the unknown. The one type, he suggests, demands critical insight or ability to correct errors ; the other type involves creativeness, invention and originality. There is, indeed, no *absolute* distinction between the two types. If there were no possibility at all of building upon the past and using the method of analogy, action would simply be unintelligible and futile. But there is the distinction, nevertheless, between the habitual and the novel and there can be little doubt that the " leap " or the " flash " constitutes in most cases a turning-point in human history.

Arthur Koestler in his book, *Insight and Outlook*, discusses the same phenomenon in a chapter entitled " The Eureka Process." " Patterns of habit behaviour," he writes, " are only broken when they prove inadequate to satisfy a given impulse, when a stress or striving cannot be relieved in the usual way. Such cases are referred to as ' original adaptations ' as opposed to the routine adaptations of habit established by past experience. In other words, a departure from habit will occur, and original behaviour will be made necessary, when a need cannot be satisfied within the framework of a given operative field." Not that a stress of this kind will always result in " an original solution of the problem set by the obstruction of the impulses "—it may " exhaust itself in disoriented trial-and-error behaviour "—but the essential point is that it " can only be relieved by departure from the original field of habit and by shifting the locus of operations to a different field." In other words, in Koestler's view the eureka process by which every advance in man's instrumental activities has been made possible " does not consist in inventing something new out of nothing, but in a bringing together of the hitherto unconnected." (pp. 248, 258.)

Summing up this brief discussion of man's conscious activities, I would say that the earliest pattern reveals a limited number of relatively uniform activities with the most notable variation manifest in the methods of feeding ; that the subsequent pattern reveals a much more highly complex association of habitual social activities, varied in minor ways by the special talents and skills of individuals ; that the most developed pattern reveals a succession of major changes having taken place in the whole behaviour-pattern of societies, a way of life based on the tillage of farms, for example, having been replaced by a way of life governed by the utilisation of industrial machines ; and that these revolutionary changes have themselves been brought about by the creative invention or original experimentation of an individual or small company who have suddenly seen the possibility of acting in such a way as to bring into a direct association with one another elements belonging hitherto to quite unrelated fields of operation. All in all, it is through the

continuing dialectic of the organic and habitual with the associa-
tive and novel that the instrumental activities, whether of society
or of the individual, maintain their efficiency and increase their
scope.

SYMBOLIC ACTIVITIES

In Chapter Five I touched upon the thorny question of the
origins of language. The theory accepted there as the most
likely to account for the emergence of symbolic words may be
regarded as a possible explanation of the development of symbolic
activities. But whatever may be said about the question of
origins there can be no doubt that every child born into the
world to-day enters a universe of experience which is a field
not only of practical but also of symbolic activity. It is
conceivable that in a rare case a child might begin its life within
a context organised in a dominantly impersonal and mechanical
fashion. No words, no gestures might be addressed to it. Its
own movements might be met by a stony silence and a cold
indifference. Even so, it is doubtful if every element of symbolic
behaviour could be eliminated from its world and in any case
such a planned experiment would remove the child so far from
ordinary human existence that it could not be regarded as having
any significance for life within the normal human environment.

The child then enters at the very beginning of its life a
realm in which symbolic activities are common. An action does
not always move towards the achievement of a determinate
visible end. The act of fondling, the kiss, the embrace, are not
employed for the purpose of leaving direct impressions upon
the infant's body ; rather they are expressions of feeling or at
least are actions symbolic of human feeling. The scowl, the
grimace, the threatened attack, are likewise gestures symbolic of
a different kind of feeling. And almost at once the child itself is
caught up into this world of symbolic gesture. It begins, in the
most elementary way, to shape its activities in such a way that
they can be seen to be more than the expression of a direct
purposeful reaction to its environment ; they are forms connected
in the first place it would appear with some feeling-situation but

repeated thereafter as symbols of an experience which may no longer be felt in all its intensity.

The symbolism of gesture may be regarded as the simplest form of symbolic human activity. Just as in the growth and development of speech elementary sounds are repeated by the child over and over again, then combined with other sounds and gradually expanded into meaningful sequences, so in the development of symbolic human activities elementary movements are repeated over and over again, then linked together to form more complex movements and ultimately built up into the series of complex gestures such as are seen in play-activities, in the dance or in the pantomime. Of these elementary movements none seem to give greater satisfaction to the child than those which are rhythmic and regular. Just as the most elementary unconscious activities are rhythmic, so too are the symbolic. In the rhythm of kicking, jumping, being rocked, and soon of crawling and walking, the child gradually gains the mastery of the fundamental human motions. Soon these can be built into more complex patterns and the child can begin to enjoy the experience of corporate movement. Through the regular pattern of steps and gestures and movements carried through in company with others the child experiences the satisfaction of that order and harmony which belongs, he instinctively feels, to the universe in which he dwells.

The construction of satisfying and enriching patterns of symbolic human activity is always a difficult task; it is a task, moreover, which can never be regarded as finished. It is difficult because the patterns must be such as to retain the interest of the participants without being so complex as to cause over-strain; the ideal is always freedom of movement within a framework which is not altogether simple and which thereby holds the attention and the interest. If the framework is too elementary and too rigid the actions become automatic and meaningless. If, on the other hand the framework is too complex and variable, the participants fail to achieve that sense of uplift and harmony which the exercise is designed to bring. This general principle holds good at every stage of individual or corporate experience. To move freely and rhythmically and confidently within a given symbolic pattern—whether at work, at worship, at recreation, or at play—gives satisfaction and refreshment to an individual at every period of life ; to share in corporate movement within a given framework—whether again at worship, at work or at play—brings health and vigour to a society at any period of history. A drab monotony on the one hand and a chaotic formlessness on the other are two of the deadliest enemies of the human race.

But the experience of rhythmic activity and ordered movement is not in itself sufficient to satisfy all the needs of the human psyche. A child from its earliest days loves rhythm and regularity ; it also loves surprise and the sudden break. It is true that a too violent surprise can inspire terror and distress. But if there is sufficient preparation and (as we might call it) " build-up," if, in other words, the surprise breaks into the rhythm of the familiar, then there comes a quite unaffected pleasure and satisfaction. This pattern continues, moreover, in children's games where the sudden break or the unexpected movement creates excitement and allows the rhythm to go forward again with renewed zest. Indeed it would seem that the non-conformist has an essential part to play at every stage of life. To break the monotony, to prevent the circle from being closed, to relax the tension even by breaking the rules, may be an achievement of the highest importance and significance. It may be, it is true, so far out of line and so destructive of the accepted pattern as to be absurd and intolerable. The idiot (i.e. the isolated individual) who behaves in ways which have no relation at all to accepted social conventions or traditions has no useful part to play in human life. But sheer corporate automatism on the one hand and sheer idiotic eccentricity on the other hand, are " sports " and perversions ; the healthy dialectic of the rhythmic and the surprising has been broken by a complete disconnectedness in one direction or the other.

I have spoken of symbolic activities in work, in worship and in play. In the first of these areas the symbolic is obviously closely related to the instrumental. Indeed in many cases work seems to be a purposive activity entirely ; its whole concentration is upon a particular end to be achieved and the activity can be said to be symbolic only in the sense that conventionally a particular type of action has come to be associated with a particular end in view. Often, however, work gains in efficiency when it is carried on within a symbolic framework. When rhythm and order are given their due place, when the workers become conscious of moving within a framework which is flexible but strong, when the individual knows that a suggestion towards change will be treated with respect and interest, then the corporate activity becomes symbolical of the universal organic process and the workers are caught up into an experience of transcendence bringing a satisfaction far beyond that which comes from achieving a limited and particular result.

Play, on the other hand, is less related to purposive activity. The participants are not concerned to make anything which is useful and enduring; their focus of interest is the present and their aim is to achieve co-ordinated activities and skilful movements within the framework of the rules of the game. At best, play becomes an artistic exercise. When a team is moving with complete inter-responsiveness and co-ordination, when the element of surprise brings momentary excitement and is then woven into the pattern of the game, when the actions of the players are graceful and relaxed and yet masterful, then both to players and spectators there comes something of the experience of the artist when the limits of space and time are transcended and for the moment a new order breaks into view. This is true both of the primitive dance and of the modern ballet, both of the ancient Olympic games and of the highly organised sport of the modern Western world.

One particular form of symbolic human activity demands special consideration seeing that it plays a significant part in the realms both of art and religion and shows by its very name that it is essentially concerned with actions and their meaning. This is the drama. " In its origins and evolution," Sir Herbert Read remarks, " drama has always been indissolubly attached to action. Aristotle was very specific about this, not only defining tragedy as the imitation of action and of life, but further indicating that its end is ' a mode of action, not a quality '—even going so far as to describe the dramatist as a maker of plots rather than of verses." (*The True Voice of Feeling*, p. 149.) In similar vein, Mrs. Langer defines the basic abstraction of the drama as " the act, which springs from the past, but is directed toward the future, and is always great with things to come." (*Feeling and Form*, p. 306.) In drama, action is raised symbolically to the highest level of intensity. Speech, indeed, has its part to play, but apart from significant action no real drama could take form. (On the other hand drama can be enacted with the minimum of words ; if certain conventions and traditions can be assumed words can be dispensed with altogether.)

As an art-form, the structure of actions which we call drama exercises immense power. It can symbolise the whole gamut of human experience in a way which is hardly possible for the other arts. It can take a section of human history and so present it symbolically that the meaning of the whole of history is revealed through it. To quote Mrs. Langer again : " Dramatic action is a semblance of action so constructed that a whole, indivisible piece of virtual history is implicit in it, as a yet unrealised form, long before the presentation is completed. This constant illusion of an imminent future, this vivid appearance of a growing situation before anything startling has occurred, is ' form in suspense.' It is a human destiny that unfolds before us, its unity is apparent from the opening words or even silent action, because on the stage we see acts in their entirety, as we do not see them in the real world except in retrospect, that is, by constructive reflection. In the theatre they occur in simplified and completed form, with visible motives, directions, and ends. Since stage action is not, like genuine action, embedded in a welter of irrelevant doings and divided interests, and characters on the stage have no unknown complexities (however complex they may be), it is possible there to see a person's feelings grow into passions, and those passions issue in words and deeds." (*Ibid.*, p. 310.)

Not only does the drama symbolise the whole gamut of human experience—it includes within its unfolding energy other forms of art. The architectural construction of the theatre, the shaping and painting of the scenery, the musical accompaniments, the poetic or historical form of the spoken words, the dance-form of the actors' gestures—each may have a significant part to play in the presentation of the drama. Yet no one of these forms can be regarded as an *essential* part of the drama. Nor can it be held that the drama is the later outgrowth or mature development of, shall we say, poetry or the dance. The only element that may be regarded as indispensable in the drama is the symbolic *act* and this act will gain its significance in one of two directions. Either it will serve to enrich and enhance and extend and fulfil life as it is ordinarily known and experienced or it will serve to resolve tension and reconcile antagonism and transcend difference and establish communion on an altogether new level of experience. These two types of drama we may, in conformity with language already employed, designate the *analogical* and the *metaphorical*. They are not mutually exclusive. Indeed the highest type of drama may be expected to lend itself to at least a degree of interpretation in each of these directions.

This division corresponds closely to the traditional distinction in the history of drama between the comedy and the tragedy. The essential characteristic of comedy is the enhancement of vital feeling through the abstraction and reincarnation for our perception of the motion and rhythm of living.[1] Laughter itself is not an essential part of comedy ; nor is the appearance of the clown or the jester or the nonsensical situation. To be sure the fact that the phenomenon of laughter is closely associated with a sense of exhilaration and expansion makes it natural for laughter-producing situations to be frequently enacted within the comic drama. Nevertheless it is not essential. Romance, heroic adventure, family life, all can provide material for the unfolding of the comedy. So long as the play succeeds in representing symbolically some triumph of vitality, some renewal of organic life, it has succeeded in its main purpose.

Looking back over the long history of man's development we see that the performance of the comic drama has been both an exceedingly common and an exceedingly significant part of his pattern of activities. Through it he celebrates life and thereby promotes life and extends life. The Comus itself (from which the name comedy is derived) was a fertility rite and it is well-known that fertility rites have always been of central importance in the eyes of primitive man. The renewal of life in fields and folds could by no means be taken for granted ; nor could it be assumed without question that the fertility of his own human stock would continue unimpaired. The one thing that could be done, however, was to perform a semblance of

[1] Cp. Langer, Op. cit., p. 344.

rebirth or of the re-invigorating of life. What, exactly, may have been the theory or intention lying behind the performance of these rites we need not inquire. What is relatively certain is that these rites promoted feelings of euphoria and confidence and hope. And with his general vitality thus strengthened man could return to his ordinary round of activities encouraged and refreshed.

The comedy, then, with all its innumerable variations—bawdiness and buffoonery, licentious dances and cruel initiations, heroic adventures and romantic episodes—is concerned to represent the continuance and the extension of life in all its forms. The essential characteristics of tragedy, on the other hand, are the coming to terms with that which threatens to destroy life completely and the representing of the emergence of life on a higher plane as a result of the encounter. Actual physical death is not an essential part of tragedy; nor is the appearance of the Fates or the Furies. Literally any human situation in which separate personalities are involved can provide material for the tragedy. So long as the play succeeds in representing symbolically some resolution of conflict, some reversal of a death-situation, it has fulfilled its particular role in human life.

As we look back into the past we find less evidence of the tragedy than of the comedy. All societies which have attained any kind of settled existence (and the historical data which we possess refer mainly to them) have been conscious of their basic communal needs, depending for their satisfaction upon the renewal of life in farm and field. But there is less evidence of the individual confronting a personal crisis or of a minority group wrestling with a hostile Fate. Yet even in the earliest days when the individual hunter was pursuing his prey or when the emigrant group was moving into enemy territory, the sense of crisis and potential disaster must often have been over-whelming. To enact a drama in which crisis was turned into conquest, almost certain death into a new quality of life, was to bring into the threatening situation a new factor of immense significance. Indeed, without the support of a symbolic encouragement of this kind it is difficult to see how primitive man could have been sustained in his journey through life. It is true that in course of time songs and stories came to fulfil the same role. Even so the tragic drama has ever remained the most comprehensive and most powerful art form in the realm of man's struggle with the forces that threaten his destruction.

History reveals a process of refining and deepening at work in the development of the tragedy as it comes to deal ever more subtly and more comprehensively with man's conflicts both with his fellow-mortals and with his divine antagonists. Man against man of another race, another culture, another capacity : man against society : man against the god of the past, the god of the present, the god of the future : man in conflict with his higher self, his fuller destiny : these are the struggles out of which the tragic situation arises, the situation which man cannot escape and which threatens to destroy his honour or his hopes, his loves and his purposes, his achievements and his supposed significances. And it is the tragic drama which gathers up these varied and variable situations into its embrace, allows them to run their course to the limit and yet, in a miraculous way, out of the extremity of the contest (the *agon*) brings reconciliation and peace. So in the tragic drama it is not so much renewal and re-invigoration that is achieved and acquired—it is resurrection, transcendence, life in an altogether new dimension. Out from the juxtaposition of two limiting situations there springs to life a new order, not unrelated to the past, yet separated by a gulf which could only have been surmounted by the leap of faith. In tragic drama art reveals its moments of intensest creativity ; in a religious setting it discloses the ultimate meaning of the relationship between the human and the Divine.

Coming finally to the realm of overt religious expression, we find that whereas the dance and the procession, the consecration and the coronation, have played an important part in man's symbolic religious activities, the most significant of all such activities within the total history of mankind have been the ceremonies associated on the one hand with the sanctification of generation and initiation, on the other hand with the reversal of degeneration and alienation. The first group of these ceremonies has normally involved some kind of water-ritual ; the second group has been associated with some form of sacrificial offering. Within the first group we include lustrations, bathings, sprinklings ; within the second group we include the offering of food, the slaying of victims, the manipulation of blood and the participation in communal feasts. Within the Christian context the first is gathered up into the drama of Baptism, the second into that of the Eucharist. To examine the origins and patterns of these dramatic symbolic forms in greater detail will be the concern of the next three chapters.

CHAPTER SEVEN

Water Symbolism and Christian Baptism

ONE OF the commonest forms of symbolic activity in the religious history of mankind has been that associated in some way with water. Descent into the waters, dipping in the water, passing through the waters, sprinkling with water—all have played a notable part in religious ceremonial. In the main these ceremonies have been related to man's desire for the constant re-invigoration and intensification of life. But they have touched human existence at many points and we shall seek as comprehensive a view as possible of the significance of Water-symbolism in human life.

IMAGES OF THE UNCONSCIOUS

Let us begin at the level of the unconscious. In the traditional ceremony of Christian initiation as administered to infants and young children the all-important element has been the contact with the water; only by being plunged beneath the water and drawn out again can the initiate be regarded as having passed through the process of rebirth into newness of life. But there is ample evidence from psycho-analytical investigation to show that water is the commonest archetypal image of the unconscious [1] and that a descent into the water is normally a symbolic description of a new penetration into those deeper and more mysterious fecundities from which a true creativity can be derived. Other elements are associated with water in this dim realm of the unconscious—the void, darkness, death, silence, loneliness—but

[1] C. G. Jung, *The Integration of Personality*, pp. 66-68.

water is the symbol which gathers all these associations together in a comprehensive way.

In support of this claim we might appeal to Day Lewis's deeply interesting final chapter in his book, *The Poetic Image*. Here we find him speaking quite naturally of " the sea of the unconscious " and telling of his own experience when he was contemplating the general subject of his book. " An image rose unbidden to my mind as a symbol of the poetic image itself : it was a whorl or vortex on the surface of a calm sea, and I received the impression that this whirlpool would draw me down into a submarine cavern from which presently I should be expelled to the surface again." In this experience he sees the outline of the rebirth pattern and he is inclined to support Miss Maud Bodkin when she takes such a poem as *The Ancient Mariner* and sees beneath it the rebirth archetype—" the process by which the spirit withdraws into a state of accidie or one of impotent frustration, a doldrum state, as an initiation into new life, going through a period of introversion before turning outward again with new vigour, descending into hell that it may rise to heaven." (p. 148.)

Or we might refer to one of the most impressive poetic achievements of modern times, the *Four Quartets* by Mr. T. S. Eliot. Beneath the surface of this poem the rebirth motif is constantly at work. Only by a descent into the dark waters can life be renewed.

I said to my soul, be still, and let the dark come upon you
Which shall be the darkness of God.

We must be still and still moving
Into another intensity
For a further union, a deeper communion
Through the dark cold and the empty desolation,
The wave cry, the wind cry, the vast waters
Of the petrel and the porpoise. In my end is my beginning.

Approaching the matter in another way, we may look back to some of the earliest ideas which have been preserved for us in inscriptions and in ancient myths and ritual-forms. Wherever

we look in the Near East—to Babylonia, Palestine or Egypt—
we find that water is associated with life-giving properties.[1] In
colloquial Arabic water is used as a name for the semen of the
male and the Koran holds that God created man out of water.
In Palestine water was early regarded as the most important of
the four elements and springs and wells came to be regarded as
" holy " places, the abodes of spirits and numens.

But it was above all in Egypt that water occupied a
dominating place in the mythology and ritual-forms of the
people. The earth, it was believed, floated on the vast waters
of the underworld, the waters out of which all life issued. Every
day the sun rose out of the waters and even the gods had
originally come forth from them. Water was associated with
birth, with purification, with rebirth after death. To be drowned
was a mark of good fortune—it meant union with the Divine.
The dry and shrivelled corpse could be revivified by being
immersed in the Nile waters. In the temples a sacred pool
symbolised the primordial waters, Nun, and out of this pool
water was drawn every day for the morning bathing of the
king. In fact " in Egyptian belief . . . the divine waters could
give life in every form in which the mind could conceive it."
(J.A.O.S., 56, p. 158.) [2]

There is still another conception in the ancient world which
may be regarded as a precursor of later symbolic forms. It is
the image of water gushing forth from a great opening which
came to be regarded as the earth's vagina. There is, for example,
a line in the Sumerian Epic of Paradise which is translated thus :
" From the place where the waters flow forth from the womb."
Commenting on this passage, Professor W. F. Albright writes :
" The mouth from which a river emerges may be regarded as the
vulva or Muttermund of the earth. This idea and its converse
that the female vagina is a well or fountain, are found everywhere and may be traced back to the beginnings of language."

[1] For example, " the ancient Babylonian alluvium fertilised the earth and
caused it to bring forth its fruits, thus giving life to all beings upon it. In order to
secure this annual outpouring of the divine lifegiving fluid the liturgy of Babylonian spring-festivals depicted the cohabitation of the god of a city with his
spouse ; the result was believed to be the abundant outpouring of the life-giving
waters." (Journal of the American Oriental Society, 56, 155.)

[2] Cp. An old Indian text which affirms : " Water, you are the source of everything and of all existence." (Quoted, L. Beirnaert, Cross Currents, 5, p. 69.)

(*J.A.O.S.*, 39, p. 69 f.) In Sumerian, for example, a spring was called a " mouth " and it is noteworthy that at a later period στόμα in Greek and *fons* in Latin came to be used as equivalent terms.

Without stressing the importance of these associations in any exaggerated way, it seems that there is enough evidence to be derived partly from ancient conceptions and partly from modern psycho-analytic investigation to justify us in affirming that

(1) Water from the heavens has been regarded as possessing life-giving properties and therefore to be sprinkled with water means to receive renewal of life.

(2) Water gushing from the earth has been regarded as issuing from the womb of the Earth-Mother and to be plunged in this water has been regarded as a means of gaining the gift of immortality.

(3) Still water, the water of darkness, has also in some way been associated with the womb : to descend into this water is to return to the source of creativity for renewal of life.[1]

Thus in and through the rite of Christian initiation there is the possibility of touching the deepest level of the " general memory " or the " collective unconscious." As Louis Beirnaert has convincingly shown, early Christian theologians delighted to speak of baptism in terms of maternal images.

" You have plunged thrice in the water," writes Cyril of Jerusalem, " and have come forth again. In the water, as during the night, you have seen nothing. In coming forth you have found yourself in the brightness of day. At the same time you died and were born, and this wholesome water has become for you both a tomb and a mother."

" O womb ! " cries Ephrem the Syrian, " which daily brings forth without pain the sons of the kingdom of heaven. They descend indeed with their faults and their stains, but they rise up pure as infants. For Baptism becomes a second womb for

[1] " The maternal significance of water belongs to the clearest symbolism in the realms of mythology, so that the ancients could say : The sea is the symbol of birth. From water comes life (Cf. Isa. 48, 1.) ; . . . All that is living rises as does the sun from the water and at evening plunges into the water. Born from the springs, the rivers, the seas, at death man arrives at the waters of the Styx in order to enter upon the ' night journey on the sea.' The wish is that the black water of death might be the water of life ; that death with its cold embrace, might be the mother's womb, just as the sea devours the sun, but brings it forth again out of the maternal womb." (C. G. Jung, *The Psychology of the Unconscious*, p. 135.)

them, which in bringing them forth makes young men out of old as the river Jordan restored Naaman to his youth."

Further, the images of the baptismal rite itself bear witness to the same association.

" May He (the Holy Ghost)," the priest prays in the Sarum ritual, " fertilise this water prepared for the regeneration of man by the secret admixture of His light that by a holy conception a heavenly offspring may come forth from the spotless womb of the divine font as a new creature, and may all who differ in sex or age be begotten by parent grace into one and the same infancy." (Quoted E. O. James, *Christian Myth and Ritual*, p. 116.)[1]

In the more sophisticated life of modern times, however, these realistic images are in eclipse and the mythic associations of the baptismal water have retreated farther and farther into the background. The font usually occupies an inconspicuous position in the Church and the use of water is highly artificial. It may, indeed, be held that it is better to have no connections with the realms of mystery and darkness and that all primordial images of the life-giving and regenerating properties of water should be rigorously excluded from the Christian sacramental system. But the power of these archetypal images is too great to be rendered null and void by any process of deliberate exclusion. If they are not sanctified within a Christian context they will almost certainly present themselves in demonic forms. To find a way of allowing Baptism to exercise its power within the Christian community at the deepest level of the human psyche is one of the most urgent tasks of our day.

But there is a second pattern of water-ritual associated with the baptism of adults or of converts from paganism. The all-important part of this ceremony is the *passing through the waters* : only by braving the flood and by triumphing over it can the initiate be regarded as having broken with his past and launched himself into a future bright with promise. It is true that in the general pattern of *descent into the water* already considered there is

[1] "O God, whose Spirit in the very beginning of the world moved over the waters, that even then the nature of water might receive the virtue of sanctification : O God, who by water didst wash away the crimes of the guilty world, and by the overflowing of the deluge didst give a figure of regeneration, that one and the same element might in a mystery be the end of vice and the origin of virtue." The prayer of *Benedictio Fontis* in the Roman ritual.

a place for the disintegration of former patterns of life and for purification from accumulated " dead works." But in general the waters are regarded as beneficent and life-giving; there may have to be the descent into the darkness, the return to the womb, the purging away of unworthy stains, but the final outcome is regeneration through the water, a new reception of life-giving properties from the water. To gain renewed contact with the waters is to gain access to the secret of the renewal of life.

But there is the other pattern of experience which cannot be ignored. It is the pattern in which water appears as threatening, opposing, malevolent, fearsome. It may be regarded as the abode of the great dragon or sea-monster; it may even be identified with some awe-inspiring living creature. That water should have this double reference is hardly matter for surprise. In Egypt flood-water may be the essential of life; in the American Middle West, flood water may bring destruction and death. Out of the primordial ocean new life may seem to arise; yet the ocean tempest may bring terrifying possibilities of death. Even in Egypt, the land to which water has seemed most precious, the action of water has not been uniformly beneficent. Professor H. Frankfort has given a vivid picture of the dual character of Egyptian life. " The sun and the Nile," he writes, " did combine to bring forth renewed life, but only at the cost of a battle against death. The sun warmed but in the summer it also blasted. The Nile brought fertilising water and soil but its annual inundation was antic and unpredictable. An exceptionally low Nile brought famine. . . . For more than a third of every year the hot desert winds, the blasting sun, and the low Nile brought the land within sight of death, until the weather turned and the river brought abundant waters again. Thus Egypt was rich and blessed in contrast with her immediate neighbours but within her own territory she experienced struggle, privations and dangers which made the annual triumph real." (Op. cit., pp. 44-5.)

But if Egypt sometimes had to battle against death in its struggle with the waters, far more was this the case in the Mesopotamian valley. Behind the myths of the great combat between the god of the bright air and the god of the dark waters, behind the legends of the great deluge which engulfed the inhabited earth, there undoubtedly lies a terrifying experience of advancing waters, of all-encompassing waters, which have threatened man's very existence. Or again, in his attempts to cross rivers and to journey over sea-inlets man has often had to struggle for his life against some unexpected movement of the waters. No wonder that water has come to be regarded as the home of demonic serpents and dragons and sea-monsters and has by a natural transition come to be personified in one of these awesome guises. In this view " the waters are the sea of death, the abyss with its devouring jaws, the retreat of monsters and dragons which in the Indo-European tradition represents a permanent danger for all formal existence." (L. Beirnaert, Op. cit., p. 69.)

In early mythology the sea is almost uniformly regarded as the enemy of ordered and civilised life. It is, in the words of W. H. Auden, " that state of barbaric vagueness and disorder out of which civilisation has emerged and into which, unless saved by the effort of gods and men, it is always liable to relapse." (*The Enchafed Flood*, pp. 18-19.) Man fears and hates chaos and desires above all else to reduce it to a proper order. Thus his myths are concerned not with the annihilation of Chaos or The Sea or The Goddess of the Waters, but with gaining so notable a victory over them that their inherent powers may be used for his own advantage. One of the most famous examples of this mythological pattern is to be found in the Babylonian story of the great struggle between the divine hero Marduk and the goddess of the waters Ti'amat. Chosen to be the champion of the gods of order against the forces of chaos, Marduk sets his battle array and rides against Ti'amat. He makes a net to encircle her and when she is caught, succeeds in shooting an arrow into her open jaws and thus pierces her heart. He then divides her dead body into two and lifts up one half to form the sky while the other half forms the earth. In each case the waters are now under control; sky-water and earth-water can now be used for the service of mankind. Gods and men can live in safety *between the waters* for the way has been prepared for them by the divine champion and saviour.

To cut a way through the waters, to gain control over the

waters, to tame or to conquer the monster inhabiting the waters
—these are constantly recurring themes in ancient mythology.
Echoes or remnants of these myths are to be found in various
parts of the Old Testament—the establishment of order out of
the primeval watery chaos in Genesis, the containment of the
sea " when it burst from the womb of chaos, when I swathed
it in mists, and swaddled it in clouds of darkness, when I fixed
its boundaries, barred and bolted it, saying, ' Thus far and no
further ! Here your proud waves shall not pass.' " (Job 38,
8-11, Moffatt), the great victory over the Dragon (or Leviathan
or Rahab) celebrated in Psalms 74 and 89 :

> Thou didst divide the ocean by thy power,
> shattering the Dragon's heads upon the waves,
> crushing the heads of the Leviathan,
> leaving him a prey to jackals.
> Thy sway is over the proud sea ;
> when the waves toss, thou stillest them.
> The Rahab thou didst cut and crush to pieces,
> scattering thy foes by the force of thine arm,

and the linking of this victory with the deliverance from the
Red Sea in the remarkable passage Isaiah 51, 9-10, where mythological images drawn from the racial memory or corporate
sub-conscious merge easily into the record of an event which
almost certainly belonged to the historical experience of the
Hebrew people. The prophet cries :

> Bestir thyself, O arm of the Eternal,
> bestir thyself and don thy might !
> Bestir thyself as in days of old,
>   in ages of the past !
> Didst thou not shatter the Rahab
>   and pierce the Dragon through ?
> Didst thou not once dry up the sea,
>   the waters of the mighty deep,
> and make the ocean-depths a path
>   for ransomed men to pass across ?

Here may be seen the transition from the primeval victory over the waters to the memorable journey through the divided waters after the exodus from Egypt. In each case there is the note of triumph, the note of a challenge successfully carried through, the note of the enjoyment of a new order of existence as the result of an encounter with the dark and threatening waters.

The image of the passage through the waters appears in other contexts both in ancient and modern poetry. There is the frequent reference to the river to be crossed before the denizen of this world can reach the land of everlasting bliss ; [1] there is the picture of the crossing of the Rubicon—a decisive step which cannot be revoked ; there is the image of life itself as a voyage over the waters towards an unknown (or dimly known) destiny. Sometimes the water is threatening and awe-inspiring ; sometimes it is merely unpredictable ; but at all times man faces the waters with some trepidation and his safe emergence on the other side is cause for relief and thanksgiving. As Mr. W. H. Auden has pointed out in the deeply interesting study of water-symbolism, the general view of the sea and of man's journeyings on it has tended to vary from age to age. Man may face the waters in a spirit of adventure, in a spirit of compulsion, in a spirit of *hubris* or in a spirit of sober determination. Always, however, the voyage separates him from his former existence ; he will emerge from it either hardened and toughened or purified and enlightened.

The early Church was not slow to lay hold of the image of

---

[1] Erich Fromm records a dream of one of his patients in which a hill appears surmounted by a beautiful city. But between the patient and the city there is a river.

"I feel that if I can only cross the river everything will be all right."

Answering the analyst's question about the nature of the river, the patient replies :

Patient : It was an ordinary river, in fact like the river in our town I was always a little afraid of as a child.

Analyst : Then there must be a bridge. You certainly have waited a long time to cross the bridge. The problem now is to discover what still hinders you from doing so.

"This is one of those important dreams in which a decisive step away from mental illness is taken. To be sure, the patient is not yet well, but he has experienced the most important thing short of being well, a clear and vivid vision of a life in which he is not the haunted criminal, but a free person. He also visualised that, in order to get there, *he must cross a river, an old and universally used symbol of an important decision, of starting a new form of existence—birth or death—of giving up one form of life for another.*" E. Fromm, *The Forgotten Language,* pp. 154-5. (*Italics mine.*)

the victory over the waters and to apply it in the context of baptism. In fact this aspect of mythic imagery seems to have been even more popular than that of the maternal and regenerative aspect. Christ was the champion who had descended into the waters of the underworld and had broken the heads of the dragons infesting them. Sometimes it is Leviathan, sometimes the serpent, but the theme is the same—the victory over the death-dealing waters. " O Lord Jesus Christ," the worshippers pray in a prayer for Holy Saturday, " who descended into the waters of hell that you might lead forth those bound in the lower depths." (Quoted L. Beirnaert, p. 73.) Christ had sounded the very depths of the abyss ; there were no hidden foes which he had not met and conquered. His baptism of death, as Beirnaert well says, can be compared " to an immersion in those terrifying and mortal waters which constituted for Hebraic cosmology the very dwelling place of death and a permanent danger for all formal existence." (Op cit., p. 73.)

The two baptisms of Christ—the first in the Jordan, the second in the waters of Sheol—are closely associated in the minds of the Fathers and in the ancient liturgies. Cyril declares that at the Jordan the dragon was in the water and by binding him there Christ made it possible for his followers to tread upon serpents and scorpions. Similarly by going down into the cavern of death He gained release for those who had been swallowed up in its evil waters. In fact by His great victory over the waters He had changed their very character and made them a source of blessing rather than of destruction.

Referring to the great event at the Red Sea, Cyril of Jerusalem cries to his catechumens : " The tyrant has pursued the ancient people even to the sea ; you too, this impudent demon and prince of evil has pursued even to the waters of salvation. The one was drowned in the sea, the other vanishes in the water of salvation." The imagery is not entirely consistent but there is at least the glad recognition that just as the ancient people of God by passing through the waters overcame their oppressor and began a new life under the rule of God, so the Christian initiates by passing through the waters of baptism become sharers in Christ's victory and heirs of His eternal salvation. To follow the Christ through the waters was to pass through a critical archetypal experience of extraordinary emotional intensity. It gave men a sense of having come to grips with their arch-enemy and of sharing in the once-for-all victory of the Divine Saviour-Hero.

THE OPEN SIGN

In addition to its mysterious life-giving properties, water possesses the more open and obvious property of cleansing and purifying. Nothing is more welcome to the dweller in hot and dusty lands than the flow of clean water over his parched skin or his soiled feet. Few experiences have such a universal reference as that of finding refreshment and deep satisfaction through bathing, washing, dipping, sprinkling in pure water.

Even the association of water with the process of purification may have roots in man's sub-conscious but in the main it is perfectly open and conscious and direct. A man sees dust on his feet; he pours water over them; the dust is removed. So the pouring of water can be regarded as a direct sign of the removal of defilement. There is nothing very mysterious about it, nothing which seems indirect or delayed, nothing which demands teaching or instruction in order that it may be appreciated and understood. It is an open and visible sign which makes an immediate and universal appeal.

It is no matter for wonder, therefore, that wherever a civilisation has grown up and regular public rituals have been established, the use of water as a sign of purification has been adopted by the community. The exact nature of the defilement needing to be removed has been conceived in many different ways. It might be a birth-tabu, affecting both the mother and the child, or it might be some form of sickness or disease; it might be a dangerous potency contracted through contact with holy objects or sacred persons, or it might be simply the defilements contracted in the ordinary daily round. In general, the impurity or dangerous infection was regarded as in some way affecting the *body* though indeed there was no clear-cut distinction between body and soul in early society. The breaking of laws of a more abstract kind was dealt with in ways other than the simple process of water purification.

Evidences of purificatory rites have been found in many different parts of the world. The Aztecs with their ceremony for the removal of the birth-Tabu, the Babylonians with their ritual forms for removing leprosy and other sicknesses, the Egyptians with their temple-fonts filled with pure Nile water, the Mandæans and the Ebionites—all in their own way accepted the fundamental principle that no one could enter the Divine presence or take part in holy things without submitting to some kind of preliminary cleansing. Similarly in the Levitical system of later Judaism special rites of lustration were prescribed in connection with the " holiness " regulations. All contact with " unholy " objects must be " neutralised " by the appropriate form of bathing the body and washing the clothes. Thus a long tradition of association between outward bodily purification and religious cleansing provided an obvious background for the early interpretation of the Christian initiatory rite.

Yet it is a notable fact that in the New Testament itself less emphasis is laid upon baptism as a sign of purification than we might have expected. It is, of course, possible that this was one of the notes which received the greatest stress in the cate-chetical instruction of the primitive Church, but of this we cannot be sure. In the New Testament we find references in the Acts of the Apostles to the washing away of sins through baptism, in Ephesians to the cleansing of the Church through baptism and in Titus to the bath of regeneration. These texts were enough to provide the Fathers with material to justify their own inter-pretations of the rite but they cannot be said to constitute the major strand of actual New Testament interpretation.

When we move into the sub-Apostolic age we find that two of the most prominent interpretations associated with baptism were those of *regeneration* and *purification*. A firm basis for these ideas was found in certain somewhat isolated yet important passages in the New Testament and a ready response to them could be elicited in an environment where the desire for *life* and for *purity* had become intense. From Egypt and the Orient had come the mystery-cults with their promises of regeneration and their practices of lustration. " Through purification to newness of life " might almost be regarded as their key-note or slogan. It was no wonder, therefore, that Christian apologists jumped at the opportunity of defining Baptism as the true purification, the true illumination, the true means of being born again into newness of life.

If, for example, we examine the earliest description of the meaning of the baptismal rite outside the New Testament, that of Justin Martyr, we find that the dominant notes in his interpretation are those of regeneration and cleansing from sin. First there must be on the part of candidates the deep desire for " the remission of their sins that are past." Then they are brought to the water and regenerated by receiving the washing which the water makes possible. " And this bath is called illumination, inasmuch as those who learn these things are being illumined in understanding. And he who is illumined is washed in the name of Jesus Christ . . . . and in the name of the Holy Spirit."[1] Again, in the case of Tertullian, who is responsible for the earliest extended treatment of the subject, we find that his leading emphasis is on " washing away the sin of our early blindness." Evidently the baptismal ceremony had been ridiculed by pagan unbelievers. How could such a simple and unadorned rite bring about the effects which Christians claimed for it ? Tertullian answers this objection in part by dwelling on the way in which God can use weak and seemingly foolish things to accomplish great ends. But he also points out that water is one of the most significant and beneficial agents known to man. It is, perhaps, the chief agent of the Divine operation in terrestrial life. The Old Testament reveals how high and important a function it fulfils in the order of creation. How much more then can water which has been sanctified by the Holy Spirit prove to be the means of cleansing and sanctifying those who are brought to it. The Spirit " rests over the waters sanctifying them from Himself ; and being thus sanctified they imbibe at the same time the power of sanctifying." Thus when man, whose spirit and flesh mutually share the guilt of sin, comes to the waters of Baptism, " the spirit is corporeally washed in the waters and the flesh is in the same spiritually cleansed."

[1] The link between washing and illumination is derived from John, ch. 9. The name ($\phi\omega\tau\iota\sigma\mu\delta s$) was early applied to the baptismal rite.

One interesting feature of Tertullian's doctrine is his hesitation about infant baptism. He recognises the presence of " original sin " in all, but does not appear to hold that this is washed away in baptism. Rather it is actual sins which are remitted through baptism and the longer the administration of the rite can be delayed, the better. Obviously, such an attitude was bound to raise difficulties and the theory was gradually adjusted until it came to be held that even in the case of infants guilt was removed through the baptismal waters. The cleansing properties of the rite had gained such general acceptance that it could hardly be doubted that *something* was washed away in baptism. And when finally Augustine propounded his doctrine of original *guilt*, the way was open for the cleansing-motif to receive an obvious and universal application. At baptism every candidate, whether adult or infant, was washed from the guilt and stain of sin (original and actual). The rite had become the open sign of purification and whatever other significance it possessed, this tended more and more to be the essential meaning attached to it in the tradition of the West.

The regenerative associations, however, were not forgotten, especially in the tradition of the East. In some mysterious way baptism was a sign of regeneration, whatever precise interpretation might be given to the idea of the new birth. But the idea of cleansing was easier to grasp. In the imaginations of the peoples of the West water was more obviously associated with the removal of dirt than it was with the reproduction of life. So at length Roman Catholic orthodoxy set the removal of the guilt and stain of sin in the forefront of its interpretation and even included the remission of punishment due to sin within the benefits of the baptismal rite.[1] But the more definite and clear-cut and universal the sign becomes, the less capable it is of reaching out into wider areas of human experience and of touching new interpretations of human life. Cleansing and purification are important aspects of the religious life and they most certainly demand symbolic expression. But when a sign of purification comes to be regarded as automatic in its effects and perfectly precise in its application, it loses its symbolic value and becomes nothing more than part of the chain which

---

[1] See O. C. Quick, *The Christian Sacraments*, p. 172, footnote.

WATER SYMBOLISM AND CHRISTIAN BAPTISM   197

holds together a rigid social whole or an instrument which performs a necessary mechanical operation.

Let us now look at the second way in which baptism has been regarded as an open sign. Our examination of early myths has made us familiar with the motif of victory over a water monster or over hostile forces associated with water. Water is the abode of chaos and darkness ; it threatens the life of man ; his salvation can only be achieved if a champion arises who can overcome the water-demons and make the land safe for his neighbours to dwell in. But as life became more settled and civilised this image tended to recede in man's consciousness and a new association took its place. Water became an open sign of *separation*. Nothing acted more effectively as a boundary than water did. It might be a stream, it might be a river, it might be the sea. On one side was territory belonging to one tribe, on the other side was territory belonging to another ; or on one side was the suzerainty of an overlord, on the other side there was the open desert and freedom. In days when artificial boundaries and frontiers were hard to create, water was the most obvious and effective dividing-line known to man.

This view of water as a sign of separation produced another idea. It was that to pass from one territory to another it was necessary to go through the water. This passage might be made by wading or by finding a shallow ford or by swimming or by constructing a boat. In whatever way it was made, it was a dramatic experience to pass from one region to another, especially if the territory to which the journey was made had never been explored before. No symbolism could more effectively portray a passage from the old to the new, from the well-known to the unknown, from the bounded to the free, as could a passage through the water. He who had crossed the water had separated himself from the old and was henceforth committed to the new.

Nowhere in the ancient world does this general pattern find more dramatic expression than in the experience of the Hebrew tribes. Imprinted on their memory was the succession of episodes which is recorded in the early chapters of the Book of Exodus. Whatever legendary accretions may have accumulated in the course of time, there is good reason to think that the essential framework of the narrative is authentic—that a band of

Hebrews was enslaved in Egypt, that under the leadership of Moses they made a bid for freedom and that their escape was dramatically sealed by a passage through the waters of the Red Sea which effectively separated them from their wretched past and opened the way to a future of promise and hope. There were other important elements in this complex of corporate experiences but nothing was so clearly the dividing line, the boundary of separation, as was the Red Sea. The fact that God had brought them through the waters was for ever afterwards connected with their beginnings as a distinctive people and with the heritage of free movement which they believed was their due.

In the later history of Israel there are other significant references to passages through the water. At the conclusion of the wilderness wanderings the event which declared that one era was at an end and that another had begun was the crossing of the Jordan. No longer were the Israelites fugitives of the desert with no certain knowledge of whence they were to derive their food and water. Now they were to be men of their own land, reaping its harvests and drinking from its springs. But the *mark* of the change, its outward and visible sign, was the passing through the waters. It is perhaps significant that according to the record this passage was made with due solemnity and with accompanying ceremonial. The priests led on and the people followed and a ceremony of circumcision was performed on the farther side. Through the waters of Jordan they had crossed the boundary. Separated from their past they looked forward once again to their future with hope and expectancy.

At a still later period in Israel's history when the unity of the nation had been broken and large numbers deported to foreign lands, the prophets often sought to renew their people's faith by pointing back to the passage of the fathers through the Red Sea and by pointing forward to the time when God would again bring His people " through the waters " and back to their own land. Moreover, when the time came for Jewish missionaries in the Græco-Roman world to present their own distinctive faith to pagans, the series of events to which appeal was constantly made was the Exodus series with its suggestive symbolism of bondage—suffering—the intervention of God

—deliverance—exodus—victory. And in this series special stress was laid upon the passage through the Red Sea which sealed and signed the emancipation of those whom the Lord had redeemed. Indeed it is not unlikely that the imagery of the Red Sea deliverance was responsible for the creation of the rite of proselyte-baptism which seems to have originated at a time not long before the beginning of the Christian era. We know that this was a time when Jewish missionaries were exceedingly active in the Mediterranean world and it is altogether possible that they found in the rite of baptism a means of showing forth dramatically the separation of a Gentile from his past and his entrance into his new heritage as a member of the people of God.

Such were the great events in Israel's history which marked their separation from one manner of life and their commitment to another. In a remarkable way they were associated with a passage through the water. Yet it must be admitted at once that there is nothing in the record of the Old Testament to show that *individual* Israelites ever passed through a water-ceremony in any way resembling the determinative experience of the fathers when they passed through the Red Sea on their way to the Promised Land. Not until the New Testament record of the mission of John the Baptist can anything of the kind be found. But there *was* a ceremony which played a notable part in the life of the nation and which later became associated in certain respects with Baptism. To this ceremony we must briefly refer.

Circumcision was in no way peculiar to Israel. Other tribes of antiquity practised it, viewing it either as a tribal mark or as a means of " putting the physical organ into the necessary condition to fulfil its function." [1] But it seemed to attain a special importance at critical times of Israel's history for great stress is laid upon it at the time of the Exodus (Exodus 12) at the time of the entry into Canaan (Joshua 5) and at the time of the return from exile (Genesis 17). When, in other words, Israel's *separation* from other nations needed to be emphasised, when its peculiar relationship to its own God, Yahweh, needed to be reinforced, then the absolute necessity of circumcision was reaffirmed and

[1] A Lods, *Israel*, p. 200.

its significance re-interpreted as a sign of the covenant which existed between Yahweh and His people. " It was during the exile," Lods says, " when the Jews came into close contact with people like the Babylonians and the Persians, who did not practise the rite, that circumcision took on in the eyes of the Israelites the character of a symbol of nationality and religion. Its distinctive nature was the more marked in that the rite had fallen into disuse about the same time among the Phœnicians and no doubt among the other peoples of Palestine ; then it was that circumcision became the sign of the covenant between Yahweh and His people (Gen. 17, 11) and was required of all, stranger or slave, who partook of the Passover." [1] Without necessarily placing the period of the religious significance of circumcision so late in Israel's history as Lods is inclined to do, we can yet accept his general conclusion that circumcision, when used as a sign or symbol, denoted *separation* from heathenism and acceptance by the God of Israel. In late Judaism the prayer used at the circumcising of a child said : " Blessed be He who . . . sealed his offspring with the sign of a holy covenant," and it was widely held that circumcision is the stamp of the covenant which entitles a man to be regarded as one of God's own people.

Thus for the individual Israelite circumcision was the sign of *separation* from the vices of heathenism and of inclusion within the covenant relationship. Actually there is a certain naturalness of symbolism in the former of these motifs for it is possible to think of the foreskin as an unholy part of the body which needs to be removed. But there is little connection with the more dramatic symbolism such as is represented on a large scale by the Red Sea crossing and possibly for this reason baptism became increasingly important in later Judaism and soon replaced circumcision altogether in early Christianity. Baptism was to be the outward mark of separation within the Christian praxis. But what are we to say of the symbolism of inclusion within the covenant ? How did circumcision in Judaism or baptism in Christianity suggest the establishment of a new relationship ?

The only possible answer to these questions seems to be

[1] *Ibid.*

provided by the image of the *seal*. In Ezekiel 9, 4-6, the Lord
commands the man with the inkhorn to " go through the midst
. . . of Jerusalem, and set a mark upon the foreheads of the
men that sigh and that cry for all the abominations that are done
in the midst thereof. And to the others he said, Go ye through
the city after him, and smite : let not your eye spare, neither
have pity . . . but come not near any man upon whom is the
mark ; and begin at my sanctuary." " This conception," writes
G. W. H. Lampe, " of a sign set by God upon His elect to mark
them as His own and protect them from destruction is a frequent
motif in Hebrew eschatology, and it exercised a profound influence
upon the Christian theory of the sealing of the faithful ' for a
day of redemption,' and particularly . . . upon the ' sealing '
of the neophyte with the sign of the Cross. . . . It is, of course,
in part this idea of a token by which God recognises and
acknowledges His people that underlies the practice of circumcision as the sign of the Covenant. Circumcision, which
acquires an immense degree of importance in the Maccabean
and post-Maccabean epochs, is itself in the nature of a ' seal
for a day of redemption ' for, according to *Jubilees*, the uncircumcised ' belongeth not to the Children of the Covenant which
the Lord made with Abraham, but to the children of destruction ;
nor is there, moreover, any sign on him that he is the Lord's
but (he is destined) to be destroyed and slain from the earth,
and to be rooted out of the earth, for he hath broken the
covenant of the Lord our God.' The uncircumcised is ἀσημος,
one who does not possess the stamp of the covenant which
entitles him to be acknowledged by God as one of His people."
(*The Seal of the Spirit*, pp. 15-16.)

Undoubtedly the idea of the seal is very ancient and is to be
found in many parts of antiquity. The practices of branding
cattle or slaves with their owner's name, of tattooing soldiers,
of inscribing a mark on the forehead of a devotee, all provide
the background for the conception of circumcision as a seal
which stamps the true Israelite with the covenant-mark of his
owner. But it is very doubtful whether anything akin to
circumcision was used in the earliest and most authentic covenant
ceremonies and it is hard to avoid the conclusion that it was
the idea of the seal which arbitrarily made circumcision the mark

of the covenant, not the pattern of the circumcision-rite which suggested it as an appropriate symbol for the establishment of covenant relationship. In any case it was clearly regarded as the covenant-seal in late Judaism and just because the symbolism was artificial and not natural it became easy to regard baptism in the same way when first, as in late Judaism, the baptismal rite was associated with circumcision, and secondly, as in early Christianity, baptism had displaced circumcision. In short, baptism shares with circumcision a certain appropriateness as a symbol of *separation*—in fact, it is far more appropriate than circumcision as a memorial of the passage through the Red Sea waters or (later) of the Saviour's passage through the waters of death. At the same time, baptism, like circumcision, is a quite arbitrary seal of the covenant ; it is true that it came so to be regarded but a water-ritual has no necessary connection with the covenant and baptism only gained its appropriateness in this connection when it included within its symbolism either the signing with the Cross or the anointing with oil. These could be regarded as the marks of God's ownership but even so they could not compare in dramatic fitness with the passage through the waters which formed the heart of the rite.

Recent studies of Baptism in the New Testament have emphasised the importance of the Saviour's own Baptism at the hands of John, of His words concerning the baptism of suffering through which He Himself would pass, and of the references to the death-and-resurrection symbolism in the writings of Paul. A single pattern emerges of the Lord prefiguring His passion through His baptism in the Jordan (identifying Himself with those who were passing out of the realm dominated by the powers of darkness into the kingdom of righteousness and truth), actualising His passion as He passed through the deep waters of suffering and death, and extending His passion as He brought men into His fellowship by the way of their passage through the waters of Christian baptism. But this pattern scarcely retained its vividness in the general thought of the early Church. Rather the emphasis came to be laid upon baptism by water as being the recognised means of entry into the Church and upon an additional signing or anointing as being the means of receiving the seal of the Spirit. Coming to the font certainly symbolised a break with the past and a separation from the vices of heathenism : receiving the consignation certainly symbolised the establishment of a fellowship with Christ in the Spirit. But the ceremony came all too easily to be regarded as the necessary and recognised *sign* of admission into Church membership and the richer and deeper notes contained in the original symbolism were either overlaid or lost.

The whole question of the meaning of Baptism was opened up afresh at the time of the Reformation and as we shall see later a particularly valuable approach to the subject may be found in the writings of Luther. It was Calvin, however, who was to have the greatest influence upon the re-formation of baptismal doctrine at the time and in the main his approach was too legalistic to make a new appreciation of the essential symbolism of the rite possible. Calvin had been trained in the processes of the law and in his day the *seal* played a most important part in legal transactions.[1] It was a colourful symbol of a deed of conveyance and by grasping it in his hands the recipient could confirm his acceptance of property or an inheritance on certain specified conditions. To Calvin this seemed to be an apt description of a sacrament. It was a seal which confirmed God's promise and gave man the possibility of embracing the gift of God by an outward and visible action.

In all his thought the covenant of grace was primary. It was this covenant that embodied the promise of God that He would be God to us and to our children. But " the sacrament is afterwards added as a seal, not to give efficacy to the promise of God, as if it wanted validity in itself, but only to confirm it to us. Whence it follows that the children of believers are not baptized, that they may thereby be made the children of God, as if they had before been strangers to the Church ; but, on the contrary, they are received into the Church by solemn sign, because they already belonged to the body of Christ by virtue of the promise." (*Institutes* 4. 15. 22.) In ancient times circumcision was the sign or seal of the covenant of grace yet to come ; in later times baptism is the seal of grace already given and waiting to be received. Both in the old Testament

[1] Calvin speaks of the seals affixed to diplomas and other public deeds and appeals to Romans 4, 11 for scriptural support.

and the New the covenant itself is concerned with cleansing
from sin by the blood of Christ and with mortification of all
fleshly desires through participation in Christ's death. Thus it
is hard to avoid the impression that in Calvin's thought this
promise of the covenant could be sealed just as well by circumcision as by baptism. So long as there was an appointed *seal* its
precise *form* seemed to be of little account.

It is true that Calvin laid great store by the *visible* quality of
the sacrament. " Yea," he says, " a sacrament is nothing else
than a visible word, or sculpture and image of that grace of God
which the word more fully illustrates . . . as soon as the sign
meets our eyes, the word ought to sound in our ears." Then
we, on our part, can make our proper response to the covenant
by embracing the sign " as a testimony and pledge of grace."
(*Commentary on Genesis*, 17, 9.) But when he tries to show how
exactly the sign represents this grace of God he is less impressive.
He suggests, for example, that the seal of circumcision showed
that whatever is born of man is polluted and that the promise
was to come through Abraham's *seed*. He declares, moreover,
that the water of baptism emblematically represents the blood of
Christ so that " at whatever time we are baptised, we are washed
and purified for the whole of life. Whenever we have fallen,
therefore, we must recur to the *remembrance* of baptism and arm
our minds with the consideration of it, that we may be always
certified and assured of the remission of our sins." (4, 14, 3.)
He points out also that baptism affords us the certain testimony
that we have become partakers of the death and resurrection of
Christ. But he leaves us with no clear conception of the relation
between the sign and the thing signified. All too easily it seems
to be implied that so long as the given seal is set forth publicly
and embraced, it is a matter of indifference whether it be circumcision or baptism or some other rite ; God's Promise and the
ordained seal of the Promise are all that really matter.

The fact that the rite continued to be administered to infants
helped to promote its interpretation as a seal or pledge for it
became increasingly difficult for Reformed theologians to think
in terms of the cleansing from original sin or of the death to sin
and rising to righteousness when infants were the subjects of
baptism. It was far easier to believe that the sacrament provided

an open seal of God's good will towards the child and that through it the child became a partaker of the privileges of the covenant. Thus in the Irish Articles of 1615 Baptism is defined as " a sacrament of our admission into the Church, sealing unto us our new birth (and consequently our justification, adoption and sanctification) by the communion which we have with Jesus Christ." In the Westminster Confession a still fuller and more explicit definition is given : " Baptism is a sacrament of the New Testament, ordained by Jesus Christ, not only for the solemn admission of the party baptized into the visible church, but also to be unto him a sign and seal of the covenant of grace, of his ingrafting into Christ, of regeneration, of remission of sins, and of his giving up unto God through Jesus Christ, to walk in newness of life." This whole view comes to clear and concise expression in the Shorter Cathechism, which speaks of Baptism as a sacrament " wherein the washing with water in the name of the Father, and of the Son, and of the Holy Ghost, doth signify and seal our ingrafting into Christ, and partaking of the benefits of the covenant of grace, and our engagement to be the Lord's."

The natural corollary of this view was that it was incumbent upon the child who had received the seal to " improve " its baptism by entering into the heritage to which it was entitled. No question could be raised about *God's* part in the transaction. He is faithful Who has promised and in the baptismal rite He openly seals His promise to the initiate. Yet it still remains possible for the child to repudiate its inheritance and to fail to make use of the promised grace of God. So it is the duty of the pastor to summon his people to " remember " their baptism and to live in conformity with the covenant to which it had admitted them openly. In the *Directory of Public Worship* of 1644 the people are enjoined " to improve and make the right use of their Baptism and of the Covenant sealed thereby betwixt God and their souls," while in *The Oeconomy of the Covenants* Hermann Witsius refers to " the extraordinary love of our God . . . that He should join us to Himself in the most solemn covenant from our tender years, the remembrance of which as it is glorious and full of consolation to us, so in like manner it tends to promote Christian virtues and the strictest holiness, through the whole course of our lives." (Quoted Schenck,[1] pp. 148-9.)

Valuable as this emphasis upon the bond or pledge or seal was in certain circumstances, it tended all too easily to make the symbolic aspect of the life of the community cold and legal and abstract. The symbolism of water, the drama of the passage through the water, the *form* of the Covenant-ceremony, the corporate character of the Baptismal rite, were largely neglected and even ignored. It is true that Calvin urged that at the time of Baptism the *whole Church* should be looking on as witnesses, and praying, but his further objection that " all the theatrical pomp which dazzles the eyes of the simple and dulls their minds " should be abjured, encouraged those who were set on making baptism nothing more than a bare and naked sign of the establishment of a legal bond. The danger which has beset the main body of Protestantism since the beginning of the seventeenth century has been that of depriving the baptismal rite of its symbolic power and significance by interpreting it as nothing more than a seal of the initiate's inheritance in Christ and an open sign of the difference between the people of God and those outside the covenant of grace.

THE EXPANDING SYMBOL

We have described some of the powerful images which belong to the penumbra of our conscious life. These are associated either with rebirth through a descent into the dark waters which typify the womb of life or with victory gained through a successful encounter with hostile forces who make the waters their habitation. We have dwelt upon the practical signs which belong to the normal and regular experiences of life : either the sign of cleansing from defilement or the seal of separation from the realm of evil, water being used in each case as the necessary matter of the sign. We come now to our final stage—the interpretation of baptism as a symbol whose range of

[1] L. B. Schenck, *The Presbyterian Doctrine of Children in the Covenant.* (Yale University Press, 1940.)

meaning can expand ever more extensively within the life of the whole Church.

In the first place we shall view baptism as *incorporation into the growing organism of the Body of Christ*. The Biblical foundation of this interpretation is twofold. On the one hand there is the Pauline teaching which finds its most vivid expression in Galatians 3, 26-9.

" For ye are all sons of God, through faith, in Christ Jesus. For as many of you as were baptized into Christ did put on Christ. There can be neither Jew nor Greek, there can be neither bond nor free, there can be no male and female ; for ye are all one man in Christ Jesus. And if ye are Christ's, then are ye Abraham's seed, heirs according to promise."

And in 1 Corinthians 12, 4-27 (of which I shall quote two verses) :

" For as the body is one and hath many members, and all the members of the one body, being many, are one body ; so also is Christ. For in one Spirit were we all baptized into one body, whether Jews or Greeks, whether bond or free ; and were all made to drink of one Spirit."

On the other hand there is the Johannine teaching which is to be found in the Gospel as a whole though certain passages in the first three chapters are of special importance.

In the Pauline teaching the Christ occupies the central position. His members were incorporated into His body through baptism, they belong to Him, they share His life, they form one man in Him, they partake of His Spirit. Care must be taken not to extend the analogy in a more detailed and literalistic way than the Apostle intended, but that he regarded baptism into Christ as *analogous* to incorporation into a human organism can scarcely be doubted. The Johannine teaching is more subtle, but its general import seems to be the same. The Messiah receives the baptism of the Spirit while He stands with John in the waters of the Jordan. He looks forward to the death of His earth-body and to the rising up of the new sanctuary of His Body, the Church. Then it is that He proclaims that only those who share His own experience through water and Spirit can become members of the Kingdom of God. The evangelist returns to the water-symbolism at various points in his Gospel and it is reasonable to infer that in his mind birth into the family of God was brought about through sharing the baptismal experience of the Messiah, though his close association of water and Spirit is a constant reminder that it is only in the sanctuary of the Spirit that water is of any avail.

Possibly the most influential later interpreter of Baptism in terms of these general categories was St. Augustine. He had been profoundly impressed by the Body-imagery of the New Testament and he returns to it again and again in his writings. Christ Himself is invisible but His body, the Church, is visible and is the outward sign of the invisible reality. Christ Himself is constantly working invisibly, but in the Church all actions performed are visible signs of His invisible operations.

" Nor has He now ceased to baptize ; but He still does it, not by any ministry of the body, but by the invisible working of His majesty. For in that we say He Himself baptizes, we do not mean He Himself holds and dips in the water the bodies of the believers ; but He Himself invisibly cleanses and that He does to the whole Church without exception. Christ sanctifies. Christ also Himself washes, Himself purifies with the self-same washing of water by the word, wherein the ministers are seen to do their work in the body." [1]

This distinction between visible and invisible, both in reference to the body and to acts performed, enabled St. Augustine to establish his famous policy in regard to heretical baptism. He would not allow that baptism duly performed was invalid. In such a baptism the real minister was Christ, working invisibly to the soul's advantage. But at the same time the fruits of this invisible operation could never be manifested visibly unless and until the initiate had become united with the visible Body of Christ. Augustine refused to adopt the heretics' own practice of re-baptism, for in his view there could be only one true Baptism. But for its benefits to be enjoyed, for its true purpose to be effected, there must be the necessary environment —namely the visible Body of Christ, the one Catholic Church. Up to a point the teaching of Augustine was valuable, but it was held too firmly within the framework of a philosophy of outward and inward, visible and invisible, body and soul,

[1] Answer to Petilian, III, 49.

to be a finally satisfying interpretation of the baptismal act. We must look to modern times for expositions which do fuller justice to the New Testament on one side and to our growing knowledge of the universe on the other.

Let us first look at the writings of Father L. S. Thornton. As is well known, Thornton regards philosophies of organism as of great significance for interpreting the Christian faith in modern terms. No such philosophy is complete which fails to find both the origin and the fulfilment of the world-organism in the Divine-human organism of the incarnate Lord. But if the world-organism be seen within this context, and if the continuing activity of God be seen in terms of the Son of His love ever taking afresh the form of a servant within the world-organism, then it becomes possible to construct a system within which the world finds its true meaning in God and God fulfils His plan of redemption through the world. Processes in the created order, processes in the life of the Incarnate Lord, and processes in the continuing life of His Body, the Church, are then seen to constitute one interlocking system and the forms of Nature can be regarded as analogous symbols of the forms which belong to the spiritual organism, the Body of Christ.

It is the great merit of Thornton's exposition that he takes the natural element, water, very seriously. Partly because of his determination to do full justice to the Biblical material, he returns to the natural properties of water again and again. He draws attention to the significance of the waters over which the Spirit brooded in the creation-story : to the passage of the children of Israel through the Red Sea waters ; to the life-giving properties of water when it is poured upon the dry ground ; to its fertilising power for seed (both of these latter properties are stressed by the prophets) ; to Jeremiah's picture of God as the fountain of living waters ; to Ezekiel's picture of the waters flowing out from under the Temple ; to the Baptism of Jesus and to the descent of the Spirit upon the new creation as He stood in the waters ; to the waters flowing from the new sanctuary of Christ's body ; to the Spirit whose coming is as water to the dry and thirsty soul ; to the baptismal waters of the new creation by whose agency men are initiated into the Divine-human organism. So from both points of view—the heavenly waters of the Spirit bringing life and refreshing to parched souls wherever they go, and barren souls gaining life and fertility as they are immersed in the waters of the Spirit—it becomes apparent how in creation, in Scripture, and in the life of the Church, water is a most suggestive and expansive symbol to denote the operations of the Spirit within the organism of the Body of Christ. Water is not just a sign of cleansing ; it is a symbol of new creation and fertilisation and refreshment and regeneration. If its natural properties are kept in view they can be used as vivid analogies of processes within the life of the spiritual organism.

The second great merit of Thornton's exposition is that he deals realistically with the time-element in world-structure. Regeneration is a process which is for ever going on in time yet which has a critical expression within time and a final fulfilment at the end of time. On the level of the created order we can constantly witness the springing up of new life after showers of rain, the growth of new life after a grafting process, the renewal of the tired and thirsty after they have partaken of draughts of water, the birth of a new individual organism after a fertilising process has taken place. But on the level of historic event " the new creation of the messianic community as a whole had its historical inauguration in the event of Pentecost. . . . The descent of the Spirit at Pentecost was that event whereby the new life of the risen Christ was precipitated into His community. By sharing the ourpoured Spirit they were re-born in Christ." [1]

If we now regard this event as the one in which " the Church of God was re-born and renewed," in which " the one organism which is the Christ . . . entered into full possession of its many members," then baptism becomes the extension of this original crisis of regeneration. " For in baptism the neophyte becomes partaker in that final ' regeneration when the Son of Man shall sit on the throne of His glory.' Moreover not only is his nature renewed by partaking of the Spirit. His baptism is also a renewal of Pentecost, in the sense that the pentecostal outpouring of the Spirit is renewed in him. At every Christian initiation the eschatological crisis enters the individual life of the

---

[1] *The Common Life in the Body of Christ*, pp. 190-1.

neophyte. Because he is in Christ, Christ is also in him. Pentecost was for the Church the dawn of the eschatological regeneration which belongs to the Last Day. In every baptism therefore
starting point and goal are one. The Last Day began to dawn
for each of us on the first day of our life in Christ." (*Ibid.*)

In Thornton's view, then, just as the creative act of generation
is continually being repeated on the level of the natural order,
so the creative act of regeneration is continually being repeated
on the level of the new order in Christ.[1] The first is an analogy
of the second. At the same time it must be recognised that the
emergence of the new organism of the Son of Man through the
Virgin Birth and the career through which He passed up to
Pentecost constitutes a determinative pattern which must control
and be reproduced in the life of the messianic community and
must be seen as the key to the character of the final purpose
of God which is to be realised in the eschaton. It belongs to
the whole doctrine of organism to speak in terms of germ and
fruition, grafting and new growth, adoption and full sonship,
earnest and full possession, firstfruits and final harvest. The
aim is to envisage the *whole* as one integrated process in which
there may be different levels or orders but only one steady
pattern from start to finish. If such a pattern can be discerned
and if a rite such as baptism can be seen to be an appropriate
symbol of an essential part of that pattern, then obviously the
rite attains an importance such as it could gain in no other way.

A third merit of Thornton's exposition is to be found in
the stress which it lays upon the *representative* character of the
incarnate life of the Messiah and in particular upon the Baptism
of Christ as *representing* the baptism of all those who are to be
incorporated into His Body. This baptism of Christ was of a
double kind ; it was a baptism of initiation in the waters of the
Jordan, it was a baptism of suffering on the hill of Calvary.
These two baptisms are not separate; yet whereas the first stresses
the notes of regeneration by the Spirit and initiation into a
particular vocation, the second emphasises the thoughts of
sacrificial consecration and purification from all defilement. In

[1] " Our sonship begins in re-birth and renewal of the Holy Spirit. Yet as
adopted sons we shall ever be new-born through the ever-renewed gift of the Holy
Spirit. The beginning is also carried through to the end. Regeneration characterises the whole of the New Life." (Op. cit., p. 194.)

two notable passages of his book, *The Common Life in the Body of Christ*,[1] Thornton discusses the meaning and implications of Ephesians 5, 26-27 and of John 1, 19-34, and shows how baptism within the Church must conform, both in pattern and significance, to the baptism by water and blood to which the Redeemer Himself submitted. In fact there is one pattern for Christ, for the Church, and for the individual member of the body. The Church is cleansed and consecrated in and through the life-pattern of the Messiah (though an element of complication enters by reason of the fact that it is the Messiah Himself who cleanses His Church) ; the individual is cleansed and consecrated as he is initiated into the Body Whose organic structure is identical with that of its Head.

Father Thornton's interpretation of Baptism is remarkably comprehensive and suggestive. He relates the symbolism of the rite to the organic processes of the created order in a way which few others have done. Sprinkling with water, affusion with water, cleansing with water, immersion in water—all become highly significant actions. The representative character of Christ's baptism is revealed, the relationship between the corporate and individual aspects of the rite is made clear, the meaning of the act within the time series of redemptive history is disclosed. There are what Thornton calls " polarities " in his system and at times these seem to involve paradoxes if not inconsistencies. But he does not attempt to avoid the double-sidedness of Christian truth when no neat integration can be achieved and it is probably true to say that Thornton's exposition provides a better foundation for re-interpreting the symbolism of baptism and for reinstating it within the practical life of the Church than any other which is available at the present time.

Nevertheless there is one aspect of baptism in particular which receives less than full attention in this tradition. It is that aspect which views baptism as marking a radical break, a renunciation, a reversal, a repudiation of the world, the flesh and the devil, a death to sin and a new life of righteousness—in fact which sees it as marking a moral crisis of quite unique importance. Baptism, in this view, signifies *the first stage in the renewal of the Covenant which God has made with His people in Christ* ;

[1] Pp. 227-9, 414-6.

it is the *first stage*, for the symbolism only gains its completion when those within the covenant seal their communion one with another in the eucharistic feast. Just as in late Judaism the full ceremony whereby a proselyte was admitted into the fellowship of the people of God included circumcision, baptism and the offering of sacrifice (though circumcision was omitted in certain cases) so in one view of Christian initiation the ceremony must be held to include both baptism and communion.[1] Only so can the full pattern of the covenant be symbolically renewed.

It is hardly possible to fasten upon one or two particular Biblical passages to provide a foundation for this general interpretation. It can, however, be pointed out that whatever variations there may have been in the precise symbolism whereby the Old Testament covenant was established and renewed, it normally included an initial mark of *separation* followed by a solemn act of *communion*. The separation might be effected by circumcision (in Exodus 12, 43-7 circumcision is demanded as a *sine qua non* for those who desire to partake of the passover); it might be effected by the sprinkling of blood (in Exodus 24, 8-11, blood is sprinkled on the people before the covenant is consummated in the common feast); it might be effected as in late Judaism by a form of baptism, a ceremony which may have been related to the event by which the children of Israel were separated from their past by the waters of the Red Sea (only when they had been redeemed from Egypt were they entitled to partake of God's manna in the wilderness). But in whatever way the separation was effectively symbolised it was the necessary first stage in the renewing of the covenant.

So in the New Testament the Servant of the Lord, through whom the New Covenant was established, began to set apart a

---

[1] There is an interesting reference to this point in an article by A. Raymond George in the *Scottish Journal of Theology*, June, 1951, p. 166. He writes: "These two sacraments were indeed in the early Church almost regarded as one Sacrament, for the initiatory rite, which we will for the moment call Baptism, though it included other items, was usually followed at once by the Eucharist, the first Communion of the candidate. Wladimir Weidle has recently contended with a good deal of evidence in *The Baptism of Art* that the Church thought of one supreme Sacrament which began with Baptism and culminated in the Eucharist. The Sunday Eucharist was a kind of reminiscent reproduction of the latter part of this, with the synaxis taking the place of the Baptism." There are similarities to this view in Thornton's exposition, though it would be truer to say that for him Baptism is the sacramental consecration of the Sacrifice which is sacramentally offered in the Eucharist.

new community in and through His own Baptism at Jordan and sealed them within the covenant through the meal in the upper room.   At a still deeper level, the covenant was established through His own baptism in suffering, and sealed when His own body was broken and His blood finally poured out for the benefit of mankind.   Thereafter, as often as a candidate passed through the baptismal waters and thereby renounced his former existence outside the covenant, as often as the community of the New Covenant joined together in eating the bread and drinking the wine and thereby sealed their communion within the covenant, the whole pattern of the new relationship between God and man was dramatically shown forth and the covenant was renewed.

So long as there continued to be a steady flow of converts from paganism into the Church, the notes of separation and renunciation never ceased to be sounded in the baptismal ceremony.   The passage through the waters, the renunciation of the powers of evil, the emergence from darkness into light, all helped to dramatise the radical nature of the change which had taken place.[1]   But the more the Church became settled and established, the less need there seemed for the symbolism of conflict and tension and critical decision.   Baptism as applied to infants was interpreted chiefly in terms of regeneration and purification and tended to be regarded as a sign of the beginning of the Christian life and no more ;   there were other important rites and ceremonies to engage the attention of *adult* Christians.   Thus we find Luther complaining that " there is scarcely anyone nowadays who remembers that he has been baptized, much less glories in it, so many other ways having been found of obtaining remission of sins and going to heaven."   It was indeed Luther who was the first to attempt to restore baptism to its place of high significance in the Christian life.

Luther's starting point was the word which he regarded as the direct promise of God ;   " He who believes and is baptized shall be saved."   Here was the promise of God ;   there was no excuse for anyone who failed to believe it and act upon it.   But the reference to baptism in the promise was in no way arbitrary ; baptism was not just a meaningless act to be performed as a

[1] Cp. G. W. H. Lampe, *The Seal of the Spirit*, pp. 149-50.

mark of obedience. Baptism is, above all, a symbol of the Death
and Resurrection of Christ and so of the believer. " When . . .
the washing away of sins is attributed to baptism it is rightly
so attributed ; but the meaning of the phrase is too slight and
weak to fully express baptism, which is rather a symbol of death
and resurrection." For this reason it is altogether desirable, in
Luther's judgment, to use the form of total immersion " for a
sinner needs not so much to be washed as to die, that he may
be altogether renewed into another creature." If this form of
symbolism be used it means that the initiate can continually
return to it in remembrance and can enter ever more deeply
into it in his experience. " Thus thou hast been baptized once
for all sacramentally but thou needest continually to be baptized
by faith, and must continually die and continually live." It is
true that Luther ran into difficulty when he sought to apply to
infants what he had first addressed to adults. The ideas of
transferred faith and infused faith seem remote and unreal and
his early exposition suffers through its dependence upon a
doubtful passage in the final section of the Gospel of Mark.
But Luther's work was of the greatest significance in that it
challenged men to consider afresh the meaning of their baptism
and in that it drew attention once again to the interpretation of
the rite as a radical death to sin and a miraculous resurrection to
righteousness of life.

In Protestant Scholasticism Baptism came increasingly to be
regarded as a sign and seal of God's covenant, as a bond and
pledge on the part of the believer. All too easily it took over
categories and terminology from the realms of law and economics;
it was held to be a first instalment, an initial bond, a post-dated
cheque, a bequest to be claimed at an appointed time. Such
images may have helped to make the baptismal rite meaningful
to a few but they are too static and impersonal for general use.
I believe that the time has come for a new interpretation of
baptism which will do justice to the various aspects of symbolism
which are involved and which will, through a rediscovery of the
essential drama of life through death, make the notes of glorious
intervention and splendid victory and radical crisis and costly
decision once again central in the whole rite. There are signs
that efforts along these lines are beginning to be made.

In any such reinterpretation, some equivalent of the symbolic act of actually passing through the water must be recovered. Millions in the Church to-day have never witnessed a baptism in which any suggestion of a critical separation or radical renunciation was included. What is there to suggest a costly encounter with opposing forces issuing in a sudden triumph ; or a toilsome struggle to surmount barriers leading to a sudden achievement ; or a tense conflict with powers of evil, without or within, and a sudden deliverance—all by the grace of God ? What is there to symbolise the plight of the sinner in contrast to the redeeming love of God ? Or of the guilt of the sinner in contrast to the justifying righteousness of God ? There is a symbol in history which suggests all these ; it is the double-sided event of Calvary and the Resurrection. Here the new covenant was sealed between a holy God and sinful mankind. But does Baptism continue to represent this symbolism in outward rite and ceremony ? In general we must admit that it does not.

Yet in early times the passage through the waters or immersion in the waters did set the mark of the Cross and Resurrection upon the initiate and indeed upon the whole Church. "Know ye not, that so many of us as were baptized into Jesus Christ were baptized into His death ? Therefore we are buried with Him by baptism into death ; that like as Christ was raised up from the dead . . . even so we also should walk in newness of life." (Rom. 6, 3-4.) The precise pattern of passing through the waters or of plunging beneath the waters may no longer be possible. But unless some symbolic forms are found to give vivid metaphorical expression to this conjunction of death and life, of sin and righteousness, of renunciation and glorification, something of vital importance will have faded out of the corporate life of the people of God.

The significance of baptism as a time-symbol has gained increasing recognition by those who have found in the New Testament what may be called a realised or proleptic or inaugurated eschatology. They have made us familiar with the idea of an event which holds a decisive importance in relation to the final issue even though a long period of painful conflict has still to ensue. From this point of view the death and resurrection of Christ is to be regarded as the proleptic realisation of the final victory of God ; the baptism of the individual believer is to be regarded as the proleptic realisation of his final deliverance from sin and his establishment in righteousness in the kingdom of God. This pattern of death and resurrection is repeated again and again in history but attains its focal expression in the complex of events which constitute the passion, death and resurrection of the Messiah. The pattern is then engraved ever more deeply upon the consciousness both of the Church and of the individual believer at each successive baptism.[1]

Finally, it is worth remarking that in two notable modern treatments of Baptism—those of W. F. Flemington [2] and Oscar Cullmann [3]—a marked emphasis is laid upon the connection between what is called the " General Baptism " of Christ and the particular baptism of the individual believer. Christ, in other words, is regarded as the pioneer or leader who by participation in a symbolic rite and by submission to an actual historical experience, provided a dramatic portrayal of the path to be followed by all who seek a share in the glory of God. He Himself took the way of the Servant, divesting Himself of all privilege and status and identifying Himself with sinful men in the waters of the Jordan ; He joined in the struggle with the powers of evil even to the point of being subjected to physical violence and a felon's death and a grave with the wicked. He rose victorious and received the name which is above every name—the Lord and Leader of mankind. Such was the " General

----

[1] Cp. " In Baptism the individual is given, so to speak, the freedom of the city of God. He is incorporated in the historic community of God's people. The significance of the action is thus described by Paul (he quotes Romans 6, 3-4). In other words, baptism signifies the re-enactment in the individual of the death and resurrection of Christ, in which the whole process of revelation in history came to a head. Let us recall that the Bible represents this fact of death-and-resurrection as giving the essential pattern of the entire history of man under the Word of God. When Abraham left Ur of the Chaldees, he was renouncing one kind of life in order to enter upon a new life on terms of God's covenant. When Israel went out of Egypt, they left a secure, though servile, way of life for the unknown perils and privations of the wilderness, in order that they might be fitted for new ways of life under God's Law. At the Babylonian conquest they died as an independent nation, with political and military ambitions, to rise again as a community dedicated wholly (in intention) to the service of religion. This is the pattern on which the purpose of God shaped the history of His people. In baptism the same pattern is applied, through Christ, to the history of the individual." (C. H. Dodd, *The Bible of To-day*, pp. 160-1.)

[2] *The New Testament Doctrine of Baptism.*

[3] *Baptism in the New Testament.*

Baptism " of the Messiah. But even during His struggle He asked those who were seeking to share His glory :

> " Can ye drink of the cup that I drink of ? and be baptized with the baptism that I am baptized with ? "

Baptism thus becomes a powerful metaphorical symbol linking the baptism of Jordan with the events of the first Holy Week and Good Friday. This meant, however, that every subsequent baptism could also find its basis of meaning in the passion of Christ. " Behind every Christian baptism," says Flemington, " there lay not only the baptism of Jesus in the River Jordan, but also his other ' baptism ' upon Calvary " (p. 123). " The outward act of water-baptism recalls, and as it were *re-presents*, that act of God done once and for all for man's salvation in the death and resurrection of Jesus Christ. Baptism thus implements that act for each successive believer " (p. 111).

Such an interpretation is entirely in harmony with the doctrine of justification by faith. The justification of the individual finds its ground in the justification of the Messiah. Though reckoned among the transgressors as He joined the multitudes which went out to the baptism of John, He was actually vindicated by the word which acclaimed Him the beloved Son of God. Though regarded as stricken, smitten of God and afflicted as He endured His cross and passion, He was still more signally justified as He rose in triumph from the grave. So, too, the individual who casts himself upon Christ, though burdened with sin and a body of death, is yet justified in and through the justification of Christ and raised to a new life in the Spirit as he rejoices in hope of the glory of God. Christ is the Leader who has established the new covenant of righteousness ; man begins to enjoy his outward privileges within the covenant when he is symbolically joined to his Leader in the waters of baptism and thereby committed to the life-pattern which the Gospel-story portrays.

There are difficulties in this interpretation. It is not easy to apply realistically to the baptism of children and it is hard to maintain an appropriate form of symbolism in which the passage through the waters occupies a central position. Even

Baptists who have done so much in other ways to safeguard the dramatic symbolism of the baptismal rite, find it hard in more sophisticated surroundings to retain the whole movement of the drama intact. Moreover, there is always the danger that by focusing attention upon the act of the individual, the all-important purpose of the ceremony—the open renewal of God's covenant in Christ with His people—will be relegated to the background or overlooked. There is need to-day for a thorough re-examination by Reformed theologians of the *form* of the baptismal rite and for a resolute facing of the question whether a passing through the waters is any longer an altogether appropriate symbol of the initial establishment of the Covenant. There is little likelihood that a widespread adoption of the practice of baptism by immersion will take place within the majority of the Churches which maintain the Reformed tradition. The question is whether any other form of initiatory rite can more adequately symbolise the great truths of the covenant grace of God and justification by faith.

In conclusion I would suggest that a way forward at the present time is to be found by holding in close relationship to one another the type of interpretation contained in Thornton's *analogical symbolism* with its emphasis upon the processes of Nature and upon the all-embracing activity of the Son of God within the world-organism, and that type contained in the *metaphorical symbolism* of Dodd and Flemington and Cullmann with its emphasis upon the events of history and upon the eschatological acts of the Christ within the time-series. Each of these types recognises fully that baptism concerns not only the individual but also the community, and of all baptismal reforms which may be needed to-day none is more urgent than that of regaining the truly *corporate* nature of the baptismal rite. Unless in normal experience it takes its place as the sacrament of the whole Church or of the gathered congregation, it fails to fulfil its proper function within the design and purpose of God.

The former of these types emphasises the relation of baptism to the natural world and our whole investigation has revealed the importance of discovering afresh the significance of *water* within the rite ; the latter of the types emphasises the relation of baptism to historical event and again our investigation has shown how important a place the *passing through the waters* must occupy within a full baptismal ritual. Within the ecumenical Church there must surely be room for both of these emphases. It is the narrow concentration upon the interpretation of baptism as an instrumental sign of regeneration or as a legalistic seal of church-membership which hinders advance in this area of Christian symbolism. Let the Church affirm afresh the place in the rite both of the community and of the individual, both of contact with the water and of triumph over the water, both of the relation to the Divine organism and of the relation to the Divine covenant, both of incorporation and of initiation—recognising that in differing historical circumstances emphases will differ—and baptism may yet recover its true significance within the expanding life of the Christian society.

CHAPTER EIGHT

The Symbolism of Sacrifice

IN THE course of man's historical experience many patterns of activity have come to possess special symbolical significance, but it is doubtful whether any has persisted over so long a period or has exercised so deep an influence as has the institution of sacrifice. Anthropological studies have shown that some form of sacrifice has been practised by primitive peoples in all parts of the world. It might be severely simple, it might involve the most elaborate pomp and ceremonial as civilisations grew and expanded. But in a strangely impressive way it has remained the central ceremony around which social life has constantly revolved. In fact the sacrificial drama must be regarded as one of the oldest and the most significant of all patterns of symbolic human activity.

When this has been said, however, certain major questions immediately arise. What was the original purpose of sacrifice? Why did men slay victims and offer gifts? Can any uniform pattern of meaning be discerned within the multitudinous forms of sacrificial activity? It has been one of the main tasks of social scientists and historians of religion to provide answers to these questions and various theories to account for the origin and continuity of sacrifice have been propounded. Some have held that it was primarily a means of offering a gift to the deity, others that it was designed to provide a means of feasting on and with the deity, others still that it was regarded as the supreme means of renewing and sustaining the life of Nature. There is probably some truth in each of these claims but it seems unlikely that any single theory will cover all the facts. I intend, therefore, to approach the matter along the lines which have been pursued the long historical record of this remarkable institution.

The earliest life of man was dominated by one main concern —how to secure adequate supplies of food and drink for himself and his dependents. Of the two needs, that of food was the harder to furnish in any regular and assured way. He might find a spring or a water-hole or a stream or a river and so long as he remained within reach of any one of them he could always quench his thirst. But the food supply was far more precarious. Some communities depended upon fruits and berries and plants but these were not always available and in some climates were not fully satisfying. Others made use of fish and animals and found that they could, by skill and cunning, be assured of a reasonably regular augmentation of an otherwise meagre diet. It is impossible to make any clear-cut distinction in this matter, but it is obvious that those who depended more upon the fruits of the earth were likely to lead a more settled life within a given area than were those who depended more upon a fleshy diet and roamed hither and thither seeking for their prey.

The great advance took place when on the one hand man discovered ways of cultivating plants to give him the vegetable food he desired, and on the other hand found means whereby animals could be tamed and either killed for food or compelled to yield their milk and their labour to ease man's own burden of toil. The gradual discovery of increasingly effective ways of co-operating with Nature so that it provided him with an abundance of palatable and satisfying food must have been one of the most exciting developments in the whole of man's history. Similarly, the sense of a growing mastery over the animal creation so that it could be made to provide him with protection and a strength greater than his own must have filled him with satisfaction and hope. Henceforth man was ceasing to be simply a food-gatherer, dependent upon seasonal crops and the uncertain results of the chase ; he was becoming a food producer, gaining in skills to cultivate and irrigate and reap better harvests and increasing in the ability to make the animals his willing slaves. Again it would be dangerous to make hard and fast distinctions.[1] Nevertheless the early distinction between fruit-gathering and animal-hunting and the later between crop-cultivation and stock-rearing are of great importance as we seek to understand the significance of the ritual activity of primitive societies.

Let us take first the societies whose primary concern is with trees and plants and cultivated crops. Clearly what matters most is that the mysterious life of Nature shall be sustained and even increased. Man early becomes aware of the changes of the seasons. Leaves are shed, fruit-bearing ceases, vegetation withers and dies. But spring comes and new life shoots forth and ultimately food becomes available again. Further, he is aware of the devastating effect of drought. Everything begins to wilt and languish and even his own energies are sapped and weakened. But once the monsoon or the rain-storm comes, everything springs to life again as if by magic, and man rejoices in the new provision for his needs. Now man who lives in close contact with Nature tends to regard his whole universe as inter-connected and as animated by one single life-force. The " life-stuff " which resides in himself and his family is the same as that which resides in Nature around him and even in the more mysterious powers which inhabit the heavenly bodies and the seasons and the storms. But he knows that his own life is sustained and intensified by the food he eats. Is he not therefore bound to give back offerings of food to the inhabitants of the natural phenomena which are found in his universe ? Can he not offer gifts to trees and stones and springs ? Can he not in some realistic way provide sustenance for the more remote spirits which dwell in the sun and the moon and the storm-cloud ?

This simple *motif* of *offering* in order to sustain and promote life is, I believe, at the root of a vast number of ritual observances in more settled societies living close to Nature. As time went

[1] Surveying primitive societies in different parts of the world, C. D. Forde has written : " The essential economies may in the broadest way be termed collecting, hunting, fishing, cultivation and stock rearing. But the adoption and practice of any one does not imply or necessitate the complete abandonment of another, nor has any people been known to rely exclusively on one alone." (*Habitat : Economy and Society*, p. 461.)

on, many new factors entered to make the ritual more complex. Man did not confine himself to simple offerings of food and water. Any objects in which the life-substance seemed to be abundant could be offered. In particular, the fruits of his own body could be offered; a living child or a slave or some victim chosen by the community could, through death, be released to increase the whole life of the universe. Blood which seemed to be the seat of life could be offered, or wine, the potent juice of the grape, or *soma*, the mysterious juice of the plant, could be brought as substitutes. From all parts of the world evidence has been gathered to show that the essential pattern of offering an object containing or representing life to pass through a process actualising or symbolising death in order to sustain and increase the total resources of life-substance in the universe, is one of the most characteristic and significant in the whole history of mankind.

Probably in no place has this primitive view of sacrifice attained such fullness of expression as in India. After the period of the early Aryan invasions, a period whose general character is preserved in the Vedic hymns, a relatively settled social order was established within which the institution of sacrifice was of paramount importance. The body of literature to which we are indebted for our knowledge of this period is the Brahmanas,[1] a collection of ritual treatises containing the most elaborate regulations for the proper performance of the sacrificial rites. According to their teaching, sacrifice is in very truth the power that makes the world go round. It was through the sacrifice of the original cosmic Man that the universe came into being, and it can only be through the continuance of regular sacrifice that the world can be sustained. At each sacrifice *Prajapati*, the Lord of creation, is offered afresh and everything done in the earthly ritual ceremony is a counterpart of that which takes place in the world of heavenly reality. There are the most detailed regulations for the place, the victim, and the officiant of the

---

[1] The Brahmanas " start with ritual and end in ritual, alluding to everything only in this light."

In them sacrifice is predominant. It is " not offered to a God in order to honour him, to win his ear or to thank him. The sacrifice stands above the power of the gods, it is sublimated magic, extremely complex in form, and all the manipulations, spells and incantations have a deeper meaning." (Quoted G. Misch, *The Dawn of Philosophy*, p. 128.)

sacrifice and any slip or mistake is held to invalidate the whole proceeding. Here, then, are the records of the behaviour of a great society in its natural environment and the pattern already outlined runs through it all, viz. : through a ritual offering which culminates in some form of death, life is renewed and expanded. This pattern has characterised the life of any society which has been attached to a particular section of land, has cared for it and cultivated it and lived on it, from the earliest times down to the present day. Through offering, unity and continuity is maintained ; through death, life is renewed.

Secondly, there are the societies whose primary concern is with wild beasts and fishes and tamed animals. Clearly what matters most is that the flesh and strength of the victim shall be secured and made available for the social group. At least in earliest times man is not immediately concerned about the continuing life of the species though ultimately that has to be taken into account. Rather, he knows that his own life and that of his kinsfolk depend upon the vanquishing and the capturing and the demolishing of the prey. He must, therefore, prepare himself for the encounter ; he must learn the ways of his enemy ; he must seek whatever assistance he can from human or superhuman powers as he goes forth to the chase ; and when success has been achieved and the living creature is in his grasp he must handle it with due caution so that the maximum potency may be derived from its capture. He may implore the assistance of superhuman power by offering a token gift before he goes. Or he may perform a dramatic ritual in which he, as it were, vanquishes his enemy before the time. His universe is not integrated in the way that the nature-dweller's is. He needs all the support that he can obtain from his own society of gods and men in order that he may be able to overcome all the hostile powers which may be arrayed against him.

The ultimate event, towards which all else is directed, is the actual feast upon the victim. At this moment the sense of achievement is at its highest and the bonds of brotherhood are made firm in the sharing of the common food. Hunger is appeased, the sense of wellbeing in the society is restored, strength is renewed, and the general exhilaration which comes through victorious achievement is enjoyed. In the common feast the tribal god is not forgotten. Often the blood of the victim is regarded as his special perquisite either because it is of mysterious potency or because being liquid it can more easily be imagined as reaching in some way the divine mouth. When fire is used it becomes easy to imagine that any parts which are entirely consumed on the altar are thereby transformed into a condition in which they may easily be consumed by the gods.

Thus the simple *motif* of *eating together* in order to sustain life and to promote fellowship is, I believe, at the root of many of the ritual observances of those more dynamic societies which have had to depend upon creatures outside their immediate environment for their food-supply. Again, as conditions changed, the ritual tended to become more complex and other motives entered in. In particular, the gradual domestication of wild beasts meant that the source of the food supply was more certain, though there may have been some reluctance to feast upon animals which had been virtually adopted as members of the tribal unit. Moreover, a system of taboos was gradually elaborated whereby, it appears, members of a clan which had formed a sacred link with one particular animal species bound themselves never to touch the flesh of an animal associated with another clan. Sacrifice was above all an occasion of communion, of covenant, of the renewal of the common life. The material of the sacrifice was not primarily an *offering*. It was a gracious *provision*. It had been secured by the hunter through the assistance of divine powers or it had been released for the use of the worshippers by an act of divine grace. Thus the essence of the sacrifice was the dismemberment and division of a victim and the manipulation of its blood in such a way that through its destruction gods and men could share in a common life and thus be renewed and sustained for the struggle of existence.

One of the best examples of the animal sacrifice pure and simple is to be found in the ritual-practices of the Arabs. " In the oldest known form of Arabian sacrifice," writes Robertson Smith, " the camel chosen as the victim is bound upon a rude altar of stones piled together, and when the leader of the band has thrice led the worshippers round the altar in a solemn pro-cession accompanied with chants, he inflicts the first wound, while the last words of the hymn are still upon the lips of the congregation, and in all haste drinks of the blood that gushes forth. Forthwith the whole company fall on the victim with their swords, hacking off pieces of the quivering flesh and devouring them raw with such wild haste, that in the short interval between the rise of the day star which marked the hour for the service to begin, and the disappearance of its rays before the rising sun, the entire camel, body and bones, skin, blood and entrails, is wholly devoured. The plain meaning of this is that the victim was devoured before its life had left the still warm blood and flesh—raw flesh is called 'living' flesh in Hebrew and Syriac—and that thus in the most literal way all those who shared in the ceremony absorbed part of the victim's life into themselves. One sees how much more forcibly than any ordinary meal such a rite expresses the establishment or confirmation of a bond of common life between the worshippers, and also, since the blood is shed upon the altar itself, between the worshippers and their god." (*The Religion of the Semites*, 1914 Edition, pp. 338-9.)

Although these are the two main types of sacrifice practised among primitive peoples, it is clear that just as no economy was exclusively agricultural or pastoral so no system of sacrificial practices was exclusively oblationary or communal. In the great settled system of India there were animal sacrifices; in the sacrifices of the Semites there were offerings of meal or fruit. At the same time it is on the face of it probable that a society bound closely to the soil and depending mainly upon crops for its food will emphasise in its sacrificial ritual different notes from those which appear in the cultus of a tribe which depends mainly upon animals, wild or domestic, to supply its needs. And what appears inherently probable is confirmed by the actual evidence we possess from many sources. It is thus possible to distinguish at the outset two main types of sacrifice.

(1) The *oblationary*, in which life-substance, natural or symbolic, is ritually offered and immolated in order that the wholeness of social life may be renewed and the individual parts of it strengthened, and

(2) The *festal*, in which life-substance, natural or symbolic, is ritually made available and divided up and distributed

In the first type the offering is the centre of the action, the feasting is an optional though desirable appendage ; in the second type the feeding is the centre of the action, the offering is an optional though desirable preliminary. Some societies have emphasised one side, some the other. Only when a full appreciation of both types is included within the attitude and outlook of any particular society can its life retain its necessary stability and its creative power.[1]

SACRIFICE IN EARLY CIVILISATIONS

For families and groups which had eked out a subsistence on wild fruits and plants it was a discovery of immense importance to find that seeds could be planted and watered and made to yield a harvest far greater in quantity than the original sowing. Natural life was not simply a mysterious and unpredictable phenomenon : nor was it just waiting to be assisted in its processes by the exercise of forms of sympathetic magic : men now realised that it was possible to plan and to employ recognised techniques in order to ensure an adequate harvest for their needs. At the same time they did not imagine that a proper technique was sufficient by itself. The mysterious principle of life-through-death had to be sustained in its operation and due supplies of water had to be made available at the appropriate times. So there grew up the complex ritual of sacrifice in which oblations of food and drink were regularly offered in order that through literal or symbolic forms of death life might be sustained and renewed.

For those families and clans which had depended on the capture of wild animals to give them their most satisfying supplies of food, it was a major discovery to find that animals

[1] " I cannot perceive any contradiction, such as Luther did, in the fact that the same entity is simultaneously received and offered. On the contrary, it is precisely the essence of all sacrifice that it should be at the same time an offering and a receiving." (G. Van der Leeuw, *Religion in Essence and Manifestation*, p. 359.)

could be domesticated and made to yield not only their flesh but also their milk, their labour, their skins, their increase. Tribes were no longer completely dependent upon the skill of practical hunters ; nor were they compelled to look for outside aid simply by carrying through ceremonies designed to bring about the conquest of the desired victim. They now began to realise that it was possible to build up families of flocks and herds, to feed upon their milk, to use their skins and wool and to have always available a supply of flesh for festal occasions. Again, however, this did not mean that all the mystery and uncertainty had gone out of life nor that the eating of flesh together could be a common and ordinary event. The fertility of animals had to be maintained and the solemn engagement of members of the tribe one to another had to be celebrated through the ritual feast. Possibly the special rites of the firstborn were associated with the former of these needs, but still the common sacrificial feast was the central ritual act of nomadic tribes whose pattern of life was dominantly pastoral in character.

It was in the great river valleys that civilisations tended to expand in size and complexity. The availability of regular water-supplies was the determinant factor in drawing together ever larger concentrations of population, but the emergence of city-life always brought fresh problems in connection with the production and distribution of food. As we saw in an earlier chapter, society began to be organised in a hierarchical way with each level finding representation at a higher level, until the summit was reached in the person of the king or emperor. In this form of organisation it is the duty of each layer of society to provide not only for its own needs but at least in part for the needs of the layer above it in the hierarchy. This means that food-supplies, or their equivalent in some form of tribute, are constantly passing through the channels which lead up finally to the apex of the organisation. But this all-important process is expressed in symbol as well as in actuality and the obviously appropriate form to be used is that of oblationary sacrifice. By making its proper offering in kind, every level of society does its part towards ensuring the harmony and well-being of the whole. Those who seem to bear heavier responsibilities in planning and statesmanship and the provision of law and order must be supported by those lower in the scale whose time and energies can be given to the more mundane and material tasks.

In particular the emperor himself, the semi-divine being who occupies a position between earth and heaven, must be provided for in order that he may maintain in unbroken harmony the whole system of relationships between gods and men. And in the house of the supreme god of any particular people constant offerings must be made to symbolise the homage of his subjects but still more to act as an expression of their fervent desire that the life of the whole universe—in Nature, in the animal world, in men—may be preserved from decay and actually increased in potency and vitality. For example, " the daily sacrifice in the great temple of Marduk at Babylon under Nebuchadnezzar was an epitome of the whole tillage of the land ; the choicest fruits, the finest produce of the meadow, honey, cream, oil, wine of different vintages, must be served. In the early ritual of an Egyptian temple, when the daily toilet of the god had been performed and he had been duly robed, painted and oiled, his table was spread with bread, goose, beef, wine and water and decorated with the flowers needed to adorn a meal." (J. E. Carpenter, *Comparative Religion*, pp. 140-1.) Still more impressively in the great Temple of Heaven at Peking it was the custom for the Emperor and his assistants to offer sacrifices to heaven and to beg for a renewal of the fertility of the earth. " The monarch, assisted by the princes and great mandarins, made three genuflections and nine adorations on the terrace. Under the Ming dynasty, while the Emperor offered the traditional lapis-lazuli, the choir chanted :

> May this offering climb into space and be known on high ! May it obtain for us what we desire ! I am come to this Mount, with my officers, to ask the August Heaven to grant earth the ripening of crops, a fruitful harvest.

Then the Emperor made nine more prostrations and the choir continued :

> By my offerings, I make my reverence known on high. May their smoke, following the path of the thunderbolt and

of the nine dragons, rise aloft, and may blessings descend upon the people. That is what I, a little child (the Emperor) ask of these offerings.

When the offerings were consumed by the fire, the choir went on :

> The tripods and the censers smoke, the pieces of flesh and silk are blazing, their smoke rises, higher than the clouds, to show the pains of the people. May our music and our chants make known the devotion of our hearts."
>
> (Account by E. Masure, *The Christian Sacrifice*, pp. 19-20.)

To take one more illustration from a source nearer to the Christian tradition, we find in the Old Testament record of Solomon's kingdom the closest parallels to the imperial sacrifices of other civilisations. It seems likely that much of Solomon's pattern of organisation was taken over from the kingdom of Tyre and this in turn was formed according to the regular model of the empires of the Near East. Solomon himself occupied a position of great splendour and beneath him were the princes and the officers of Israel and beyond them the rulers of many of the surrounding tribes. A vast organisation of tribute was built up so that a constant stream of animals and food-supplies flowed towards the royal court. Peace was established over a wide area and for a period there seems to have been general satisfaction with the system of give and take which united a large population within one integrated whole. Each made his offering towards the centre and received in return good government and the blessings of an established order. All this was gathered up into a great sacrificial cultus at the high place in Jerusalem. There Solomon, as representative of the whole people, offered large numbers of oxen and sheep as burnt offerings and peace offerings and made supplication for the peace and prosperity of his people. In part the sacrifices provided food for the great festal banquets in which the worshippers joined, but their primary purpose seems to have been to express outwardly the combined devotion of the whole people and to seek the renewal of the blessings of heaven on which the continued prosperity of the empire so clearly depended.

The oblationary sacrifice, symbolising the devoting of the whole of the life of Nature and man to God and the receiving of the renewal of vitality and strength for the whole universe, established itself as perhaps the outstanding religious institution of early civilisations. But it soon became clear that there were grave dangers of perversion in its practice. These were of a double kind. On the one side there was the danger of over multiplying and over elaborating the sacrificial acts, either as a means of appeasing the higher powers or as a way of increasing the prestige of the offerer. As social levels within the hierarchy came to be more rigidly defined it was customary for any member of a lower rank to approach his superior with deference and awe. Often this expressed itself through a gift offered half as a mark of respect, half as a means of gaining some advantage. All too easily, then, an offering could become the means of winning special favours or of avoiding penalties due to the suppliant on account of some misdemeanour of which he had been guilty. Once such considerations became prominent, it followed that the larger the gift the greater the benefit that could be expected. Sacrifices were multiplied and an elaborate system was constructed in which every breach of social duty had to be atoned for by an appropriate offering.

It needs little imagination to see how easily sacrifice, when viewed in this way, can become an unworthy and degrading practice. In addition there was the danger that the superior person who had the right to demand the payment of goods for the carrying on of the sacrificial system, would steadily enlarge his demands for the sake of his own vanity or prestige or simply as an indirect way of increasing his own wealth. Indeed history seems to show that there is always danger when sacrifices are multiplied and elaborated. As a symbol of the oblation of the individual and of the community the offering can be altogether worthy. When it becomes the mechanical means of winning favours or of establishing prestige it degenerates into a base and degrading institution.

I spoke of a second danger. This has been the concentration of interest upon the precise efficacy of the act of offering apart from any relation to the whole context in which it is set and the whole symbolism of which it forms an essential part. The moment of offering is always a time of great solemnity. It is the climax of long processes of preparation, it is the symbol of the ascent from earth to heaven, it is the prelude to enhanced vitality and richer blessing. The official to whom the responsibility of this special action is committed stands at the centre of the universe, as it were, and by the performing of the rite lifts earth to heaven. Once the oblation has been made the material offered can no longer be regarded as a common substance. Either it has been consumed or etherealised or transported into another realm or given some heavenly character. All this means that the act of oblation comes to be regarded as the central point of the whole ceremony and to be invested with a significance greater than that attached to any other part of the service.

The obvious danger is that the act will come to be regarded as automatically efficacious and that the change in the character of the material of the oblation will be regarded as having been automatically produced. Men desire the preservation and enhancement of life. They believe that the way towards its attainment is the ritual offering of appropriate symbols of life. So long as the symbolic actions are performed with technical correctness, it seems that the desired result must follow. If it does, it means that the symbols offered must themselves be charged with new potency and that they can themselves impart new vitality to those persons or things which come into contact with them. Thus the desired result is attained simply through the central act of oblation which lifts earth to heaven and thereby brings heaven to earth. The process of reasoning is plausible and up to a point its validity may be allowed.

Yet the more impersonal and mechanical a rite becomes, the less it retains of religious depth and the less capable it becomes of embracing widening areas of human experience and of the world's life. For if the desired result can be achieved entirely by means of mechanical activity, then man or his representative becomes simply an automaton in the whole proceeding. Moreover, its specifically religious character vanishes, seeing that religion only survives within a context of living relationships between gods and men.

Yet again, if the worshipper can become partaker of the divine life simply by receiving an object or substance into his body through physical processes then he becomes a mere cipher in an automatic process and all sense of significant religious relationship disappears. If the universe is nothing more than a vast mechanism controlled by some remote superhuman power then there is no reason why that power should not sustain it in motion by stimulating man to perform certain mechanical acts and by allowing him to receive certain automatic injections of a divine soul-substance for the reinforcement of his own vitality. But if the universe is not a soulless mechanism controlled by a mechanical brain then a place must be found for free and personal factors to operate in all relationships between Nature, man and God, and this means that there is no final place for an automatic mechanical rite in a universe in which man is made in the image and likeness of the Divine. The more formal and impersonal and stereotyped the act of oblation becomes the less the system of which it forms a part retains any vital religious values and the less the men who participate in the act are brought into any living relationship with the Lord whom they desire to serve.

What, then, is to be said of the developments which have taken place in the practices of more nomadic and pastoral tribes ? It stands to reason that there have never been great concentrations of population amongst these peoples as has been the case with the river-valley civilisations. The normal manner of growth in size and complexity has been through the inauguration of leagues and covenants whereby various tribes band themselves together within a loose confederacy, often under the leadership of one outstanding chief. Here the basic principle of social life is exchange or reciprocity. Two tribes would not come together unless there was some mutual advantage to be gained by so doing. Through solemn agreements they pledge themselves each to the other to share their resources in a common purpose. This means that food supplies in particular are shared through the processes of barter and exchange and the great symbolic expression of the strengthening of the common life is the covenant sacrifice with its accompanying communal feast. On these noteworthy occasion gods and men join together to seal their union in a single purpose through solemn pledge and joyous participation in a common meal.

At all times the leader occupies a position of importance. Ideally, as we saw in Chapter Four, he is a little ahead of his contemporaries—in foresight, in skill, in courage, in personal imagination. He it was who led them in their forays, whether in search of food or of new territory or of fresh conquests. So, having gained the confidence of his own people and having won the respect of other tribes, he is in a position to lead the way in more constructive enterprises—the extension in particular of the area of exchange so that his own people may profit by the acquisition of goods at present denied them. Normally any such extension of the area of common existence is inaugurated by a solemn covenant in which after an exchange of valued possessions all join together in a great communal feast.

The exchange of possessions takes various forms. Perhaps the most significant of all is the exchange of blood. This can be effected by drinking, by smearing, by sprinkling, by mingling or by using some appropriate substitute such as wine. The respective leaders may taste each other's blood or may slit open their own arms and mingle the blood in a common flow. Or the blood of animal victims may be used, some being sprinkled over one party to the covenant and some over the other. Another common method of effecting the reciprocal relationship is through the exchange of breath in the kiss or through the exchange of clothes which are regarded as virtual extensions of the body. Indeed in early conceptions many articles of possession are looked upon as extensions of a man's own personal existence and so become natural symbols to use in establishing mutual agreements. Thus the objects of exchange become almost unlimited in their variety—blood, breath, clothes, weapons, tools, amulets, charms, animals, cereals, fruits and merchandise of all kinds. But whatever the precise nature of the interchange may be, the motive of the action remains the same : to take a symbolic part of one's own total existence and so to relate it to a similar symbolic part of the total existence of another that a new symbolic totality comes into being, a totality which may not represent present fact but which points to the goal towards which future purposes and activities will move.

As the early stage of hunting came to be superseded by the stage of shepherding and stock rearing, the scale of values of nomadic tribes gradually changed. The leader, as we see from the narratives of the Book of Genesis, was the great shepherd or flock-master. The most treasured possessions were flocks and herds. Hence when it became desirable to inaugurate a covenant, the natural procedure was to take victims from the flock or herd and to use them first for the solemn ceremony of exchange and secondly for the common feast. In this way the sacrificial action served a double purpose; it provided blood for application to the respective leaders (sometimes in a general way to the covenanting parties) and flesh for the communal meal. Through this twofold ceremony the covenant was firmly established, though it was customary to renew the covenant by similar ritual actions when it seemed to be losing its original vitality and force.

There is abundant evidence in the Old Testament to show that the covenant procedure was regarded as appropriate not only for leaders and their followers but also for the god himself. He might inaugurate a covenant with an individual leader as representing a family or tribe or in certain circumstances he might relate himself to the whole community. In any case the ceremony followed the same pattern—a mutual exchange of vows and gifts followed by a common meal. It is true that when the god was one of the partners in the covenant, man's gift tended to be overshadowed by that of the deity and in the common feast the feeding activities of the god had to be imagined rather than actually witnessed. Nevertheless the general pattern persisted, and (except in the heyday of the monarchy and in late Judaism) the normal conception of sacrifice in Israel was that of a covenant-inauguration or renewal, with Yahweh symbolically relating Himself to His people, and with all sealing the relationship through participation in a common feast. The most notable examples of this general pattern are to be found in the account of the establishment of the Sinaitic-covenant as given in Exodus 24 and in the remarkable record of the Abrahamic-covenant contained in Genesis 15. The exact significance of the symbolic actions may not be always easy to discern but that there was some mutuality of interchange and some community of participation through eating and drinking seems reasonably clear.

When we come to consider the dangers involved in this type of sacrifice we find as before that they are twofold. On the one side there is the danger that the feast itself, with the intensified sense of " togetherness " which it creates, will come to be regarded as the be-all and end-all of religious experience. In the lonely places of Arabia, hungry men flung themselves in a kind of common ecstasy upon the quivering flesh of the camel ; in the mountains of Thrace the votaries of Dionysus behaved in similar fashion and wherever men have sensed hardness and deprivation and loneliness, the opportunity to satisfy their physical and social needs in a supreme experience of common participation has brought with it a feeling of heightened emotion and even of ecstasy. What more natural than that the emotion itself should come to be regarded as the supreme good of existence ? So long as the feast itself seems to stimulate the desired feeling, it tends to retain its place of importance in the life of the society. But if other ways can be found—common singing, common bodily movements, common exhortation, common contemplation of visual images—then the feast comes to be regarded as unessential and the heightened emotion which originally accompanied it is sought for its own sake. Thus a concentration of interest upon the feast itself leads ultimately either to a crass materialism in which togetherness is experienced through an orgy of eating and drinking or to a rarified spiritualism in which togetherness is achieved through a temporary withdrawal from individual bodily experience and an absorption into a mass collectivism of an emotional kind.

The other danger is, in a sense, a corollary of the first. Once the concentration of interest is upon the experience of mass-togetherness, the covenant-bond, upon which that experience really depends and which was originally designed to govern the character of the experience, tends to recede into the background and almost to be forgotten. The actual inauguration of the covenant may still be remembered ; its original purpose may still be recognised ; but it ceases to be actively celebrated in any dynamic symbolic form and it fails any longer to exercise a controlling influence upon the pattern of the actions designed to promote the togetherness of the community. Thus unless the wholeness of the covenant-ceremony be regularly maintained

—a symbolic renewal of mutuality through committal to a common way of life and a symbolic re-establishment of togetherness through participation in a common meal, whose character is determined by the particular way of life to which the committal has been made—the society will degenerate and become either the feeble relic of a glorious past or the fevered pursuer of experiences of mass-emotion which only debilitate and ultimately destroy.

Each of the dangers just described is a form of the peril of embracing unreservedly a philosophy of dualism. This peril threatens every dynamic and revolutionary group, for it is consciously seeking to escape from a rejected past into a better future, it is seeking to transcend the hard, material conditions of its present and to attain a new standard of living in which social euphoria is desired even more than material prosperity. These aims are laudable and are the inspiration of social advance. But if they become so exaggerated that they lead to a form of dualism in which the past in the time-series and the material conditions of life in the present are either neglected as unimportant or are repudiated as harmful, then the universe splits asunder and man's existence within it becomes ultimately intolerable. Thus nothing is more important than a retention of the true pattern of covenant-sacrifice in which there can be constant renewal of reciprocity and a participation through symbolic means in a common good. Through sacrifice a dynamic society can anchor itself to the past historic event through which its own existence became possible, and can enjoy a foretaste of the future good on which its hopes are set. Sacrifice, in fact, is the symbol by which groups separated from one another by differences of character, and generations separated from one another by long intervals of time, are brought together and held together within a common embrace.

OTHER THEORIES OF SACRIFICE

In attempting to give a straightforward account of the origins and development of the institution of sacrifice I have laid the chief emphasis upon the economic factors operating in human history. Man's constant need for food and drink, his dependence upon the animal and vegetable realms, his recourse to barter and exchange—these are powerful factors in his development and their influence upon the evolution of sacrificial rites can be confidently assumed. At the same time I am well aware that other factors have been at work, particularly those of a more inward kind. Man must eat and drink to live, but he does not live only by eating and drinking. There are inward psychical urges which demand satisfaction, especially in the realm of inter-personal relationships, and it has been claimed that at least in an indirect way some of these have found expression through the sacrificial ritual. Some reference must therefore be made to the leading theories in which this general position is maintained.

Possibly the most famous attempt to expose the psychological " drives " which govern the outward practice of sacrifice is that of Freud. The general ritual-pattern which is common to all forms of sacrifice can easily be made to correspond to the general psychical pattern which, Freud believes, is normal in all human growth and development. The child, desiring a sexual relation-ship with the mother, inwardly wills the death of its rival, the father. But this death-wish, being suppressed, must find its outlet in an appropriate symbolic form. Analysis shows, how-ever, that the father is constantly identified in the child's unconscious with an animal. What, therefore, could more powerfully express the slaying of the father than the ritual slaughter of an animal ? Here, Freud claims, is to be found the initial *motif* lying behind the sacrificial action.

But this is not all. It is an integral part of Freud's general theory that the son who desires the murder of his father also desires to be identified with him and to share his strength. Indeed he never loses his feeling of admiration and affection for his father, even when he is consenting to his murder. The result is that all the time there is a certain *ambivalence* (in Freud's ter-minology) which needs to find expression in outward ritual. And, paradoxically enough, the very ceremony which provides the symbolic expression of the death-wish provides also the symbolic expression of reconciliation and satisfaction. The totem-meal can be regarded as a means of reconciliation through communion with the father-substitute ; or the sacrifice can be regarded as offering satisfaction to the father for the outrage inflicted on him. Freud allows for development in the history of the attitudes expressed through sacrifice but insists that the primary " drive " which brought this form into existence was the urge towards parricide; the ambivalence of the son's relationship to the father subsequently issued, however, in the instinct of affection also finding satisfaction through the sacrificial act.

Freud bases his conclusions on the evidence of myth (particularly the Œdipus-myth), on the records of totemism, and on the evidence derived from psycho-analysis. His theory constitutes a brilliant attempt to uncover the origins of man's sacrificial practices and there is little doubt that he has laid his finger upon some of the psychological factors which are constantly operative. That a child often projects the fear of its father on to an animal seems to be a well-established fact; that the dual attitudes of affection towards and revulsion against the father are often to be found struggling with one another within the child's psyche also seems relatively certain; that the myth of Œdipus is striking and suggestive is plain—though whether it should be interpreted in the Freudian way is another matter; that the theory of parricide followed by a desire for communion gives a plausible explanation of the taboos and practices of totemism may also be allowed. But that sacrifice in *all* its later forms and meanings stems from the one original parricidal act is a large claim and one which cannot be regarded as finally proven by the evidence which Freud supplies. The Œdipus myth, for example, is certainly patient of other explanations and it is a big assumption to make that tendencies operating in particular children in relation to their parents to-day were necessarily present in a primal horde of sons as they lived with their father and with one another in the remote past of antiquity. The most convincing points in Freud's theory are the symbolic identification of the sacrificial animal with the father, the symbolic acquisition of the father's strength through participation in the sacrificial meal and the symbolic expression of the ambivalent attitudes of love and hate by means of the double-sided ceremonies of the sacrificial act. These *motifs* may have operated at various times in certain forms of sacrificial practice.

But I believe it is too much to claim that they have been the motivating " drives," mainly, if not solely, responsible for the formation and development of this many-sided institution.

Before leaving Freud's theory, let me quote one striking paragraph in which he refers to the stage in the history of religion when the clan deity has emerged and the sacrifice is performed in his presence. " In the scene of sacrifice before the god of the clan," he writes, " the father is in fact represented twice over as the god and as the totemic animal victim. But in our attempts at understanding this situation we must beware of interpretations which seek to translate it in a two-dimensional fashion as though it were an allegory, and which in so doing forget its historical stratification. The two-fold presence of the father corresponds to the two chronologically successive meanings of the scene. The ambivalent attitude towards the father has found a plastic expression in it, and so, too, has the victory of the son's affectionate emotions over his hostile ones. The scene of the father's vanquishment, of his greatest defeat, has become the stuff for the representation of his supreme triumph. The importance which is everywhere, without exception, ascribed to sacrifice lies in the fact that it offers satisfaction to the father for the outrage inflicted on him in the same act in which that deed is commemorated." (*Totem and Taboo*, p. 150.)

A less spectacular though more widely applicable theory is to be found in the writings of Jung. Instead of the repressed libidinous satisfaction being expressed in a " substitute gratification " (Freud), it is, in Jung's theory, transferred through the medium of symbolic forms to the furtherance of some cultural purpose. Freud's theory looks mainly to the past with some reference to the present ; Jung's, while drawing upon the past, looks with special interest towards the future. In an important statement, Jung defines his general view thus : " Psyche is transition, hence necessarily to be defined under two aspects. On the one hand, the psyche gives a picture of the remnants and traces of the entire past, and, on the other, but expressed in the same picture, the outlines of the future, inasmuch as the psyche creates its own future." (Quoted E. Fromm, *The Forgotten Language*, p. 88.)

The unconscious of man, then, holds together the archetypal

experiences of the race in a state of creative potentiality and out of it may come forms and symbols, full of significance for man's cultural development. Man's libidinal energy moves outwards from the unconscious and returns to it again and may in the course of this movement carve out symbolic forms besides flowing through more ordinary channels. The process is well described by Frieda Fordham when she writes, " Libido is natural energy, and first and foremost serves the purpose of life, but a certain amount in excess of what is needed for instinctive ends can be converted into productive work and used for cultural purposes. This direction of energy becomes initially possible by transferring it to something similar in nature to the object of instinctive interest. This transfer cannot, however, be made by a simple act of will, but is achieved in a roundabout way. After a period of gestation in the unconscious a symbol is produced which can attract the libido, and also serve as a channel diverting its natural flow. The symbol is never thought out consciously, but comes usually as a revelation or intuition, often appearing in a dream." (*An Introduction to Jung's Psychology*, p. 19.)

What, then, is the essential meaning of the symbol of sacrifice ? What cultural purpose is the flow of the libido through the channel of sacrificial ritual serving ? In a word, through sacrifice man comes to terms with death. By means of a passage through a symbolic death man is renewed in his own inner life and at the same time his own energy is dedicated to the service of the social order in which he dwells. Energy of the libido which, flowing freely through instinctive channels, would bring about destruction and death can, by being diverted through the channels of symbolic death—that is through sacrifice in its many forms—bring about creativity and life.

There is a passage in Jung's *Psychology of the Unconscious* in which he describes this general process within the context of the rising and setting of the sun. His view of sacrifice will become clearer if I quote this passage in full :

" The sun, victoriously arising, tears itself away from the embrace and clasp, from the enveloping womb of the sea, and sinks again into the maternal sea, into night, the all-enveloping and the all-reproducing, leaving behind it the heights of midday and all its glorious works. This image was the first, and was profoundly entitled to become the symbolic carrier of human destiny ; in the morning of life man painfully tears himself loose from the mother, from the domestic hearth, to rise through battle to the heights. Not seeing his worst enemy in front of him, but bearing him within himself as a deadly longing for the depths within, for drowning in his own source, for becoming absorbed into the mother, his life is a constant struggle with death, a violent and transitory delivery from the always lurking night. This death is no external enemy, but a deep personal longing for quiet and for the profound peace of non-existence, for a dreamless sleep in the ebb and flow of the sea of life. Even in his highest endeavour for harmony and equilibrium, for philosophic depths and artistic enthusiasm, he seeks death, immobility, satiety and rest. If, like Peirithoos, he tarries too long in this place of rest and peace, he is overcome by torpidity and the poison of the serpent paralyses him for all time. If he is to live he must fight and sacrifice his longing for the past in order to rise to his own heights. And having reached the noonday heights, he must also *sacrifice the love for his own achievement*, for he may not loiter. The sun also sacrifices its greatest strength in order to hasten onwards to the fruits of autumn, which are the seeds of immortality ; fulfilled in children, in works, in posthumous fame, in a new order of things, all of which in their turn begin and complete the sun's course over again." (C. G. Jung, *Psychology of the Unconscious*, pp. 390-1.)

Whether or not we accept Jung's theory of the unconscious and of the flow of the libido through symbolic channels, there can be little doubt that he has focused attention upon important elements in the inner psyche which bear an evident relation to the general movement of the sacrificial ritual. The notes of *recuellir pour mieux sauter*, of withdrawal in order to return, of suffering as a way to release new energies—all these have some connection with the symbolic act of sacrifice. Man has the mysterious inward urge to renounce as well as to grasp, to hold back as well as to rush forward, to accept suffering as well as to seek pleasure. As Durkheim has impressively written : " It is by the way in which he braves suffering that the greatness of a man is best manifested. He never rises above himself with more brilliancy than when he subdues his own nature to the point of making it follow a way contrary to the one it would spontaneously take. By this, he distinguishes himself from all the other creatures who follow blindly wherever pleasure calls them ; by this, he makes a place apart for himself in the world. Suffering is the sign that certain of the bonds attaching him to his profane environment are broken ; so it testifies that he is partially freed from his environment and, consequently, it is justly considered the instrument of deliverance. So he who is thus delivered is not the victim of a pure illusion when he believes himself invested with a sort of mastery over things : he really has raised himself above them by the very act of renouncing them ; he is stronger than nature, because he makes it subside." [1] And no pattern of symbolic behaviour expresses this renunciation more dramatically than does the institution of sacrifice, at least in its more developed forms.

Summing up the contributions of Freud and Jung to our understanding of the motifs which find expression in and through sacrificial forms, we may say that whereas Freud emphasises the symbolic behaviour which derives from repressions within the individual's relationship to the father, Jung gives greater prominence to the patterns through which the individual transfers his excess libidinal energy into social usefulness. Sacrifice may exist in crude and debasing forms, but in the main an institution which enables man to come to terms with his death-wishes and his death-fears, his repressed hates and his instinctive desires for comfort and calm, may be regarded as of immense benefit for the psychic health of mankind.

Another contribution to the understanding of the place which sacrifice plays in the life of society has been made by Dr. Rachel Levy in her two books, *The Gate of Horn* and *The Sword from the Rock*. Her primary aim is to study the religious conceptions of the Stone Age, especially as they are revealed in the art of the ancient cave-dwellings. Taking into account the various strands of archæological evidence, she concludes that the

[1] *Elementary Forms of The Religious Life*, p. 315.

paintings could not have been executed just to produce æsthetic delight in the painter and his companions ; they are situated in deep recesses of the caves, often in little side-chapels. Moreover, although it is highly probable that in many cases magical ends were in view—the stimulation of fertility in the animal-herds or the bestowal of skill upon the huntsman—this motive could not always have been dominant. In regard to the conquest of the animals, for example, " such conquest would not require this beauty ; symbols would have sufficed as they did with the instruments of death—and symbols were known to them long before they had achieved artistic mastery. It is hoped in the course of these chapters to show that reciprocity was their aim, a participation in the splendour of the beasts which was of the nature of religion itself and so required this elaborate separation from normal activities ; that the perfected forms which flowered in the pitch-dark solitudes were types by which ritual called up the species ; that exactitude was desired for the sake of closer attunement." (*The Gate of Horn*, p. 20.)

To *participate* in the splendour of the beast (and the " beast " of Stone Age religion seems to occupy the very same place in tribal regard as is occupied by the totem in the religion of hunting tribes in more modern times), to have communion through him with the ancestors and with other members of the tribe—this was the object of the ritual-forms of prehistoric times. " The primary group-relationship known to us was not that of blood, but of a willed participation in a life both physical and non-physical, which stretched through time to include the dead and the unborn." (*Ibid.*, p. 35.) And this participation was attained through representation of the form of the beasts in paintings and carvings, through masked dances and through sacrificial ceremonies. The dominant motif in the sacrifice seems to have been the desire for communion with the totem. By eating portions of the animal (though sparingly) men could capture something of its life-energy [1] and be strengthened in their relationship with one another. Dr. Levy finds many parallels between Stone Age religion and the totemistic systems which have been investigated by modern anthropologists and

---

[1] This is inferred though Dr. Levy allows that there is no positive evidence of ceremonial or sacrificial consumption in Palæolithic times. p. 45.

she has produced impressive evidence in support of the theory that the earliest religion practised by man was some form of totemism in which through ritual acts (including sacrifice) he sought to maintain an abiding relationship with the divine totem-animal and to share in its mysterious potency.

With the coming of the Neolithic Age and the changes of social habits consequent upon the development of pasturage and nomadism, the forms and motifs of sacrifice also changed. The new characteristics of this Age were its concentration on cyclic recurrence, its recognition of the decay and renewal of vegetation, its observance of the regularities of the heavens, its establishment of rhythmic forms in social life. Sacrifice had its relation to all of these. It became more regular, more intimately associated with the cycle of Nature, more allied to the developing patterns of social life. At all costs fertility had to be maintained. Through ritual action man had constantly to re-identify himself with the rhythmic movement of the universe. The actual victim took on many forms : sometimes the offering consisted of the first-fruits or of an effigy composed of the newly-cut seedlings of corn or rice ; sometimes the victim was the first-born of the flock ; sometimes it was the reigning chief whose natural vigour showed signs of waning and who, being the source of fertility, must himself pass through the renewing process of death ; sometimes it was a substitute—a royal prince or a mock-king.[1] But whatever the nature of the victim the general pattern of the sacrificial movement remains the same ; only through death, actual or symbolic, can life be renewed and sustained.

One other theory of sacrifice which deserves mention is that of Professor G. Van der Leeuw in his book, *Religion in Essence and Manifestation*. He accepts the basic conception of sacrifice as a gift but insists that " gift " must be interpreted in a much more profound way than is usually the case. Taking the Latin word *dare*, he affirms that it " does not mean merely to dispose of some arbitrary object with a quite indefinite intention ; the word *dare* means, rather, to place oneself in relation to, and then to participate in, a second person by means of an object, which however is not actually an ' object ' at all, but a part of one's own self. ' To give," then, is to convey something of oneself

[1] Cp. E. O. James, *The Beginnings of Religion*, pp. 88-90.

to the strange being . . . the gift allows a stream to flow, which from the moment of giving runs uninterruptedly from donor to recipient and from receiver to giver. . . . To offer somebody something, then, is to offer someone a part of oneself ; similarly, to accept a thing from another person is to receive some portion of his spiritual being, of his soul." (pp. 351-2.)

Van der Leeuw's chief concern is to emphasise the facts that through the interchange of gifts the stream of life and power is kept flowing and that through the sacrifice, giver and receiver commune with one another in symbolic interchange of their very selves. Ideally sacrifice is not a matter of barter or even of homage ; certainly it is not a matter of bribery or of buying favour. Men truly meet one another *in the gift*. God meets man and man meets God in the *gift*. Through the sacrifice a channel is formed whereby in a reciprocal movement the life of God can flow to man and the life of man can flow to God. This is a valuable idea and although I do not find in Van der Leeuw's interpretation any clear explanation of the place of *death* in the sacrifice, yet there is surely a place for his theory in any comprehensive consideration of the sacrificial ritual.

Summing up this evidence derived from various lines of inquiry, it has become clear that sacrifice is one of the most widely-practised and diversely-interpreted religious activities in the history of mankind. In its developed forms the motivations can be defined with greater confidence though they cannot be regarded as independent of the psychological and environmental needs which led originally to the emergence of sacrificial rites.

Far back in the recesses of the consciousness of mankind two fundamental urges may be discerned. On the one side there is the urge to accept death, to be immolated (symbolically) in order that the current of life may continue to flow ; on the other side there is the urge to grasp life, to slay (symbolically) a victim in order that its life may be made available. Deep down these two urges interact and both find their appropriate outlets in and through the varying forms of sacrificial ritual.

As social patterns develop and become more stable, these streams of sacrificial motivation find expression on the one side in the *oblation*. This is the channel through which the flow of total life is continuously renewed by passing through symbolic death. On the other side there is the *sacred meal* which forms the occasion at which the life of a particular society is enhanced by its members sharing in the life of a victim which has been handed over to death. These two types of sacrifice contain possibilities of almost unlimited development and elaboration, possibilities, however, which can lead all too easily to distortion and to a decline of symbolic power. In the next chapter I shall examine the way in which sacrificial practices and interpretations have been taken up into Christianity and used both in the search for wholeness and in the striving for that final reconciliation which is the goal of Christian faith.

CHAPTER NINE

Sacrifice and the Eucharist

VERY EARLY in the history of the Christian Church the language
of sacrifice came to be applied to the central act of its worship,
the Eucharist. In the New Testament the background of the
rite is provided by the Jewish Passover, a sacrificial ceremony
which belongs to the second category of Chapter Eight rather
than to the first. Its roots go back to the nomadic life of the
ancestors of the Hebrews and there is little doubt that in its
earliest form the note of communal feasting was predominant. In
the course of Israel's history, it gathered to itself more of covenant
significance and came to be celebrated as the sacrifice which
recalled the blood-bond made between Yahweh and His people
and which sealed afresh their mutual relatedness through the
common feast. Other sacrificial motifs were doubtless in existence in late Judaism and these may well have exercised a
considerable influence upon the views which early Christians
took of their common eucharist. But in the main it was the
passover and covenant pattern which governed the development
of early eucharistic theology, and only in the second century did
the ideas of oblation and of life-giving food come prominently
into view.

From this time onwards the double emphasis upon the
eucharist as the great oblationary sacrifice of the Church and
upon the consecrated elements as the food of immortality
became ever more conspicuous. The dangers of which we have
already spoken began to manifest themselves and few would
deny that in the millenium between A.D. 500 and A.D. 1500 many
abuses arose through an over concentration upon the act of
offering itself. Masses were multiplied and were regarded as

almost automatically efficacious ; the elements which had been offered in sacrifice were treated with almost superstitious awe and veneration. When at length the great reaction and revolution came in the sixteenth century, it was against the whole idea of sacrifice that the attack of the Reformers was directed. Seeing the institution of sacrifice only in its one-sided and perverted form, they judged that it was worthy of absolute condemnation and for a while little attempt was made to separate the good from the bad. In their view the slaying and the offering of the Christian sacrifice had taken place once for all at Calvary. They could recall it to remembrance by celebrating the eucharistic rite. They could show their gratitude by offering praise and thanksgiving (which might include a token material oblation) for their redemption. But to offer the sacrifice of the Mass and to make devotions before the consecrated elements were to them dangerous and even blasphemous practices.

In one important respect the Reformers returned to the pattern of the Covenant sacrifice. They insisted that the Eucharist must be the central occasion for the *communion* of the people. In the late medieval Church either the ordinary worshipper did not communicate at all at the Mass or he received communion in one kind only. In the sixteenth century, however, new forms and regulations were provided to ensure that the climax of the service should be the actual participation of the worshipping congregation in the symbols of the body and blood of Christ. The breaking of the bread and the outpouring of the wine were solemn actions which represented symbolically the impaling of the body and the shedding of the blood of man's Redeemer. Now these gifts were made available by God to all men so that they might receive them with thanksgiving and be bound together within the one mystical body as they experienced afresh their sense of fellowship in Christ.

Since the sixteenth century the struggle has continued, both within Catholic and Reformed Christendom, to discover a more adequate view of the relation of the eucharistic rite to the time-honoured practice of sacrifice. For a long time this was made difficult by the fact that on the one side Roman theory tended to be built almost exclusively upon ideals of sacrifice drawn from the religion of ancient Rome while on the other side Reformed theory tended to be dominated by the system of Levitical sacrifices described in the Old Testament. This meant that the determinative idea on the one side was that sacrifice was a means of satisfying or propitiating God and that it must at all costs be maintained in due and regular order if the well-being of the community was to be ensured. On the other side the leading idea was that sacrifice had been ordained by God as a foreshadowing of the sin-offering to be made by Christ Himself and that since the one full, perfect, and sufficient sacrifice had been offered at Calvary, the all-important matter was to keep the Christian community continually reminded of that fact. This might be accomplished by the preaching of the word but even more vividly by the actions of the eucharistic feast. Thus in the Reformed view sacrifice as such had been abrogated, but a remembrance and reflection of it could be retained through the offering of praise and thanksgiving by lip and by life.

Gradually, however, new ideas of sacrificial worship began to appear. Various reasons may be suggested for this change. In the first place a better acquaintance with the tradition of the Eastern Church revealed that in the Greek Fathers and in the writings of those Latin Fathers who were acquainted with Greek philosophy, there was less emphasis upon sacrifice as a quasi-legal rite ; it was not regarded primarily as the paying of a fine or a due. Rather there was the idea of the sacrificial rite gathering up into one symbolical act the devotion and the homage of the whole community. The gifts in kind were outward expressions of an inward movement towards God and through sacrifice they were conveyed into His Presence, sanctified, and made available to the worshipping church. In the second place a growing acquaintance with the religious ideas and practices of other peoples of the world revealed the fact that a great variety of sacrificial forms existed and that it was not always easy to be sure of the motive behind the ritual in any particular culture. In some cases there seemed to be the idea that through sacrifice an altogether magical transformation could be effected while in others exalted ideas of costly self-oblation to the deity seemed to be suggested. At least it began to be evident that no single theory of sacrifice could cover all the facts. In the third place, the developing study of the Old Testament led to a radical revision of the accepted view of the whole Levitical sacrificial system. Much of this, it was seen, really belonged to post-exilic Judaism and reflected an elaboration and complication of sacrifice unknown in the early days of the history of Israel. Might it not be, therefore, that some of the motifs here enshrined were importations from other sources and did not belong to the original genius of Mosaic and prophetic Judaism? To determine the exact time when new ideas and theories enter into a people's purview is an exceedingly difficult and often impossible task. But at least it could be asserted that the emphasis upon sin-offerings and trespass-offerings belonged to a late stage of Israel's development and did not really represent the eucharistic note of the early sacrificial rites.

Other influences may also have been at work but the final result has been that new theories of the essential meaning of sacrifice have emerged and these have been used as principles of interpretation of the saving work of Christ. This work has been conceived as embracing his whole activity—in His incarnate life, in His death and resurrection, in His heavenly existence and in His continued manifestation through His Body, the Church. All may be included within the one category of sacrifice if the successive stages in the general pattern of oblationary sacrifice are carefully followed. A noteworthy attempt to use the sacrificial category in this way was that of Bishop F. C. N. Hicks in his book, *The Fullness of Sacrifice*, while more recently Father L. S. Thornton, in his book *Revelation and the Modern World*, has indicated that sacrifice is the event in which the whole process of revelation and redemption finds its focus. In Roman Catholic theology one of the most interesting attempts to reinterpret sacrifice in the light of new knowledge is that of Canon Eugene Masure in his book, *The Christian Sacrifice*. While there is no general agreement amongst Catholic theologians about the precise way in which the passion and death of Christ is to be regarded as a sacrifice or about the way in which the Christian eucharist can rightly be designated a sacrifice, yet we are now in a position to sketch a general view of sacrifice and its fulfilment as held by many Catholic writers at the present time.

MODERN INTERPRETATIONS OF SACRIFICE

I propose to begin with an extended section from Masure's book ; I shall then make certain comments on it and show how small differences of emphasis may be seen in other writers. After a careful inquiry into the practices of ancient people and into the definitions of sacrifice offered by S. Augustine and S. Thomas, Masure propounds his own definition thus :

" Sacrifice is a sensible sign (or rite) in which under the symbols (or species) of a victim, man, to pay his dues to God and so to realise his end, bears witness that he renounces sin which is his evil (immolation), and that he turns to God who is his good (oblation)—hoping that the divine acceptance, sanctifying his offering, will win for him the heavenly alliance at which he aims and that the victim will bring him by communion the guarantee of it."

After explaining that the bracketed words only reinforce the meaning and could be omitted without injuring the sense, the author goes on to say :

" Sacrifice is thus the gesture symbolising man's return to God, in which he expresses his desire and will for union with the Creator. This internal movement and external action presuppose that an intelligent adoring creature refuses to make itself its final end. In the state of sin this renouncing becomes a purifying in suffering and expiation, which the gesture represents and at the same time realises. Then it is for God to welcome this return, to sanctify the victim by His acceptance. The victim can now come down again to men to be the sacrament of their communion.

" More simply, sacrifice is the expressive, and, if possible, efficacious sign of the deliberate and suppliant return of man to God, who receives him. That is why there is *action* in sacrifice, as S. Thomas constantly repeats. Something is changed. There is movement, activity, a great stirring of mankind towards its Master, turning deliberately heavenwards to reach the end without delay. Creation finds success, fulfils itself. Before sacrifice there was nothing achieved. After sacrifice order has appeared. Man has recognised God—*adoration*; has given himself to Him—*love and homage*; he has respected God's eternal rights—*religion and reparation*; the disquiet which is our very definition has been now appeased—*requiescamus in Te.*" (pp. 78-9.) The author concludes by pointing out that oblation and immolation are to be regarded as the positive and negative sides of a single undertaking—man's restoration to a true integration in and with God.

What immediately strikes me in this whole exposition is the large place accorded to *man* in the sacrificial activity. Man appears to take the initiative. Man renounces sin and cuts himself off from it through the symbolic act of immolation. Man turns to God and offers his homage through the symbolic act of oblation. Man desires to attain God; man, through sacrifice, rises towards God; man finds his true end and his perfect rest in God. Only after the full performance of the sacrifice—in which man is not only the offerer but also in a very real sense the victim—can he hope for the Divine acceptance and the blessing of Divine communion. Many Catholic theologians would doubtless insist that whatever man does in this way is in reality the work of the Holy Spirit or the result of prevenient grace and that it is only thus that God in and through man returns to God. It is a weakness of Masure's exposition that he makes no explicit reference to the Spirit or indeed to the Trinitarian framework within which, presumably, his theory is set. However, even if we allow that this prompting and stirring of the Divine Spirit turning mankind towards its Maker may have been an implicit assumption, it still remains true that this definition as it stands is one-sided and lays too great an emphasis upon the initiative and activity of *man* without any explicit recognition of the initiative and activity of God.

The second striking thing in the exposition (and the earlier pages of the book makes this even clearer) is the emphasis laid upon the action of deliberate renunciation. Man, we are told, has become bewitched by the goods and possessions and creatures which have been given to him by God for his benefit. He has made them his end, he has become absorbed by them, he has become attached to them as partial goods, he has set them in the place of God Himself. It is in sacrifice that a surgical opera-

tion takes place. Man renounces his false ends, cuts himself off
from the treasured possession and commits it into the hands of
God. He immolates himself, he offers himself " since these
riches which I have relinquished were the extension of my
personality, of my enjoyment of ownership. Let us say simply
that those riches are immolated in so far as they leave me, and
offered in so far as they reach God." (pp. 37-8.) But *can* man
suddenly decide to immolate himself, to cut himself off from
treasured things, to perform a surgical operation on himself?
Can he renounce his partial goods at will? Again it may be
said that it is God who works in him and gives him the will
or that the institution of sacrifice is already in existence to
encourage man to make the all-important break. These considerations are important and true, but again it seems that even
if these assumptions are implicit, the exposition as it stands
does not recognise fully enough the *Divine* activity in sacrifice,
the activity which alone can bring man to the point where he is
willing to renounce his pride and his selfishness and to yield
himself a living sacrifice to God.

Still further, it is noteworthy that there is no explicit reference
to the pattern of *community* relationships or of *communal* activity
which sacrifice represents. Sometimes it appears that individual
man is the chief actor, sometimes that mankind as a whole is
involved in the general activity of sacrifice. It is true that
Masure tends to speak of man in generic terms and he would
probably allow that no man can act entirely alone when he
engages in the sacrificial act. Yet there is a danger in concentrating attention overmuch upon sacrifice as consisting in a
transaction between man and God through the manipulation of
things or *creatures*. Certainly, man is related to the material
order and ever needs, through some symbolic activity, to relate
that whole material order to God. But even more important,
man is related to the *social* order and needs through some
symbolic activity to relate his social order to God. Thus a
one-sided emphasis upon the manipulation of goods and treasured
possessions in sacrifice is dangerous. It needs at least to be
complemented by a wider view of the place which sacrifice holds
in the whole complex of man's social relationships. Nevertheless,
as representing one strand of thought and one possible approach

value. In particular his sketch of the essential pattern of *oblation-immolation+transformation-impartation* needs constantly to be borne in mind when considering any form of symbolic activity within a relatively settled society.

In modern interpretations of sacrifice in which the emphasis lies on its oblationary aspect, a large measure of agreement will be found with the essential pattern which Father Masure presents. In *The Fullness of Sacrifice*, for example, the regulations of the Pentateuch are analysed and the institution is shown to consist of six main stages. The offerer " draws near " and lays his hand on the head of the victim. In this way he declares his intention of making an *oblation* and identifies himself closely with the victim which he dedicates to this solemn purpose. Thirdly, he slays the victim—the stage which may be described as *immolation*. The priest now comes into the picture as he performs some ceremonial manipulation of the victim's blood.[1] Fifthly, the flesh or part of it is placed upon the altar and burnt —a process which symbolises the acceptance and the *transformation* of the offering by God Himself. Finally, portions of the victim are returned to the sacrificer for his consumption. By partaking of holy flesh *impartation* of the divine life is made possible. It will be seen at once that this pattern is substantially the same as that of Masure, except that in the latter's exposition no special emphasis is laid upon the blood-ritual or its significance. Oblation-immolation followed by transformation-impartation seems to describe the normal sacrificial practice of post-exilic Judaism.

There is one other interpretation of sacrifice in which a somewhat greater stress is laid upon the psychological aspect of the matter. In a paper on the Eucharistic Sacrifice, Professor Cyril C. Richardson has a section entitled the Meaning of Sacrifice. In this he lays it down as a fundamental principle that sacrifice is the acting out of the drama of salvation in the sense that those who participate in it are thereby returning to the centre of their being in God and becoming holy or " whole " even as He is holy. Man's whole existence is concerned with

[1] " The uses made of the blood" the author writes " vary in the different classes of offerings. But in substance the principle is the same. It is taken by the priest into the presence of God." (12).

dying to self and its false values in order to be reborn into the true life of God. And the supreme way in which this transformation can be effected is through participation in the symbolic or dramatic act of sacrifice. Dr. Richardson links this idea with primitive practice in the following way :

" Ancient man," he writes, " chose the best of his herd in order to destroy it and save himself. By laying his hands on it, he identified himself with it. There followed the slaughter of the animal with all its vivid concomitants of the flowing of the blood and the burning of flesh, and, in this dramatic action, what happened to the animal happened to the worshipper. We shall not appreciate the inner meaning of sacrifice until we grasp this mystical unity between the offerer and the offering. What the worshipper is doing is enacting out the destruction of the ego in order to gain the creative powers of the deeper self. The action is of central importance for without it the movement of the soul cannot occur so surely and efficaciously. The offerer, to realise his essential nature, has to make himself objective, as it were, to live out the truth of his being through powerful symbolic actions which have been consecrated by tradition and which have behind them the religious power of the community. He cannot gain his harmony and wholeness by reflection—he has to *act it out*—a point which the modern use of psycho-drama well illustrates. Finally, there comes the feast on the animal, which is the feast on and with God. This is the moment of grasping the new life, of the welling up of the creative powers of wholeness through the previous destruction of the ego. The part has been sacrificed for the whole, and in some measure, the offerer has become holy."[1] There may be elements of idealisation and of rationalisation in this interpretation, but it provides a striking parallel in more psychological terms to the pattern we have already considered. Self-oblation and self-immolation followed by self-transformation and self-integration—this, Richardson affirms, is the age-long motif and purpose of sacrifice.

On the other side there is the covenant or communal interpretation of sacrifice. Here we are confronted with a difficulty

[1] *Anglican Theological Review*, January, 1950, pp. 53-68.

in that the violent reaction of the Reformers against all forms of sacrificial interpretation of the central eucharistic action made their descendants hesitate to think of Christian worship in sacrificial terms at all. Hence there has been little attempt so far on the part of modern Reformed theologians to reinterpret sacrifice in any comprehensive way or to show how the Lord's Supper is to be regarded as a sacrificial rite. A book of brilliant originality which has exercised a wide influence was Robertson Smith's *Religion of the Semites*, but he did not use it to build up a revised eucharistic theology. He did, as we have seen, propound a theory that the essence of early sacrifice was communion with the deity, but other scholars have had little difficulty in showing that this single motif was not universal. Moreover, his assertion that the sacrificial meal was a means of feeding on the deity has also been questioned, though it is probable that amongst certain totemic tribes this idea held sway. There is, then, no full exposition of sacrifice available in terms of the more dynamic forms of the life of restless and pioneering peoples. I shall therefore draw together some of the points of our earlier discussion and attempt to define sacrifice in more covenantal and communal language.

Let us first try to frame a definition which will be comparable in some respects to that of Masure and yet which will emphasise the other realm of experience which we have in mind.

" Sacrifice," we may say, " is a sensible sign (or rite) through which under the symbol of a slain victim, God, to redeem His people from destruction and to lead them into the blessedness of His eternal kingdom, binds them into covenant-relationship with Himself as He looses them from their guilt and estrangement ; at the same time He makes provision for all the demands of their future pilgrimage by giving them, through the victim's broken body, the symbol of His own essential character which accepts suffering and death in order that the life of others may be renewed."

In this definition, it will be noted, there are two main parts, as was the case in the former definition. The first part covers the complex process of covenant and cleansing. In the classic passage which deals with God's new covenant,[1] the assurance

---

[1] Jeremiah 31, 31-4.

is given that in establishing the new order of mutual fellowship God will remove all the sins and iniquities which at present make any true relationship impossible. Just as it is futile to discuss the exact chronological order of the oblation-immolation complex, so it is equally unprofitable to analyse priorities in the covenant-cleansing complex. Each involves the other. Covenant implies reconciliation ; guilt implies estrangement. To remove one is to establish the other. In the actual symbolism the blood was spilled and applied in some way to each party in the covenant. But this action could imply not only the binding of both parties within the one covenant relationship but also the covering of one party from the wrath of the other or the loosing of one party from the debt owed to the other. Through the slaying and dividing of the victim and through the manipulation of its blood, the pattern of covenant-cleansing or of loosing-recon-ciling was vividly set forth. It was for the stronger party in the transaction to take the initiative ; in the context of the relations between God and man, therefore, it is God who is to be regarded as the chief actor in the sacrificial rite.

The second part of our definition covers the complex process of communion and glorification. Here there is a close parallel to the transformation-impartation complex of the first definition but the emphasis is a little different. There it is implied that the gifts of men are lifted up upon the altar of God and transformed through the symbolic destruction which ensues. In symbol, they are then given back to man so that he may partake of the life which has passed through death. The food of immortality is imparted to him. In the second context, however, it is implied that the sacrificial victim, having passed through the fires of the altar, is made available to men for their use in a common feast. But the strength they derive from it is no general or *ordinary* strength for body or mind. It is strength to be transformed into the same pattern of sacrificial life and thereby to be changed from glory to glory within the sacrificial fellowship. In other words, those who receive the symbols of the victim's broken and burned body and feed upon them, are thereby brought into a fellowship of common sacrifice, and are committed to win glory only through the way of service and sacrifice. God spreads a table for His covenant people, but it is furnished with symbols of His own essential character, the pattern of the one who seeks not to be ministered unto but to minister and to give His life a ransom for many.

It may be objected that in this definition insufficient attention is paid to *man's* part in the sacrificial action. Does he not bring the victim? Does he not slay it? Is he not responsible for taking and eating the flesh provided for his needs? Is it not man's will which must respond to the implications of the sacrifice? These are valid questions and call for a reference to the Holy Spirit such as we suggested was necessary in the first case. It is the Spirit of God working in man Who prompts him to transcend his own immediate interests and bring the victim for the communal feast. But now, as it were, man stands back and waits for God to act. Though the prompting to sacrifice was there, man knows that he is altogether unworthy to take part in the great purpose of God. He is unclean, fettered, estranged. Only as God in His mercy takes of the victim's blood and uses it to unite man to Himself can any real fellowship be established. And only as God grants a new bestowal of strength for sacrifice can man hope to continue in the divinely-appointed path. Such a view spells death to man's pride and self-sufficiency. But again through the prompting of the Spirit he overcomes his pride and humbly accepts the Divine provision for his future manner of life. In all this it is the Spirit whose character is dramatised in the outward events, it is the Spirit who is inwardly at work in the consciences and imaginations of man. Man is not a cipher nor an automaton. He belongs to a community and by that very fact is related in some way to the Spirit Who has entered into the historical experience of mankind. So he is moved by the Spirit and, supremely in the act of sacrifice, responds to the Spirit. Obviously his own sacrifice is never perfect or complete. Only in the case of the Son of Man who was full of the Spirit and who accepted the Cross for the sake of the fellowship was the pattern of sacrifice completely fulfilled and the true nature of God's essential character made manifest.

Again it might be urged that within this definition no place is given to man's need to repent and to renounce his false goods ; it might appear that the act of reconciliation was effected by a sheer exercise of the Divine fiat declaring man to be loosed

from his sins. Or it might be urged that little attention is given
to the symbolism of the victim itself. When the focus of interest
is the slaying of the victim or the breaking of the body, how
can a true interpretation be given of the order of being which
the victim in itself represents? These objections also have force
and though I might urge that a reconciliation effected by *blood*
must inevitably lead man to repentance and that the death of
the victim cannot ultimately be thought of apart from the nature
of the victim itself, yet I should readily allow that these particular
emphases are more obviously covered by the first definition of
sacrifice than the second. It is indeed my whole contention that
neither of these definitions is adequate if it is separated entirely
from the other. Both of these patterns of sacrifice have existed
within the historical experience of mankind, though it is very
doubtful whether one type has ever existed in complete independence of the other. Each emphasis is needed if there is to be
a true representation of ultimate reality and if man's life in
relation to Nature and society is to be kept healthy and strong.
Happy is that society which can find room within its range of
symbolic activities for both of these types of sacrifice.

One further word on sacrifice in general remains to be said.
It may seem that we have narrowed our attention unduly in
speaking of sacrifice as the major symbolic activity of mankind.
I recognise that there are innumerable symbolic actions which
do not seem at first sight to have any special connection with
the ritual of sacrifice. Yet I believe that when they are analysed
they will be found to fall within one or other of two main
categories and these two categories correspond to the sacrificial
patterns which we have discussed. For are not man's symbolic
activities mainly of two kinds? On the one hand he desires to
ascend *upwards*. He wishes to grow. He aspires to a higher
standard of living. He hopes for a more exalted position from
which he can exercise a wider range of responsibility. He
desires to lift his dependants, his possessions, his powers to
higher levels of existence than they at present occupy. So in
his ritual activities he *raises, lifts, offers*. But concurrently he
repudiates, renounces, annuls. He separates himself from the low
and the downward-dragging in order that he may rise to the
high and upward-rising. In his architecture, in his art, in his

ritual activities, this is the pattern which we find expressed again and again. In his inward spirit man cries :

> Lift every gift that Thou Thyself hast given
> Low lies the best till lifted up to heav'n,

and in his outward symbolic activities he takes of the things of earth and offers them up to be purified and sanctified and charged with new vitality and meaning that they may serve for the glory of God and may promote the true life of mankind.

On the other hand, man desires to move *forwards*. He wishes to advance. He yearns for a better country, for a better order of society. He feels the pull towards the future. He craves the companionship of others in this common quest. He would fain experience even now the glories of the coming age. He is ready to respond to the leader who can direct the way to the promised land. So in his ritual activities he yields himself to his leader and to his companions in the pursuit of the common purpose ; but concurrently he turns away from his former existence and attachments and commitments. *He dies to the past in order that he may live to the future.* He leaves behind those who are content with things as they are and participates already in the essential pattern of the life which is yet to be. He chooses to be united with his leader in some form of death so that he may attain to the resurrection of the dead. Thus dying, he lives ; chastened, he is not killed ; sorrowful, he always rejoices ; poor, he makes many rich ; having nothing, he already begins to possess all things. Into all his relationships and activities the principle of life-through-death enters to establish true mutuality and reciprocity and to move towards the fulfilment of all things in the Kingdom of God.

THE CHRISTIAN EUCHARIST

Having sketched a general theory of sacrifice within which the Christian Eucharist may be set, let us now examine the rite itself in rather more detail. Here is the central and the most significant symbolic rite of the Christian Church. Its origins lie far back in the realm of ritual oblations and covenant ceremonies. It gathers up into itself the essential nature and activity of the incarnate Son of God. It reaches out to touch and affect every aspect of human life. It performs its function in and through the symbolic form which is at once the most comprehensive and the most compelling known to man—the drama. The Eucharistic drama is the symbol *par excellence* of the Christian Gospel.

The essential pattern of the Eucharist is severely simple. It is derived from the New Testament records of the institution of the Lord's Supper in the upper room, from lesser references to or echoes of the celebrations in the primitive Christian Church contained in early Christian literature and art, and from the earliest fragments of developing liturgical forms. From these we learn that certain simple actions were performed, certain simple words were said. There has indeed been wide divergence of opinion about what can be regarded as authentic details of the original form or forms of celebration, but it would be generally agreed that in the most solemn part of the rite bread was taken, blessed, broken and given ; a cup of wine was taken, blessed, and given ; words were spoken in relation to the bread, " This is My Body," and words were spoken in relation to the cup, " This is My Blood of the New Covenant." A series of actions with a loaf of bread and a cup of wine ; a series of words referring to Body and Covenant-Blood—we may at the least assume that these constitute the central image (it may, of course, be a two-sided image) of the Eucharistic drama.

When this is said, however, we find ourselves at the end of agreement concerning the form and significance of the Eucharist. Not unnaturally this central image has been made the ground-pattern of a host of dramatic forms, though amidst this multiplicity and diversity it is possible to discern certain groupings which are of special interest. In the main the groupings represent particular cultural traditions, it being always remembered that just as cultures tend to overlap and even to merge into one another, so eucharistic symbolic forms constantly reveal influences derived from varying traditions and cultures. It will, however, be of value to attempt to isolate rather sharply the separate groupings or families of symbolic forms. When this has been done it becomes easier to see how in the life of contemporary Christendom existing rites show the influence of more than one tradition.[1]

1. *The Greek cultural tradition.* Two axiomatic principles have governed the attitude and outlook of the typical Greek in every walk of life. One is the principle of *analogy* ; the other is the principle of *organism.* I call these principles " axiomatic " for they are not so much argued or debated—they are assumed and implied. They constitute what have been called the " dogmas " or fundamental presuppositions which govern the approach which any members of a particular culture make to the problems of life.

Through the principle of analogy men express their fundamental conviction that the world of the senses is not the only and not indeed the most important world. Except in extreme cases (where the analogical principle is virtually abandoned) men do not despise or abandon the world of the senses. All that is seen and felt and heard is in the highest degree interesting. But it is interesting not because of what it is in its isolated self-existence but because of what it indicates and implies about an inner or a higher world, however precisely the other world is imagined and described.

In the process of receiving his sense-data man should ever be seeking to discern significant forms and ordered sequences and important classifications. The Greek was well aware of the endless variety that exists in the universe, but he was also fascinated by the regular patterns which may be seen in the external world of Nature, in the experience of the individual, and in the life of societies. These patterns suggested permanence in the midst of flux, unity in the midst of multiplicity. Once he had succeeded in giving an ordered account of the forms which his investigations revealed, the way was open for an

---

[1] In concentrating attention upon broad features of form I am not suggesting that form can be separated from significance. It is not the fact that a single original meaning can be taken and expressed through all kinds of varieties of art-forms. Rather is it true that meaning and expression live and move in a constant dialectical relationship with one another. Meaning seeks an appropriate form but there can be no guarantee that the chosen form will adequately or permanently express the original intention and meaning. A particular form may imply different *nuances* of meaning in different places and ages. Thus the interplay between meaning and form must forever continue. Form is the easier to describe, but it is never independent of the meaning which it seeks to express.

adventure *beyond* these forms to their perfection in some changeless and unified sphere of being. Such an adventure was made
by the method of analogy. By extending the discovered pattern
to its limits, by *raising* it to a higher plane, by imagining the
perfection of that which was imperfectly manifested, it was
possible to move towards the world of perfect forms which is
the origin and motivation of all that earth reveals.

How, then, did the Greek express his ideas in outward
symbolic forms ? In general by seeking ever to produce such
symmetry, such proportion and such harmony as could be
regarded as a worthy approximation to the ideal forms which
existed in the world of his imagination. His temple was the
symbol of the ideal dwelling-place ; beautifully proportioned,
four-square, stable and secure. His statues provided the symbols
of ideal human types ; without passion, without flaw, harmonious
in gesture, the perfection of some bodily excellence. His games
were the symbol of rhythmic and smooth-flowing human
activity ; his dramas were the symbol of the triumph over every
disturbing and disruptive force, the idealisation of superb
magnanimity and effortless calm. Objects and activities and
attitudes belonging to the common life of mankind were considered, compared and their essential form abstracted ; this
essential form was extended, purified, perfected ; it was expressed
outwardly in artistic creations which forever raised men's eyes
to the heavenly ideal.

The second axiomatic principle was that of organism.
According to this principle man's whole life, individual and
social, constitutes a living, growing organism within which
every part has an essential function to perform. Just as man
seeks the health and perfection of his physical body, so he should
seek the health and the harmony of the social whole to which
he belongs. But how is the pattern of its harmonious functioning
to be discerned ? To this question different answers were given,
but there was general agreement that it was the duty of men of
wisdom to inquire and discuss and compare so that the essential
pattern of the ideal state might be formulated in the mind and
expressed in outward institutional forms. In short, the controlling image of the State was the human body ; the symbolic
forms of Greek society were the idealisation of those structures

These two principles of analogy and organism, characteristic of the Greek way of life, have had a profound influence upon the symbolic development of the Christian Church of the East and of those Churches which have inherited, at least in some measure, its tradition. In the present context we are concerned only with the Eucharistic drama, but the influence may be traced in the whole complex of rites and ceremonies. Pre-eminently these rites were concerned with the sanctification of every part of the world of experience by bringing it into the context of the heavenly world, the general pattern of which had been revealed to the Church in and through the career of the Logos of God. Through His birth, His baptism, His miracles, His transfiguration, His suffering, death and resurrection, He had identified Himself with the essential experiences of human life. Now through the symbolic re-enactment of these events, the imperfection and the ordinariness of their character as normally experienced could be transformed and the secular, this-worldly situation could stretch out towards its real quality and pattern as it exists within the heavenly design.

In the Eucharist this sanctification of life reaches its fullest expression. On the one hand it is assumed that in the Eucharist the whole Church, the living and the departed, participates in the sacred actions of the sacred drama. In other words the Eucharist is the action of the *totus Christus*—the whole Body of Christ, the complete social organism of the Church. By participating in the Eucharistic actions the Church is caught up into the Divine pattern of reality and becomes thereby ever more closely conformed to its true nature.

In particular, in the Eucharist man's dependence on the fruits of the earth for his daily sustenance, his dependence upon the breath of God for his continuance in life, his need for a medicine of immortality to overcome his inevitable subjection to the processes of corruption and decay—all receive notable emphasis. In the middle of the fourth century we find Cyril of Jerusalem praying God to " send forth His Holy Spirit upon the gifts lying before us that He may make the bread the body of Christ and the wine the blood of Christ." By partaking of the " divine, holy, immaculate, immortal, heavenly, life-giving, awful, mysteries of Christ " (*The Liturgy of St. Chrysostom*) the worshippers are strengthened with heavenly food and made partakers of the life which is eternal. The whole setting and performance of the liturgy—the building, the furnishings, the music, the vestments, the movements of the participants, the actions of the worshippers —are designed to symbolise the worship in heaven. Nothing on earth can be a perfect representation of the heavenly reality. But the essential pattern of the heavenly archetype can be displayed on earth and those who take part in the earthly drama can, in the very act of their participation, stretch out towards the perfect and receive a foretaste of eternal bliss.

The ancient Greek view of the organic nature of society and of the need for the earthly *polis* to be ever seeking to mould its forms according to the pattern of the ideal city-state was taken over quite naturally by Eastern Christendom and expressed in its Christian form in the doctrine of the Church as the Body of Christ. In its essential form the Church *is* the Body of Christ : yet in its daily experience the Church is seeking ever to participate more fully in the life of the Body of Christ. And the Liturgy is the central means by which the essential form is symbolised and the eternal life is shared. It is, as it were, the focusing image of the whole panorama of the Divine Life. " Partaking of the Holy Gifts," writes a modern interpreter of Eastern Orthodoxy " is only a part of the Eucharistic service, the content of which is an expression of the whole Orthodox faith. Not only those present, but the whole Church—the living and the departed—share in the Eucharist ; it is an unbloody sacrifice offered for the whole world as the realisation here and now of the Saviour's sacrifice on Calvary. Eucharist pre-supposes the communion of saints, the prayerful participation in it of the Mother of God, the co-ministration of angels." (L. Zander, *Vision and Action*, pp. 152-3.) In other words, within the tradition which stems from Greece the Eucharist may be regarded as the analogical symbol of the oblationary sacrifice of the Eternal Divine Son and of the mystical participation of all the faithful in the life of the Body of Christ.

2. *The Roman cultural tradition.* Two axiomatic principles

have governed the attitude and outlook of the typical Roman in every walk of life. One is the principle of *instrumentality* ; the other is the principle of *hierarchy*. Through the principle of instrumentality the Romans expressed (explicitly or implicitly) their fundamental conviction that the existing world is not fixed or final in its form. There are agents—divine and human— who have it in their power to impose patterns of order and regularity upon that which is confused and unpredictable, to manipulate efficiently that which is deficient or inoperative. Indeed the Romans had, it was assumed, been entrusted by the gods with the special task of managing the world and reducing it to order. Through the improvement of techniques in the realms of agriculture, military operations, road-making and building, the Romans showed themselves to be the outstanding technicians of the ancient world ; through the organisation of government, the civil service, the army, the labourers, they showed themselves to be the most competent administrators that the world had yet seen.

It is not surprising that this highly efficient and practical people should have focused their attention in religious matters upon rites and ceremonies which would assist in the task of establishing order and promoting the smooth efficiency of social life. Of these rites and ceremonies none was so extensive in its use and efficacy as the *sacrificium*—a rite which by its very title suggests a definite end to be achieved by a specified form of activity. It was the handing over to the deity of gifts of food and animals, thus making them " sacer ", and ensuring that prosperity and increase would be continued in the life of the farms. A second rite, the *lustratio*, included the offering of sacrifices but seems to have been designed with special intent to cleanse a particular area from evil or to protect it from harm. The *piaculum* again included an act of sacrifice but was pro- pitiatory in intention and normally involved the shedding of the blood of the victim. Thus in all these ritual performances the emphasis lay upon particular forms of sacrificial activity ; once the precise need had been defined the sacrifice could be offered with particular intention and with the confidence that through the act of handing over certain objects to the deity (accompanied by appropriate prayers) the required end could be achieved. The gods and their human agents could constantly co-operate in the task of maintaining regularity and efficiency in the whole social life of mankind.

The second principle was the hierarchical. From the simple beginnings in the family life of the agricultural communities, where the *pater familias* was the central figure, there gradually emerged a highly developed social organisation in which the Emperor occupied the place of honour at the summit of the pattern with other groups or classes arranged, as it were, on successively lower levels surrounding him. We may, indeed, conceive the model of Roman social organisation in either of two ways. We may imagine it as a pyramid with the broad base representing the slave-workers and successively smaller squares representing higher classes of officials rising towards the Emperor at the peak. Or we may imagine it more in accordance with the plan of the Roman temple which stood on some kind of eminence and was normally approached by a flight of steps. Within the temple were the cellae devoted to the gods and there was thus no sharp division between gods and men. Society, in fact, could be envisioned as a series of hierarchies, rising up from those occupying the lowest step of the temple stairway, up to the Emperor occupying the exalted place next to the gods themselves. Such an organisation, broad-based, rising by successive but diminishing stages towards the summit, is perhaps the most simple and stable, both architecturally and sociologically, of all the patterns which men have discovered in the course of their historical experience.

This same hierarchical structure regulated, in large measure, the organisation of the religious activities of the State. In the days of the Republic the calendar of festival days was carefully followed and various classes of religious officials had their particular duties to perform. There was at the lowest end of the scale the order of the *Flamines*, each of whom was attached to a particular deity with the responsibility of kindling the sacrificial fire. Higher orders of priests performed prominent functions on special days of the sacred year while above them the famous colleges of the Augurs and the Pontifices dealt with matters of divination and ecclesiastical law respectively. Thus, under the final authority of the Emperor, the established hierarchies, both in civil and religious affairs, kept the manifold processes of the imperial life running smoothly and dealt effectively with breaches of law in the realms both of the secular and the sacred. Technical efficiency within a hierarchical social organisation was the hallmark of the culture of Ancient Rome.

Just as the Greek tradition has exercised a profound influence upon the development of the symbolic life of the Churches of the East, so the Roman tradition has deeply influenced the symbolic character of the great Church of the West. At the centre of the ritual life of this Church there have ever been the few simple actions and words derived from the records of the Upper Room. But in the interpretation of these actions and their application to the wider life of mankind the primary emphasis has always been laid upon the instrumentality of the actions, the efficacy of the words and the general sacrificial character of the rite of which they form the determinative core. Just as the ancient Romans offered sacrifice at every notable religious celebration, so the Western Church has made the sacrifice of the Mass the central feature both in its regular and its special worship, though it has tended to give a greater uniformity to the pattern and meaning of the sacrificial act than was the case in the older State-religion. In and through the actions of the Mass the whole of human life is sustained, repaired and fulfilled.

It is important to notice that in the Latin tradition little stress is laid upon the precise symbolism of the bread and the wine. Their associations with the fruits of the earth and with the processes of organic life and with the wholeness of the created order are regarded as of secondary importance, if indeed they are mentioned at all. The all-important matter is that by the instrumentality of the sacred words of institution these earthly creatures *become* (in some sense at least) the body and blood of the Lord. " The priest pronounces over the bread certain words that signify (i.e. are a sign of) the body of Christ ; and forthwith the thing signified is also accomplished ; the bread is no longer bread ; it is the Body of Christ. Similarly the words spoken over the chalice signify the presence of Christ's blood in the chalice ; and forthwith, instead of wine, the Blood of Christ is present in the chalice. How does it all happen ? The change is made, of course, by the power of God, but not by the power of God acting in a purely arbitrary manner. The power of God is bound, so to speak, to the words in question (provided the necessary conditions are fulfilled), so that as often as they are employed, so often they are effective. And how does the power of God come to be attached in this way to the words of consecration ? The answer is—because Christ instituted them as a sacramental sign, to carry out what they signify." [1] In fact the sacred words constitute a sign by whose instrumentality Christ is made present upon the altar at every Eucharist.

There is, however, the further aspect of the Eucharist, viz. : the offering of the sacrifice. Again little stress is laid upon the precise symbolism of the act of offering. Its association with the universal principle of the renewal of life through death or with the common experience of expansion through costly surrender receives little attention. The all-important thing is that the prescribed actions of the sacrifice must be repeated at each Mass in order that in a quite outward and visible manner the sacrifice of Christ upon the Cross may be represented and commemorated. " The sacrifice He left was the sacrifice of Himself—a sacrifice to be offered by us in a manner that would represent and commemorate His own offering of the same sacrifice on the Cross. He Himself offered . . . by the shedding of His blood unto death. The separate consecration of His body and blood is the sign He has instituted to represent and commemorate that offering. . . . What the priest does and says at the double consecration signifies . . . not only the presence of Christ's body and blood, but also the offering of Christ's body and blood as a sacrifice. And just as it effects or accomplishes the presence of Christ's body and blood because it signifies it, so also it effects or makes the *offering* of Christ's body and blood because it signifies it." (*Ibid.*) There appears to be room for some difference between Roman Catholic theologians about the precise way in which the actions performed by the priest in the Mass constitute the sign of Christ's sacrifice. But it is agreed by all that the actions do constitute the sign by whose instrumentality Christ is offered to the Father. Though other benefits may accrue, this sacrifice is offered primarily on each occasion for the propitiation and expiation of the sins of mankind. In short,

[1] *The Mass : What is it ?* William Moran, p. 25. (Catholic Truth Society.)

the Mass is the instrumental sign of the propitiatory sacrifice of Christ. Only in the manner of offering does it differ from the sacrifice of the Cross. The effects of the sacrifice are the same.

What, then, is the importance of the *hierarchical* principle? Throughout the long history of the Latin Church the central concern has been the establishment and maintenance of *order*. No structure, in the view of the Latin theorists, can ever take the place of the pyramidal structure in which, under the suzerainty of Christ the King, the supreme pontiff holds sway at the apex, with descending orders at lower levels, until the broad base of the ordinary lay-folk is reached. This is the essential structure so far as all law and order is concerned. Every rank in the hierarchy is pledged to obey his superior and to uphold both the dogmatic definitions and the moral codes which have been promulgated by due authority. To gather the whole of mankind into the embrace of this Divinely-ordained structure is the goal of all hoping and striving.

What, then, prevents the establishment of this firm, ordered, all-embracing society? It is sin—sin of thought and word and deed—which prevents the realisation of this harmonious order. But there is an instrument committed by Christ to His Church through His accredited representative and His successors—it is the instrument of the Mass by which all may participate in the one great sacrifice in which He wrought the redemption of the world. The actual right to use this instrument is committed to a wide circle, to all, in fact, who are priests. They stand to act on behalf of the great circle of those who are below them in the hierarchy; their authority to act in this way they derive from those who are above them in the hierarchy. Ideally, then, the whole Church is to be conceived as acting through its accredited representatives, taking part in the one great sacrifice of Christ by which the world is being redeemed, offering constantly through the ordained sign the effective sacrifice by which the aberrations and disobediences of men are propitiated and by which the whole world is being reconstituted under the sovereignty of God.[1]

[1] As a final comment on the Latin tradition it may be pointed out that just as in the ancient Roman sacrificial system the actual feeding upon the consecrated elements was not an essential part of the ceremony—it only took place comparatively rarely—so in the developed eucharistic system of the Latin Church

3. *The Hebraic cultural tradition.* Two axiomatic principles governed the attitude and outlook of the ancient Hebrews—the men of the desert encampment, the shepherd, the nomad, the lover of the open spaces. One is the principle of *metaphorical conjunction*: the other is the principle of *covenant relationship*. The first principle determined their attitude to the universe around them and to the conditions of life which governed their daily existence; the second principle regulated the pattern of their social relationships, both internally and in their contacts and dealings with other groups.

Nomads who journey to and fro over monotonous tracts of steppe and upland pay little attention to the characteristics of their immediate and day-to-day environment. They are, indeed, quick to detect marks of direction or significant changes in the landscape. But in the main they are men who dwell " between the times." They look back to some notable event or chain of events in the past; they look forward to a consummation or a destiny in the future. The present is never final. Only rarely is the present stimulating and exciting. Life is activated by memory and by hope.

I have called the principle which determined their general attitude to life that of " metaphorical conjunction " because, as has been shown in earlier passages of this book, the essence of metaphor is the daring and unexpected bringing together of two seemingly disparate entities. When the general structure of a situation seems dark and meaningless some element in it is suddenly seized and related to an element in a quite different context. Immediately a shaft of light illuminates the situation. This light is so dazzling that it seems to be out of all proportion to the conjunction which actually caused it to shine. But the illumination is unmistakable and the creative energies which are released by the metaphorical leap are as powerful as any known to men.

Thus it was with the ancient Hebraic patriarchs, leaders,

the reception of the body and blood of Christ is not the central part of the service and in many instances is confined to the priest alone. The words and the actions are essential : distribution and reception are not. The essential work to be done is that of redemption and this is achieved through the instrumentality of the appropriate signs : the reception of the host is important and may be desirable, but even if none besides the priest receives, the all important *opus* is still effectually accomplished.

prophets, seers. They were men who forever refused to be daunted by the threats of an immediate situation or to be lured by the specious finality of an attractive pattern of settled life. Some element in their existential experience they associated with a signal event of their past or with a hoped-for event in their future. During the patriarchal period, for example, the altar of stones—a seemingly puny pile in the vast stretches of flat desert—was probably associated with the great event in the past when a theophany took place in some remote mountain region. In the period following Moses' activity, the fire—a seemingly transient phenomenon—was associated with the fire on the remote mountain side which burned unceasingly while the bush was not consumed. The annual paschal feast was linked with the dramatic deliverance from the bondage of Egypt, the offering of sacrifice with the formative covenant established at Mount Sinai. In this way, however drab and unpromising the immediate temporal circumstances might seem, the power of the past coming into the present through the metaphorical conjunction of two widely disparate clusters of events, enabled men to gain new courage and confidence and to go forward into the future refreshed and renewed. The evidence suggests that the associations made between sacred objects or actions in the present and places or events in the past were not always identical; the sabbath or circumcision were given different references at different times. Nevertheless the general principle remains unchanged; that in the authentic Hebrew view of any present configuration special elements are seized and related to determinative experiences of the past in such a way that new creative forces begin to work and the present becomes potentially transfigured in the light of this revelation.

But this principle did not only operate in relation to the past. The succession of men in Hebrew history, who are usually designated " prophets," made it their special aim to turn men's eyes to the future. By taking some ordinary object in daily life —a basket of summer fruit, an almond rod, a boiling pot—and relating it to coming events in history, the prophet made a leap of faith which not only portrayed the future but in at least a minimal way helped to bring it to pass. Even more was this so with the series of miniature *dramas* which are described in the prophetic writings of the Old Testament. Elijah's activities on Mount Carmel, Elisha's acted parables, Isaiah walking barefoot and Ezekiel using tile and pan to enact the siege of the holy city, are all in their way metaphorical conjunctions between present situations and future events. They are not merely illustrations of ways in which the Divine activity will be manifested in the future. They are means by which the present situation can be caught up into the future goal of the Divine purpose and be thereby transformed (or at the least begin to be transformed) into the pattern of the eschatological *dénouement*.

As I have already suggested, prophetic symbolism was particularly directed to the future and yet not exclusively so. An attitude which expects a precise supernatural event to happen in the future as the direct result of a dramatic activity performed in the present can only be called magical. But this was not the prophetic attitude. Their confidence concerning the future was not unrelated to their insight concerning the past. They had discerned the special ways in which God's judging and saving activity had been manifested in the past. They were certain that this kind of activity would be openly manifested again in the future. But the obvious structure of the present situation seemed utterly opposed to any such confident faith. Their task, then, was to select a particular object or event or series of events from the existing situation and to project it into the imagined future without doing violence to the pattern of the reforming acts of God which they had known through the past. The symbolic act is related to the past, performed in the present and metaphorically joined to the future which will transcend and fulfil it.

The second principle was the *covenantal*. The structure of the social life of the Hebrew peoples had been built up and maintained by a succession of covenants (or renewing of covenants). The covenant might be between two families or two tribes or two collections of tribes. Normally, representative individuals acted as principals in the covenant-making ceremony, but the ultimate result was to bring groups which had hitherto been separate from one another and even hostile to one another into a relationship within which they shared with one another their common resources and moved together towards a common goal. As I have written elsewhere : " The very word covenant suggests a coming together, the bridging of a chasm, the transcending of a dualism, the creating of an intimate union. It is implied that two parties have been standing over against one another in separation and uncertainty and that now a new relationship is being established which will bring them together in a union of a permanent character. But just because the antecedent tension has been so sharp and painful, the new communion cannot possibly be achieved lightly and easily. The actual coming together constitutes a critical occasion of unusual solemnity and is normally marked by symbolic words and actions designed to bear witness to the irrevocable character of the new relationship thereby established." (*The Structure of the Divine Society*, pp. 33-4.) Thus the metaphorical symbol takes its place within the social context and operates in conformity with the pattern of social relationships which have been characteristic of Hebrew culture from its earliest days.

In spite of the later development of Jewish ecclesiasticism, the characteristic principles which belong to the Hebrew cultural tradition have never been completely lost within the history either of Judaism or of Christianity. Just because these principles, however, do not depend upon the maintenance of unbroken continuity but allow for " leaps " to be made between different sets of circumstances in history or between different groupings of men within the wider social context, they have tended to receive special or renewed emphasis at critical turning-points of history. Moreover, they have usually been associated with creative leaders who have themselves made the " leap " of faith in a new way and in time made clear to expanding groups within society what the implications of the " leap " necessarily are. The fact that centuries may go by within which no particular appeal is made to the metaphorical or prophetic principle does not detract from its validity or its power when it comes to be reapplied within a new set of historical circumstances.

For those whose general attitude to social history is governed by the two principles of this particular tradition the words and actions of the Eucharistic rite have been invested with peculiar significance. The Covenant associations of the Last Supper relate it determinatively to the great reformation of the Divine

society at Sinai after the exodus from Egypt; the eschatological
associations lift it forward to the great marriage supper of the
Lamb. Here in symbolic form the new Covenant is established;
here the fellowship of the finally reconciled society is pro-
leptically enjoyed.

In regard to the precise symbolism of the acts performed at
the Last Supper it would be precarious to relate these in a too
detailed way either to the past or to the future. But in harmony
with the general character of Hebrew prophetic symbolism it
may be inferred that Jesus' breaking of the loaf bears some
resemblance to Jeremiah's breaking of the earthenware flask.
(Jeremiah 19.) There is little justification for associating the
bread with the life of agriculture and the work of mankind any
more than there would be for associating the earthenware flask
with the life of industry and the art of mankind. The loaf
represents a wholeness of life *which is to be broken.*[1] But from the
very beginning this has constituted the central feature of the
covenant-making symbolism. A wholeness of life—a human
victim, an animal victim, a cereal model—is taken and cut
asunder, broken, divided; it is between the sundered parts of
the divided victim that the two parties of the covenant are
joined together into an indissoluble union. In and through the
broken bread, God and man are reconciled in one body. And
moreover, just as Jeremiah was actuated by the faith that out of
the brokenness of the immediate form God would bring renewal
of life to His people, so out of the brokenness of the body which
could not fail to be associated with the historic people of Jesus'
own time (Cp. especially John 2), there would come into being
the new Body, the resurrection-body, the Body which is the
Church.

Again, " the blood of the new covenant " or " the new
covenant in my blood " cannot fail to be linked in our imaginations with the blood-shedding which had from time immemorial
been associated with the most binding of all human covenants.
To be united with another *through blood* was to be bound within
a union which no changes or chances of this mortal life could
ever be allowed to destroy. The blood of the two covenanting

---

[1] " We ought carefully to observe that the chief, and almost the whole energy
of the sacrament consists in these words : ' It is broken for you ; it is shed for
you.' " Calvin, Institutes, 4, 17, 3.

parties might be mingled together openly and publicly; the blood of an animal victim might be sprinkled on the two parties; or the wine, connected by a metaphorical " leap " with blood, could be drunk together and thus shared in a new way. To identify wine with blood and to drink it was indeed a startling innovation. But it was a new covenant that was being inaugurated and in this amazingly expressive and impressive act God and man were bound together, in symbolic form, within the everlasting covenant of blood.

Thus the metaphorical conjunction of the breaking of the bread both with the dividing of the victim in the early covenant ceremonies and with the rupture of the flesh-body of the Christ upon the Cross; the conjunction of the offering of the cup both with the blood-sharing of the covenant ceremonies and with the blood-shedding on the cross; the conjunction of the bread with the body which shall have passed through death and the wine with the life-blood of the new community—all these serve to bring into creative relationship events which seem at first sight strangely unrelated to one another and serve at the same time to extend and universalise the social pattern of cove- nant relationships already expresssed in a limited way within the Hebraic cultural tradition. In the life of the Christian Church the Eucharist may be viewed as a metaphorical symbol of the reconciliation of God and man and as the realisation on successive occasions within time of that perfect communion which is from beyond time—the communion of man with man within the everlasting covenant of God.

4. *The Jerusalemite cultural tradition.* Two axiomatic principles govern the attitude and outlook of the Jew of the developed Jerusalemite culture. One is the principle of the *confirming sign*; the other is the principle of the *binding contract*. Accord- ing to the first, special objects, events, activities in the world of human experience may be regarded as given seals which remain in perpetuity as marks of the mighty acts of the living God. According to the second a definite constitution has been given by God to men and man's whole life—religious, ethical and political—must be carried forward within this contractual framework.

The records of the Old Testament show that this conception of the relations between God and man gradually developed from the time of the settlement of the Hebrew tribes in Palestine. The exigencies of the historical situation virtually compelled the children of Israel to adopt the social organisation of the tribes amongst whom they settled. A king, judges, priests, civil officials—all became necessary if a strong and stable national life was to develop. Yet for a long time the old Hebrew culture of the free open spaces retained its influence and the constant calls to battle kept the close contact between leaders and their fellow-tribesmen intact. Jerusalem, however, grew in importance, both because of its association with the great king David and because of its strategic position as an enclosed city presenting a formidable obstacle to attacking forces. In all the time of troubles after the death of Solomon, Jerusalem retained its position of eminence and the temple became the centre of the growth of a new and distinctive cultural tradition.

This tradition which may be designated either the Deutero-nomic or the Priestly stood for the organisation and reorganisation of social life on the basis of given *law*. Numerous codes were promulgated at different times in Israel's history, but whatever variations there might be, the underlying premise remained the same : that Yahweh had revealed His law to Moses, the law governing the religious, the ethical and the social life of His people, and that it was incumbent upon the people to obey this law in every detail. The law, originally given to Moses directly, had been encoded first on stone tablets and then in a more developed written form. Thus the book of the law was the primary seal or sign of the unchanging laws of God though other outwards signs commanded by the law were also regarded as seals confirming God's attachment to His people and their allegiance to their God.

Corresponding to the conception of the Divine provision of the seal of His will in outward and visible form, there was the belief that God had bound a particular people together by a covenant. This covenant came increasingly to be viewed as a strictly defined contract whereby God had bound Himself to provide for and protect His chosen people on condition that they on their part remained faithful to the provision of the solemn treaty or agreement. Failure to keep the covenant would inevitably lead to retributive action on God's part; a steady determination to walk in the way of the Lord would certainly lead to prosperity and blessing.

These ideas, which had begun to win acceptance in the temple circles at Jerusalem before the great disaster in which the city was sacked and the majority of its citizens led away into exile, became firmly entrenched in the minds of those in Babylon who struggled to discover the meaning of the nation's past, present and future. It is true that prophetic voices sounded even amidst the misery of the exile, encouraging the people to expect a new manifestation of the power of God as in ancient days and the birth of the people of a new covenant who would know God from the least even to the greatest. But the more acceptable voices were those which interpreted the events of history in accordance with a strict law of retribution and reward within a contractual relationship. God had redeemed His people from slavery and given them a new law; this law they had failed to observe; let them now resolve afresh to obey it in every detail and He would grant them a fresh deliverance and establish them as a faithful and purified community within their own land.

When permission was granted for a large band of the exiles to return to Jerusalem, it seemed that this doctrine had received a signal outward vindication. Now the teachers of the law could seek to make its regulations better and better known and to build up a new society in which the whole of life would be subject to the given law of God. The words of the Law were to be in men's minds day and night. The Book of the Law was to be the constant seal that God had chosen them as the people to show forth His promise. But in addition the sabbath was to be a seal of God's gracious provision of rest for His people; their keeping of the sabbath was to be a sign of their obedience to His command. Circumcision was to be a seal of God's separation of His people from the heathen; their faithfulness in the use of the sign was to be a mark of their continued consecration to God alone. The sacrificial system was to be an outward provision for man's need of cleansing and access to the Divine presence; by a careful attention to the details of the sacrificial ritual man could be assured of gaining the benefits which he desired. Thus the general character of post-exilic Judaism may be described as that of a society concentrating its attention upon the outward signs and seals of salvation and confident that at length this scrupulous attention and obedience would lead to the final vindication of the Jews in the eyes of the whole world. The final salvation would be an outward sign to the heathen of God's faithfulness to His people; it would also be a sign of their faithfulness within the covenant relationship.

In the history of Eucharistic interpretation this general tradition has had a notable influence especially in post-Reformation Protestant scholasticism. Men fastened upon the idea of the covenant but in all too many cases it was interpreted in conformity with the outlook of post-exilic Judaism rather than in line with the early Hebrew prophetic tradition. This was not, it is true, surprising. The supreme rediscovery of the Reformation was a book—the book, as it seemed, which revealed the truth and proclaimed the moral law of God. What more necessary than that men should submit themselves to that book in all its provisions and thereby prove themselves to be in very truth the heirs of the covenant of God? There were, indeed, other outward signs—in particular the Sacraments of the Gospel —but these were to be regarded as seals of the promises of God and pledges of the final salvation which His own people were destined to inherit.

The keynotes of Eucharistic theology within this particular tradition have ever been " in remembrance of Me " and " till He come." An examination of the records of the institution of the Lord's Supper reveals the fact that even if the Supper was not a passover meal it was surrounded by passover associations. If, then, it can be regarded as a new passover, its function within the Christian Church must, it is argued, be akin to that of the passover in the Jewish Church. But was not the Paschal Feast the supreme memorial of redemption? When the son in the Jewish household makes the well-known inquiry concerning the *raison d'être* of the rite, he is told that the lamb is eaten " because God passed over the houses of our fathers in Egypt "; unleavened bread " because our fathers were redeemed from Egypt "; bitter herbs " because the Egyptians embittered the lives of our fathers in Egypt." The great redemption of the past is called to remembrance in the present through the sign which recalls particular aspects of the event in its original setting. So the new passover, according to this interpretation, calls to remembrance the great redemption from sin through the signs of the broken body and the shed blood, each of which recalls particular aspects of the death on Calvary.

But not only was Passover night a time of solemn remembrance, it was also a season of great joy. For " at the Passover the deliverance from Egypt is the prefiguration of the even greater redemption to come. Thus it was said by Joshua ben Hananiah (*circa* A.D. 90) that Passover night was the night on which the Jews had been redeemed in the past and on which they will be redeemed in the future." (A. J. B. Higgins, *The Lord's Supper in the New Testament*, p. 47.) So the Lord's Supper has been regarded as the supreme pledge of that final salvation which will be granted to all who remain faithful within the covenant. At every Eucharist they show forth the Lord's death till He come, they renew their loyalty to Him and rededicate themselves to His obedience. To all such the word of the promise is confirmed that they will eat and drink with their Lord in His Kingdom. The feast below is the pledge of a joyful participation in the feast of the Kingdom of Heaven.

This interpretation of the Eucharist is accepted in many of the Churches of Western Christendom. It is simple and direct, it serves to confirm and strengthen the souls of those who have responded in faith to the word of the Divine promise. The sacrament is regarded as " an holy ordinance instituted by Christ ; wherein, by sensible signs, Christ, and the benefits of the new covenant, are represented, sealed, and applied to believers." (The Shorter Catechism.) Normally the sacrament follows the proclamation of the word for, as Calvin puts it, " God has been pleased to add to His Word a visible sign by which He might represent the substance of His promises to confirm and fortify us by delivering us from all doubts and uncertainties." There is, in this way of thinking, no place for change or adaptation in relation to new conditions of life. The word of God's redeeming grace has been spoken once and for all : this word has been sealed, represented, exhibited, in and through a particular sign; now whenever the sign is duly repeated the word of God's salvation is confirmed; those who receive the sacrament in faith gain fresh assurance that they have been saved through the offering of Jesus Christ once and for all and that they will be saved for ever in the final consummation of the Kingdom of God. In other words, the Eucharist is a sign and seal of redemption through the Cross and a pledge of final salvation in the age to come. The word of God's Promise is primary. The sacrament serves to strengthen and confirm the faith of those who have been brought within the covenant of grace.

I have tried to give some account of the four leading cultural traditions within which, it seems to me, the normative acts of the Eucharistic drama have been expressed and interpreted. I have tried to bring out the noteworthy positive principles which have operated in each of these traditions and to show how they have been applied within the context of Eucharistic meaning. It is only natural that any particular observer or writer will have his own particular sympathy and, coupled with that, a better chance of understanding a particular tradition. At the same time it is of great importance that in a day of renewed interest in the ecumenical Church every effort should be made to appreciate the positive contributions of traditions other than one's own.

It will be obvious from the whole argument of this book that my own sympathies lie in the direction of the third and the first of the traditions described in this chapter. I believe that the danger of rigidity and inflexibility are never far away from the second and the fourth. Mechanical efficiency can be purchased at too high a price. Unquestioning acceptance of clear-cut signs may result in social petrification. Nevertheless there are real values to be found in each of these traditions if they can be held within the embrace of the wider whole.

It is surely one of the great tragedies of Christian history that the institution of Sacrifice and the sacrament of the Eucharist have been so often interpreted in narrow and limited ways. The original pattern of the Eucharist, there is every reason to believe, was severely simple. But it was set within a particular symbolic context which was important though not to be regarded as final and dogmatically determinative. There is more than one sacrificial context; there is more than one way of making a memorial. Inflexible liturgies and unchanging ceremonial-patterns are not worthy settings for the Lord's own symbolic acts; inflexible dogmatic formulations and unchanging verbal definitions are not edifying interpretations of the Lord's own symbolic words. It is idle at this stage of the world's history to seek after uniformity. But the tradition which will set itself to understand the symbolic structure of another tradition and in particular to appreciate its interpretation of the Eucharistic drama, will both enrich its own inner life and at the same time more adequately manifest to the world the true nature of the Divine sacrifice.[1]

[1] A notable expression of this new understanding and appreciation may be seen in the Report of Section 3 at the Edinburgh Conference on Faith and Order in 1937. Cp. the following section.

"We believe that, if sacrifice is properly understood, as it was by our Lord and His followers and in the early Church, it includes, not His death only, but the obedience of His earthly ministry, and His risen and ascended life, in which He still does His Father's will and ever liveth to make intercession for us. Such a sacrifice can never be repeated, but is proclaimed and set forth in the eucharistic action of the whole Church when we come to God in Christ at the Eucharist or Lord's Supper. For us, the secret of joining in that sacrifice is both the worship and the service of God; corporate because we are joined to Christ and in Him to each other (1 Cor. 10: 7); individual, because each one of us makes the corporate act of self-oblation his own; and not ceremonial only but also profoundly ethical, because the key-note of all sacrifice and offering is Lo! I come to do Thy will, O God."

CHAPTER TEN

Are the Traditional Christian Symbols Outmoded?

WITHIN THE tradition of Catholic Christendom—Eastern and Western—signs and symbols have always occupied a place of major importance. The roots of Catholic culture extend far back into the ancient symbolisms of Greece and Rome and it has ever been the aim of the Catholic Church not to destroy but to purify and hallow the symbolic forms which belong to the age-long consciousness of mankind. Whatever variations there may have been in the interpretation of symbols or in the retention of particular symbols, there has rarely been any disposition to discount the necessity of or to minimise the significance of symbols for the initiation and the development of the Christian life.

Yet even in Catholic circles there are evidences of disquiet and apprehension concerning the general decay of traditional symbols in the modern world. Only a few years ago that a Monsignor of the Roman Catholic Church, speaking at a Conference on rural church life in the state of Vermont, described the great town churches of his own communion as perilously like efficiently run sacramental filling-stations. In other words, the general mechanisation of urban life has invaded and influenced the churches to such an extent that the ancient symbolic forms, though continuing to be employed, no longer relate themselves powerfully to the whole structure of human life.

The subject has been considered in its widest context in Father Gerald Vann's book, *The Water and the Fire*. He begins by deploring the loss both of our roots in Nature and of so much that the word " home " has meant to mankind through the ages. How many moving symbols have been associated with the home! Yet, he goes on, " it is not only the loss of *this* symbolism we have to deplore; it is the loss of symbolism in general. Down through the ages humanity has learnt something at least, consciously or unconsciously, of the meaning of life through the great universal symbols as they come to him in myth and legend, in drama and folklore and fairy-tale. He has learnt something, for instance, of the meaning of the ' dark journey '; the night-journey through forest or caverns or sea, wherein the hero must meet and conquer dragon or serpent or sorcerer, and in the end, out of the darkness, attain to rebirth, to fullness of life. For primitive man no doubt these things make up almost the whole of the psychological life, apart from the immediate necessities of every day; and in the great ages of civilisation they still loom large, in art and poetry and drama, joining with philosophy and science to the creation of a rich and deep psychological life. But we, for our part, live in a lopsidedly cerebral age; the vast triumphs of science have caused us to neglect and perhaps to deride the other avenues to knowledge; we make use of symbols, of course, but for the most part they are strictly practical and utilitarian, like the road sign or the barber's pole; the rest is largely lost " (pp. 15-16).

In view of the serious state of unbalance which this loss of symbolism has produced, Father Vann sets to work to suggest ways in which some of the great archetypal symbols of mankind may be recovered. The Hero-King, the Fire of Life, the Woman, the Bread and the Wine—these, he believes, have an essential part to play in a rich and fully human existence. " Once you lose the water and the wood, the wine, the oil; once you make love a question of sophisticated glamour and work a question of a dull uncreative routine; once, in other words, you forget your roots in human nature, in mother-earth, in the cosmos, you doom yourself (or are doomed) to unreality " (pp. 156-7). His deep concern is that modern urban man, living as he must in constant relationship to machines and technical devices and uniform structures may yet, through his life in the Church, regain health and sanity by being exposed to the traditional symbolic influences which have nourished the deep inward experiences of humanity.

But if there are evidences of concern in Catholic circles over the increasing impoverishment of man's symbolic life, the situation within Protestantism is even more serious. The early revolt against the forms and institutions of the medieval Church has all too easily led to a general rejection of *all* symbolic forms which seem to stand in the way of the soul's direct communion with God. This recoil from the use of outward signs and ceremonies has been specially violent within the realm of the order of Nature. Time-symbols and verbal-symbols have been recognised as necessary, but nature-symbols and human-symbols have been regarded as either irrelevant or dangerous. No Protestant thinker has uttered more urgent warnings on this subject than has Professor Paul Tillich. " The decrease in sacramental thinking and feeling," he writes, " in the churches of the Reformation and in the American denominations is appalling. Nature has lost its religious meaning and is excluded from participation in the power of salvation ; the sacraments have lost their spiritual power and are vanishing in the consciousness of most Protestants." (*The Protestant Era*, p. xxiii.) It is not perhaps surprising that one who grew up under the conditions which he describes so graphically in his autobiographical introduction to *The Interpretation of History* should feel as he does. Attached as he was to the soil, the sea, the sights and sounds of Nature, it was natural that he should himself gain a sense of relationship with Nature, of communion with Nature, even of reverence for Nature, which would in time make the development of a sacramental interpretation of Nature possible if not inevitable. But the " Churches of the Reformation " have become increasingly churches of the city and the " American denominations " have adopted in the main the view of Nature which I suggested in Chapter Two was characteristic of the New World. If Nature waits simply to be mastered and utilised, then its power as a symbolic medium is reduced to a minimum. Nature, in fact, " hast lost its religious meaning."

So convinced is Tillich of the seriousness of the situation that he returns to it in other parts of his writing. " The solution of the problem of ' nature and sacrament,' " he writes, " is to-day a task on which the very destiny of Protestantism depends." (*The Protestant Era*, p. 112.) Or again : " Are we still able to understand what a sacrament means ? The more we are estranged from Nature, the less we can answer affirmatively. That is why, in our time, the sacraments have lost so much of their significance for individuals and Churches. For in the sacraments Nature participates in the process of salvation. Bread and wine, water and light, and all the great elements of Nature become the bearers of spiritual meaning and saving power. Natural and spiritual powers are united—reunited—in the sacrament. The word appeals to our intellect and may move our will. The sacrament, if the meaning is alive, grasps our unconscious as well as our conscious being. It grasps the creative ground of our being. It is the symbol of Nature and spirit, united in salvation." (*The Shaking of the Foundations*, p. 86.)

Thus the decay in the understanding and use of symbols is widespread. Man in general in the modern scientific and techno-logical age either seeks to dispense with symbols altogether or grasps despairingly at symbols which seem to promise some temporary satisfaction. As Ira Progoff remarks in his exposition of Jung's psychology : " Fundamentally, Jung's diagnosis of the modern man is that he is suffering from a starvation of symbols." [1] And he continues : " It is the deadening of images which once had a vital power that lies at the source of the confusions in modern consciousness. The question is whether the occidental peoples can continue to live as they now are with only a morgue of symbols to supply them with the meaning of life. From Jung's point of view, this is impossible ; periodic confusion, paralysis of spirit, and ultimate breakdown are bound to result." (*Ibid.*) And once again : " With regard to the con-temporary situation, he (Jung) finds many signs of the regression of energies, the relentless introspection of modern literature and psycho-analysis, the searching for new religions and exotic doctrines in distant corners of the world, the total questioning of intellectual and moral values and the search, throughout Western civilisation, for the meaning of life. Jung interprets all of these as signs that the traditional symbols of Western civilisation are ceasing to be operative, that they are becoming

[1] *Jung's Psychology and its Social Meaning*, p. 292.

less and less able to hold together the personality of the Western individual, and that therefore new symbols must soon come to the fore." (Op. cit., p. 231.)

Perhaps Jung's most notable insistence is upon the necessity for a continuous interplay between the conscious and the unconscious layers of life—both in individuals and in cultures—if psychic health is to be maintained. The dynamic forms of the unconscious cannot, it is true, be allowed free rein; at the same time the more static forms of the conscious cannot be allowed to become merely conventional and inflexible. There is little doubt that in many parts of Christendom the latter eventuality has happened and the result has been a frightening outburst of energies from beneath, directed towards symbols which were thought to have been buried in the past. It is hard to see how the Christian Church can make any impact upon the modern world unless it can discover new symbolic forms which, while related to the archetypal symbols of former ages, are also relevant to the technological age in which we are living to-day.

If we turn to yet another field—that of the artist—we find the same recognition of the problems which arise through the change in man's attitude to his traditional symbols. In his autobiography, Stephen Spender tells how André Malraux affirmed one day that poetry was superannuated as a great art. "It was only—he argued—in an environment where a few simple objects could be immediately apprehended as spiritual symbols, that it could be a major art. The forest, the lion, the crown, the cross; when the actual, lived reality of these was invested with inner significance which men immediately recognised, then the poet could make use in his poetry of these clearly recognisable symbols of a lived poetry of sacraments, figure-heads and beliefs, within the world. But in our day of many inventions rapidly superseding one another, the most powerful poetic symbols of the past had been driven out by symbols derived from machinery, which had an overwhelming and disturbing force, but lacked the transparent, spiritual meaning of the symbols which had been superseded. Moreover, the phenomena of industrial civilisation symbolised totally different things for different people, so that the modern poet was not

Some European poets like R M Rilke deliberately sought to be obscure

only preoccupied with his own poetic vision but also with establishing the validity of his symbols. Hence poetry inevitably became over complicated and obscure, because it was trying at the same time to make statements and establish the terms for making them." (*World Within World*, pp. 239-40.)

Such a diagnosis of the general human situation and such an analysis of the poet's task may seem over gloomy and pessimistic but it clearly indicates the magnitude of the problem which confronts anyone who attempts to use symbolic forms in the contemporary world. The simplicities and the unities have gone, perhaps for ever. The new symbols may be bewilderingly complex ; they may be frighteningly powerful. How long they will endure, none can say. And meanwhile the struggle to retain the traditional symbols and to reinterpret them into successive ages can never be abandoned unless man dismisses the whole of his past as irrelevant to the problems of the present age. I still believe, however, that the ancient and traditional symbols are not finally outmoded and this conviction I shall seek to substantiate in the final section of this book.

II

In the course of our inquiry about the symbolic forms which man has employed during the period of his historical existence, I have had occasion more than once to emphasise the broad distinction between societies on the one hand which make a permanent settlement within a particular locality and societies on the other hand which are restless and mobile, ever seeking fresh worlds to conquer. Within the former category may be included communities engaged in agriculture and simple forms of manufacture, within the latter category communities engaged in hunting and simple forms of trade. Obviously there have been communities within which each of these forms of activity has had a place ; the agriculturists may seek expansion of his domain, the hunter may seek to establish his rights within a particular area. But this does not affect the fact of the existence of the two general types, each possessing its own characteristic and distinctive symbols.

In communities attached to particular localities symbols related to settlement and regularity and orderliness have been all-important. The home or the sanctuary—often a small-scale model of the universe itself ; the jar or bowl or pool of water— representing the ' deep,' the great universal source of the waters : the image symbolising the Earth-Mother or the Sun-Father : the mythological poem or liturgical text symbolising the great regularities within the universal process : the ritual actions representing birth or re-birth and the growth of the life of Nature. This classification allows for innumerable variations and developments, but the general context and the dominant motifs remained unaltered through the centuries.

In communities which are predatory and adventurous, symbols related to the object of the chase, to memorable events, to social purpose have been all-important. The encampment with its central mound or stone or tree : the spring or well of water : the totem symbolising the leader : the story or song recalling dramatic events in tribal history : the ritual actions associated with blood and later with the fire, representing both the reception of and the renewal of the life of the sacred species. In spite of all manner of variations and associations with the symbols of the more settled type of society, this general pattern of symbolism has repeated itself again and again through the period of man's historical existence. Thus the ingathering sanctuary and the place of periodic meeting ; the pool and the spring : the parent and the hero : the water-ritual and the fire-ritual : the sun and the moon : the sacred plant and the sacred animal : these pairs have provided the time-honoured symbols throughout the greater part of man's historical existence.

But now, as André Malraux suggests, a radically new development has taken place. The new scientific and techno-logical age has produced new patterns and processes which have taken shape in a succession of symbolic forms. So rapid has been the movement, moreover, that before one symbolic form has had time to establish itself another has taken its place. The clock, the machine, the engine, the battery, the valve—each in turn has been the characteristic instrument of an age. But the age has been short-lived and symbolic expressions of the new conditions of life which these instruments have made possible have been largely stillborn.

Yet that man has been living in an increasingly technological age as distinct from an agricultural or a hunting age is altogether evident. The symbolic significance of the home decays; it becomes simply a dormitory in which the tired industrial worker can relax and sleep. The symbolic character of the meeting wanes; it becomes simply the occasion for determining the respective policies of management and labour in the industrial realm. The symbolism of water disappears; it is hidden in tanks and pipes and drawn from taps when needed for particular purposes. The parent plays an ever-diminishing role in social life; the nursery-governess and the teacher-instructor assume the responsibility for the training of the child. Myth is replaced by the scientific description of the processes of the universe, story by the scientific recording of the events of history. The symbolism of fire loses its appeal; fire is now chiefly the hidden agent to release energy for industrial processes. Birth and death and rebirth have little significance within a dominantly mechanical context.

All this is true. And although it might have been claimed until comparatively recent times that there were still vast areas of the world where the agriculturalist and the hand-worker, the herdsman and the small-trader, were in secure possession and therefore still open to the appeal of traditional symbols, the rapid mechanisation of agriculture and of animal husbandry, the squeezing out of crafts and of small-business enterprise by standardisation and large-scale planning, above all the spread of modern means of communication, have meant that the patterns and purposes of the technological age have laid hold of the human mind and imagination to an extent which would have seemed unthinkable fifty years ago. Can the distinctively Christian symbols, therefore, closely associated as they are with the environments out of which they originally emerged, survive in the altogether changed environment of the mid-twentieth century?

III

Two major phenomena of the twentieth century lead us to ask afresh whether the patterns of the past are as completely outmoded as they seemed in danger of becoming in the heyday of mechanisation and of more rapid communication. Man has for centuries recognised his dependence upon Nature for the food and water without which he cannot live. But now it seemed that by applying his mechanical skills to the processes of agriculture he could ensure an ever-expanding food supply and a regular control of water resources. Great areas were cleared and put under intensive cultivation; water sufficient for immediate needs was brought from any convenient reservoir. For a while it appeared that spectacular results could be obtained by manipulation and mechanisation in this realm as well as in that of the production of manufactured goods.

Such a prospect, however, has already received severe checks and the whole conception clearly needs serious qualification. The dramatic symbolic denial of the omnicompetence of the process of mechanisation is the phenomenon of soil erosion—though the problem of the world's food-supply is of a far greater complexity than can be symbolised by any single phenomenon. Yet soil erosion has produced the first major danger signal, warning man that the universe in which he dwells cannot simply be used and exploited without regard to the forms and processes which belong to its *organic* wholeness.

Thus, as far as the layman can judge, the present period is one in which a major effort is being made in the scientific world to restore a sense of proportion and balance which had almost been lost. The efficiency of the machine is undoubted; the use of mechanical energy for the production of goods is likely to increase rather than to diminish. But mechanical processes cannot be allowed to operate in isolation from the rest of life. The health (wholeness of body and mind) of the operator must be considered; the optimum number for the health of a community must be determined; the rhythm of the crops, the health of the soil, the conservation of water, the relation of every part to the whole—all must be taken into account. In other words, the so-called physical sciences cannot be allowed to occupy the seat of final control. The biological sciences, chemistry, psychology, each must be allowed to make its particular contribution to the ordering of man's handling of his natural environment. If man is to survive he must discover—or rediscover—the meaning of organic wholeness in his relations with Nature in the world of to-day.

In the second place, corresponding to man's early attempts to gain possession of desirable objects from regions more remote —either by direct hunting with the aid of weapons or by more indirect methods of planned enterprise or exchange—we have seen in recent history the organised struggle to secure control over the resources from which energy can be obtained. To this end a vast network of communication has been constructed. The personal agent engaged in prospecting must be able to move quickly from one place to another; he must then be able to communicate quickly with his base; means must be found of sending the raw goods or sources of power quickly to the centre of industry; exchange of possessions must be practicable without friction or delay. In the whole realm which is loosely described as the improving of man's standard of life, it has proved to be imperative to employ the most efficient means of communication which are available. And for a while it was believed that the processes of competition, carried on through ever improved means of communication, would lead ultimately to the optimum standard of living for all mankind.

Such a prospect, however, has also received severe checks and cannot any longer be entertained without serious qualification. The dramatic symbolic denial of the unlimited extension of the use of rapid means of communication to attain particular ends is to be found in the phenomenon of mass destruction in modern warfare. Man's struggle with his fellow man has always involved a certain risk, but he has engaged in it because of his conviction that the struggle was directed towards a worth-while end. Normally, moreover, it has been at least possible to resolve the struggle into a new form of co-operation with a view to the realisation of a common good.

But with the advent of the possibility of unlimited mass-destruction through the use of rapid means of communication and of remote control, the whole situation has changed. In a short space of time man can bring death and destruction to vast numbers of his fellow-men. His most delicate and beautifully precise instruments can be used to annihilate large sections of the world's population and to gain nothing by so doing.[1] The fact is that during the past century the processes of inter-communication have been developed increasingly within an impersonal context. Man has travelled hither and thither, seeking objects of uncertain value, grasping them without regard to the intricate personal relations involved in a real give-and-take, hoarding them in isolation from his fellow-men, or providing for their distribution in predominantly impersonal ways. He has searched for information, knowledge of techniques, scientific data, and these have been stored in increasingly impersonal ways (files, libraries, etc.), until now the electronic brain has made possible the accumulation of vast stores of information which can be called upon through intricate pro-cesses of selection to solve the most complicated problems as they arise. But just as the mechanisation of the means of production out of the context of the organic wholeness of Nature can lead to disastrous results, so too the acceleration of the means of communication out of the context of the delicate complex of inter-personal relationships in society can bring about terrible consequences. In other words the science of tele-communication cannot by itself be allowed to determine man's actions and destiny. The science (if it be a science) of social relations must be allowed to guide man's use of his information and his potential energy. If man is to survive he must discover the meaning of true relationship, the deep implications of the dialectic of give-and-take, for the ordering of social life.

[1] It can indeed be argued that he gains by delivering himself from the threat of a cruel tyranny : or at worst, that he gains room for his own expansion. These gains, however, which are purely hypothetical, cannot possibly justify *aggressive* use of these weapons.

Man's supreme need at the present time is to become related to powerful and meaningful symbols. They must be such as to integrate him into the *wholeness* of the natural environment to which he belongs : such as to bind him to his fellow-men by ties which are deeply *personal*. They must on the one hand be flexible enough to allow for an expanding knowledge of the universe ; they must, on the other hand, be of such a pattern as to make room for a continually extending dialectic between man and man.

If it be granted that man cannot exist as man without symbols, that they are, as Whitehead wrote, " inherent in the very texture of human life " (*Symbolism*, p. 61), the question still arises whether every successive age needs new symbols or whether the most powerful symbols are those which have been established for long ages in the life of mankind. To this question there is, in my judgment, no single answer. The whole argument of this book will have suggested that certain archetypal forms correspond so harmoniously with the very structure of human life in society that it is almost unthinkable that they could ever be entirely superseded. They may, indeed, become over-formalised and inflexible and in this case their function will be to cramp rather than to promote the expansion of life. But where men are alive to the need for constant adaptation and extension the ancient symbolic form can exercise an ever-deepening influence upon the life of humanity. At the same time it has been the contention of this book that it may happen at any time that a new symbol arises to capture the attention of at least a section of mankind. It will not be new in the sense that it has no connection with patterns already in existence ; it will be new in the sense that it brings together into vital relationship forms or symbols which have never been associated with one another before. Such a conjunction always stands in danger of becoming fantastic and absurd. But where men are alive to the need for keeping the new symbolic association firmly within the context of living personal relationships, it can become a most powerful inspiration to new purpose and progress.

In the light of these general principles what may be said about the place of the traditional Christian symbols in the life of to-day? In our discussion of baptism we have emphasised the life-giving and body-cleansing properties of water. These have in no way grown less through the passage of the centuries. In fact, in rural areas throughout the world to-day it is fully recognised that while water is essential for every stage of growth and development, in the *beginnings* of individual existence—whether of the infant or the suckling animal or the plant or the tree— water and liquid food are beyond all necessary for the establishment of the rhythmic processes of life. Moreover, in all forms both of preventive and curative medicine, the need for cleansing by water is being constantly stressed.

There is thus no reason why the traditional initiatory rite of the Christian Church should not continue to be employed with increasing effectiveness in the vast areas of the world where the nature of organic processes is recognised and appreciated. But its effectiveness will grow only if attention is directed more and more towards the water and the water-ritual rather than towards the non-essential additions and developments which have become part of the baptismal service in the course of Christian history. All revisions of the baptismal liturgy should be in the direction of *simplicity*. Nothing is essential save the symbolic initiation *through water* into the organism of the Triune God—Father, Son and Holy Spirit—Who creates and sustains and purifies and enhances the life of the whole universe. The precise mode of the water-ritual may vary. But that *water* may be openly recognised again as a sacramental element; that some dramatic action may again be performed with the *water*; these are matters of supreme importance if the baptismal rite is to recover its symbolic importance in the organic world-picture which is opening out before men's eyes.

In the great urban and industrial areas of the world the situation is far more difficult. Within this general context water has become an almost hidden or highly artificial element. In the majority of churches—both Catholic and Protestant—the baptismal rite has become a traditional sign or an arbitrary seal with little living symbolic power. It may be that with the gradual growth of the consciousness of the need for relationship to the

wholeness of the natural order, the need for balance and proportion in living in contrast to the exaggerations and enormities
of mechanised societies, the water-ritual will regain something
of its earlier significance. But the immediate prospect in the
megalopolis is not bright.

It seems rather that the symbol should be such as to provide
a pattern of decisive movement from one condition of life into
another. Pairs of conditions exist in various forms of
polar relationship to one another ; life within the home over
against life in the outside world ; life under some kind of tutelage
over against a life of personal independence ; life under some
kind of restrictive bondage over against a life offering particular
freedoms ; life without meaning over against life which is
caught up into an integrative purpose ; life without any sense
of the living activity of God over against life which seems to be
pulsating with the Divine energy. When such pairs of conditions
exist alongside one another in the social order the need becomes
urgent for a symbolic form to provide the dramatic externalisa-
tion of the passage from one condition into the other. Time and
again in history this symbolic form has been provided by the
drama of the passage through the waters. It is doubtful, however, whether such a symbol any longer possesses any compelling
appeal to the human imagination. Even a change of clothes,
which at certain periods of history has marked a decisive movement into a new condition of life, no longer carries any special
significance except in very limited circles.

Probably in modern society the most widely used means of
commitment is simply the personal registration of the name.
This registration of the name for entrance into a particular
community or for commitment to a particular purpose is in the
main the means of initiating a new process of inter-communication. Once the name and address and telephone number and
identification mark are listed on the records of a particular society,
the flow of communication begins ; the initiate is made aware
of his new responsibilities and privileges ; he is caught up into
the complex of relationships which the new context contains.
Many of the initiate's *organic* ties still hold him tightly to
his former context. But his *name* is definitely and decisively
committed to a new social environment. The name which

is the symbol of his personal identity is now part of the complex of the life-in-relationship in which the new society consists.

Applying this procedure to the Christian realm we can readily see that where there are large concentrations of population or much mobility of habitation, the most natural way of commitment to the Christian cause is by the registration of the name upon the roll of a particular congregation. This registration may be dramatised by the familiar baptismal ceremony or by confirmation or by reception into church membership; it may be preceded by some form of dramatic break with the past through the very process of going forward to register the name. But once the name is enrolled, the initiate is committed to share in the common purpose of the Christian community. His name is now linked in covenant with *The Name*. His own past is slain in and through the death which The Name includes; his future is assured in and through the resurrection-life which The Name implies. In fact, this commitment by man and this apprehension by God may be regarded as another form of the early Christian " baptism into the name." The water symbolism is altogether less prominent and may be absent. Yet it may be claimed that if the initiation is clearly directed into the Name of the Lord Jesus, it is genuine Christian initiation. Its precise form may change from age to age according to the changing patterns of society. This need not cause alarm, however, for the very structure of human life seems to necessitate a symbolism both of continuing organic existence and of critical dialectical inter-relationships. A water-ritual continuous in form with the past and a commitment-into-the-Name-ritual, varying in form from age to age, each has a place within the full life and praxis of the Christian Church.

v

In our discussion of the Eucharist we have emphasised the life-through-death and the sustenance-through-food symbolism of the bread and the wine. This symbolism is still vivid and meaningful, especially in the great rural areas of the world. The

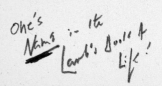

corn of wheat must still fall into the ground and die or it abideth alone; the fruit of the vine must still be crushed if it is to be transformed into the wine which maketh glad the heart of man. Moreover, whatever refinements and elaborations man may make in his diet, it still remains true that some form of bread or baked cereal is the most widely used article of food in the world to-day. Thus there is no reason why the traditional Eucharistic rite of the Christian Church should not continue to be employed effectively even in areas which have little direct contact with the processes of Nature. Men are becoming increasingly aware of the peril of mass-starvation which hangs over the world and of the need to bring all available land under cultivation. They are also becoming more aware of the rhythm of life-through-death which controls all organic processes. The symbol which enacts this rhythm and has at its heart the bread which sustains the life of mankind is not outworn. There are signs that man is ready to respond to a symbol of sacrifice with new devotion and hope.

But again it needs to be emphasised that the effectiveness of the Eucharistic symbol will depend in no small measure upon the recovery of *simplicity*. It is a striking fact that the great Roman communion which has traditionally been associated with pomp and splendour of ceremonial has been seeking in recent times to bring this sacrament to the people in conditions of great homeliness and simplicity. Even the factory-worker, living in the mean streets of a great city, who sees the bread which is to be consecrated to God, who watches the solemn offering, who gazes upon the hallowed bread now made available for his nourishment, cannot fail to gain some sense of the true Divine order to which his life belongs, by which it is sustained and within which it finds its meaning. In the course of an imaginary address for a simple Mass as it might be celebrated in a slum-room by a priest-worker, Father Gerald Vann says:

" So in the Mass, the greatest of all symbols, we learn to live, we learn to be wise; and then we learn to understand, long for, receive not only the fullness of human life, but the life which is divine; and so we return to our roots not only in the universe but in God. Through the bread and wine we become rooted again in Nature; through the bread and wine we begin to live a divine life because we begin to be possessed by God." (Op. cit., p. 159.)

I have already urged that there are signs of a deepening understanding of the organic processes of Nature and of the need for man to discover his responsibilities within the whole organism to which he belongs. He is steadily learning how better to promote organic balance and growth. May he not be ready to respond in a new way to the central Christian symbol which bears witness to the rhythm of organic life and to the inter-relatedness of every part of the organism with great simplicity and power ? If the Eucharist can only be restored to its true place at the centre of every sectional grouping within the social whole, it may yet become the greatest integrating factor of our time.

But can the Eucharistic symbol carry meaning even in the conditions of modern city life ? It must be admitted that it is far from easy to establish any vital connection between this symbol and the complex system of intricate communications which the average city represents. By focusing attention upon man's family life, his rare contacts with Nature, his daily food, it is possible to find some elements of symbolic association with the bread and the oblation. But large areas of his existence remain virtually untouched and the question arises as to whether these must be regarded as irredeemably profane and secular.

In my judgment, just as the organic life of Nature is lifted up and sanctified within the symbolic offering of the fruits of the earth ; and just as this sanctification takes shape within the organic life of man himself, man being a part of Nature and dependent upon Nature and yet at the same time a priest for Nature and lord over Nature ; so a system of communication can be directed towards its proper goal by being related to a symbolic constellation of communication having a definite direction ; and this constellation is, in fact, formed by man in relation to his fellow-man, man meeting his fellow in such a way that each renounces a measure of his own autonomy for the sake of the achievement of a common good. In other words, the only way in which the vast network of modern communi-cations can be redeemed is by bringing any and every part of it into relationship with some creative meeting of persons whose pattern forms the symbol of judgment for the whole complex.

A creative meeting of persons normally resolves itself into a common aim and purpose—a common *direction*. Two apparently conflicting aims are suddenly fused together as each renounces his own ambition in order that the richer common good may be realised. This common aim now sets the direction for the whole network to which the *persons* of the creative meeting belong. It becomes the symbol which controls and judges all communicating agencies and saves them from degenerating into soulless machines, operating only for the profit of a single individual or for the aggrandisement of a single community.

What, now, is more worthy to serve as the determinative symbol for all systems of communication than the drama of the New Covenant? Since the very dawn of human history the covenant form has been used to symbolise the overcoming of suspicion and antagonism between two parties, the cementing of the new togetherness within a common bond of peace. Both the giving and the receiving have been sacramental. Often some form of blood-symbolism has been employed—blood which constitutes the most vivid and even startling conjunction of life and death, of self-giving and self-replenishing, of individuality and community. The precise blood-symbol has varied in the course of historical development—the actual blood of the covenanting parties, substitute blood, animal blood, wine—but the underlying pattern of the action has remained constant. By sharing symbolic blood, the symbolic death of the one party is united with the symbolic death of the other while at the same time the symbolic life of the one party is united with the symbolic life of the other. This is the pattern which is to govern henceforth the whole system of inter-relationships within which the two parties will move.

So far as the traditional Christian symbol is concerned, the important matter is the continuance of the common participation in the cup of wine. That this has become difficult in many contexts is obvious. The fact that wine is produced in only relatively small areas of the world, the fact that fermented wine is obnoxious to many folk to-day, the fact that grave hygienic objections have arisen to the sharing of a common cup, the fact that the symbolic connection between wine and blood is no longer immediately apparent—all these factors have caused serious questioning about the continuance of the new covenant symbolism in its traditional form. Even the ceremony of the loving cup is rarely practised in modern life and the toast is no longer a familiar gesture.

Now I have suggested more than once in the course of this book that whereas the symbolism which operates within an organic or analogical context must maintain a general continuity of pattern, that which operates within a dialectical and metaphorical structure is not bound in anything like the same way. Its very genius is to make new associations and new conjunctions. In principle, therefore, it would seem entirely possible that some new covenant symbol might be discovered, more appealing and more compelling to our modern industrial society. But is there any blood-symbol of giving and receiving, of personal meeting and personal commitment, of common devotion to a common aim which is widely used in contemporary life? It is difficult to think of any such, even in the trades-union groups which are probably the most powerful social organisations of modern life.

Until a new and compelling symbol of meeting presents itself, therefore, we may claim that the Christian Church is justified in continuing to use the traditional pattern of the new covenant as its determinative symbol of communion and commitment. Even to eat a common meal together can still be a sacramental experience; a recovery of the solemnity of drinking as a company from the one chalice of the blood of the covenant might do more than any other single thing to bring a new sense of direction to the industrial and technological age in which we live. The place for this is not necessarily in church. Wherever men and women now meet together for any assertion of common purpose—this is the place which cries out to be redeemed by being related to a symbolic form which will direct the impulses of this new age towards a worthy goal.

On the one hand to-day the cry is for more abundant production in order that standards of life in all countries may be raised even higher; on the other hand the cry is for more efficient communication in order that processes of scientific development may advance ever more rapidly. But what is the criterion of a *higher* standard ? What is the criterion of *real* progress ? Where are the symbols to express these criteria powerfully and meaningfully ?

To-day the world at large depends mainly upon the *sign*. The " sign " is the clear witness to order established, to efficiency achieved, to law defined, to status guaranteed. And it is true that man cannot live except in a context which contains at least a measure of order and regularity. Yet this very necessity constitutes his greatest danger. History is full of instances where the " sign " has become the chain rather than the guide, the final security rather than the stage for further advance. Possibly no phenomenon in human history is more ambiguous, more ambivalent, than the " sign " and our own civilisation is in grave peril of sacrificing all other goods for the sake of the efficiency and the security which the " sign " represents.

How great, then, is the need for the *symbol* which reaches down to the depths of the racial unconscious, yet stretches up towards the heights of the transcendent, which comes to terms with the past estrangement yet leaps towards the future reconciliation. Wherever such symbols exist to-day life is still open, progress is still possible. And because God has not left Himself without witness, they do in fact exist in many forms and in many contexts. Yet in the last resort the Christian still finds the only symbol of unlimited expansiveness in Him Who gathers up the whole structure of organic processes within His own sacred body and in the power of the eternal Spirit offers it without spot to God, still finds the only symbol of unbroken relatedness in the sacred conjunction of the Christ with His followers in the covenant of blood which is the promise of the final reconciliation of all things in the perfect Kingdom of God.

APPENDIX

Appendix

AQUINAS ON BAPTISM

PERHAPS the combination of the regenerative and purificatory aspects of Baptism referred to on pages 194-7 can best be seen in the developed theory of Thomas Aquinas.

" The generation of a living thing," he writes, " is the change of a lifeless into a living being. Now man is deprived of his spiritual life in his origin, by original sin, as we have already stated, and whatsoever sins a man commits in addition to this, deprive him of life. Hence it was necessary that Baptism, which is spiritual birth, should have the power to remove original sin and all the actual sins a man has committed. Now the sensible sign in a sacrament should be adapted to signify the spiritual effect of that sacrament; and water is the easiest and handiest means of removing dirt from the body. Therefore Baptism is fittingly conferred with water, hallowed by the Word of God. Moreover, since the generation of one thing is the corruption of another, and since that which is generated loses its previous form and the properties resulting therefrom, it follows that Baptism, which is spiritual generation, removes not only sins which are contrary to spiritual life, but all guilt of sin ; so that it not only washes sin away, but removes all debt of punishment." (S.C.G. IV. 59.)

In this exposition there is no indication that the water-imagery is in any way associated with the actual processes of the generation of life. It provides an open *sign* of the removal of dirt and so of corruption. There is no indication that it also acts as a sign either of spiritual *seed* or of the waters of the womb out of which natural life is generated.

Thus in Western Catholicism the tendency has been for baptism to be regarded as first and foremost the open sign of the removal of birth-sin or original sin. Sometimes this is extended to include the removal of original guilt and even the debt of punishment. Whatever variations there may be, however, in the conception of that which is removed, the basic image remains the same—that just as ordinary water removes dirt from the body, so the baptismal water removes all corruption and defilement from the soul. If no resistant barrier stands in the way, the sacrament operates *ex opere operato* and the outward act is the effective sign that the inward process takes place. In a vaguer way the rite is also associated with generation or re-generation, but at least in the West the symbolism has been far less precise or direct. The traditional connection between water and birth from above is retained, but there is little in the ceremony itself to show what this connection is. Traditionally and officially baptism is an effective sign of rebirth, but it is hard to interpret this statement otherwise than in a purely instrumental if not a mechanical fashion.[1]

[1] *The Catholic Encyclopaedia* defines the effects of baptism thus :
(*a*) It remits all sin, original and actual.
(*b*) It remits all penalties due for sin before God whether temporal or eternal.
(*c*) It bestows sanctifying grace and the infused virtues.
(*d*) It imprints a " character " or indelible mark on the soul.
(*e*) It makes the recipient a member of Christ and of the Church and makes it possible for him to receive the other sacraments.

CALVIN ON BAPTISM

ALTHOUGH, as has been indicated on page 203, Calvin found the seal-imagery exceedingly congenial, his own teaching is rich and comprehensive and not confined to any one image as the following quotation amply illustrates :

" Now that the end to which the Lord had regard in the institution of baptism has been explained, it is easy to judge in which way we ought to use and receive it. For inasmuch as it is appointed to elevate, nourish and confirm our faith, we are to receive it as from the hand of its author, being firmly persuaded that it is himself who speaks to us by means of the sign ; that it is himself who washes and purifies us and effaces the remembrance of our faults ; that it is himself who makes us the partakers of his death, destroys the kingdom of Satan, subdues the power of concupiscence, nay, makes us one with himself, that being clothed with him we may be accounted the children of God. These things, I say, we ought to feel as truly and certainly in our mind as we see our body washed, immersed and surrounded with water. For this analogy or similitude furnishes the surest rule in the sacraments, viz. : that in corporeal things we are to see spiritual, just as if they were actually exhibited to our eye, since the Lord has been pleased to represent them by such figures ; not that such graces are included and bound in the sacrament, so as to be conferred by its efficacy, but only that by this badge the Lord declares to us that he is pleased to bestow all these things upon us. Nor does he merely feed our eyes with bare show ; he leads us to the actual object, and effectually performs what he figures." (*Institutes IV*, 15. 14.)

But the fact remains that very soon the precise symbolism of the baptismal rite tended to become a secondary matter in Confessional Protestantism and ultimately almost a matter of indifference. The all-important thing was that there should be a sacrament of initiation into the fellowship of the people of God which would serve to *seal* the covenant of Grace and to act as an outward mark of the profession of a Christian man.

Bibliography

Barbour, I. G., *Myths, Models and Paradigms*, SCM Press 1974

Beirnaert, L., *The Mythic Dimension in Christian Sacramentalism*, Cross Currents, NY 1953

Bevan, Edwyn, *Symbolism and Belief*, Allen & Unwin 1938

Bourdillon, M. F. F. & Fortes, M. (eds), *Sacrifice*, Academic Press 1980

Brandon, S. G. F., *Time and Mankind*, Hutchinson 1951

Burkert, Walter, *Homo Necans*, University of California Press 1983

Caird, G., *The Language and Imagery of the Bible*, Duckworth 1980

Callahan, J. F., *Four Views of Time in Ancient Philosophy*, Harvard University Press 1948

Cassirer, Ernst, *The Philosophy of Symbolic Forms*, New Haven 1955

Collingwood, R. G., *The Idea of Nature*, OUP 1945

Cope, Gilbert, *Symbolism in the Bible and the Church*, SCM Press 1959

Cullmann, O., *Baptism in the New Testament*, SCM Press 1950

Dillistone, F. W., *Traditional Symbols and the Contemporary World*, Epworth Press 1973

—— (ed), *Myth and Symbol*, SPCK 1966

Dix, G., *The Shape of the Liturgy*, A. & C. Black 1945

Douglas, Mary, *Natural Symbols*, Barrie & Jenkins 1970

Duncan, H. D., *Symbols in Society*, OUP, NY 1968

Eliade, M., *Myths, Dreams and Mysteries*, Collins Fontana 1968

—— *Patterns in Comparative Religion*, Sheed & Ward 1963

Emmet, Dorothy M., *The Nature of Metaphysical Thinking*, Macmillan 1945

Fawcett, Thomas, *The Symbolic Language of Religion*, SCM Press 1971

Firth, Raymond, *Symbols: Public and Private*, Allen & Unwin 1976

Flemington, W. F., *The New Testament Doctrine of Baptism*, SPCK 1948

Foss, Martin, *Symbol and Metaphor in Human Experience*, Princeton University Press 1949

Freud, S., *Totem and Taboo*, Routledge & Kegan Paul 1950

Fromm, Erich, *The Forgotten Language*, Gollancz 1952

Geertz, Clifford, *The Interpretation of Cultures*, Hutchinson 1975

Gombrich, E. H., *Symbolic Images*, Phaidon Press 1972

Goodenough, Erwin R., *Jewish Symbols in the Graeco-Roman Period* (10 vols), OUP 1968

Gray, G. B., *Sacrifice in the Old Testament*, OUP 1925

Hicks, F. C. N., *The Fullness of Sacrifice*, Macmillan 1938

Holloway, J., *Language and Intelligence*, Macmillan 1951

Hook, Sidney (ed.), *Religious Experience and Truth*, New York University Press 1961

Hubert, H. & Mauss, M., *Sacrifice. Its Nature and Function*, Routledge & Kegan Paul 1964

James, E. O., *Origins of Sacrifice*, John Murray 1933

Jung, C. G., *Man and his Symbols*, Aldus Books 1964

Knights, L. C. & Cottle, Basil (eds) *Metaphor and Symbol*, Butterworth 1960

Langer, Suzanne K., *Philosophy in a New Key*, OUP 1942

—— *Feeling and Form*, Routledge & Kegan Paul 1953

Leeuw, G. Van Der, *Religion in Essence and Manifestation*, Allen & Unwin 1938

Lewis, C. Day, *The Poetic Image*, Cape 1947

Maccoby, Hyam, *The Sacred Executioner*, Thames & Hudson 1982

McFague, Sallie, *Metaphorical Theology*, SCM Press 1982

Masure, E., *The Christian Sacrifice*, Burns Oates 1947

Neumann, E., *The Origin and History of Consciousness*, Routledge & Kegan Paul 1954

Parker, Robert, *Miasma*, OUP 1983

Pederson, J., *Israel* (2 vols), OUP 1926

Progoff, I., *Jung's Psychology and its Social Meaning*, Julien Press 1953

Rahner, Karl, *Theological Investigations IV*, DLT 1955

Ramsey, Ian T., *Models and Mystery*, OUP 1964

—— *Models for Divine Activity*, SCM Press 1973

—— *Religious Language*, SCM Press 1957

Ricoeur, Paul, *The Symbolism of Evil*, Boston 1970

—— *The Rule of Metaphor*, Routledge & Kegan Paul 1978

Robinson, H. Wheeler, *Inspiration and Revelation in the Old Testament*, OUP 1946

Sanders, B. G., *Christianity after Freud*, Geoffrey Bles 1949

Smith, W. R. Robertson, *The Religion of the Semites*, A. & C. Black 1927

Storr, Anthony, *The Dynamics of Creation*, Secker & Warburg 1972

Swiatecka, M. J., *The Idea of the Symbol*, CUP 1980

Tillich, Paul, *The Protestant Era*, University of Chicago Press 1948

—— *Systematic Theology* (3 vols), University of Chicago Press 1958–1963; reissued SCM Press 1978

Toynbee, A., *A Study of History*, OUP 1934–54

Tracy, David, *The Analogical Imagination*, SCM Press 1981

Turner, Victor, *The Ritual Process*, Ithaca Press, NY 1977

—— *Dramas, Fields and Metaphors*, Cornell University Press 1975

—— *Symbolic Action in Human Society*, Ithaca Press, NY 1974

Wainwright, Geoffrey, *Eucharist and Eschatology*, Epworth Press 1977

—— *Doxology*, Epworth Press 1980

Whitehead, A. N., *Symbolism*, CUP 1928

Yerkes, R. K., *Sacrifice in Greek and Roman Religion and Early Judaism*, A. & C. Black 1953

Young, Frances M., *Sacrifice and the Death of Christ*, SPCK 1975; SCM Press 1983

Young, J. Z., *Doubt and Certainty in Science*, OUP 1951

—— *Programs of the Brain*, OUP 1978.

Acknowledgments

Grateful acknowledgment for permission to quote material from other publications is extended to the following:

Oxford University Press and the Harvard University Press for passages from *Philosophy in a New Key*, by Suzanne K. Langer: Mr. Walter de la Mare and Faber & Faber for the lines reprinted on p. 96: Burns, Oates & Washbourne Ltd. for the passages from *The Christian Sacrifice* by E. Masure: Faber & Faber for the passages from *Four Quartets* by T. S. Eliot which appear on p. 184: Mr. Stephen Spender and Hamish Hamilton Ltd. for the passages from *World Within World*: Princeton University Press for passages from *Symbol and Metaphor in Human Experience* by Martin Foss: Hodder & Stoughton for the passages from the Moffatt Translation of the Bible: Victor Gollancz Ltd. and Rinehart & Co. for the passages from *The Forgotten Language* by Erich Fromm.

INDEX